Key Concepts in
Body and Society

Recent volumes include:

Key Concepts in Sport Psychology
John Kremer, Aidan Moran, Graham Walker and Cathy Craig

Key Concepts in Sport and Exercise Research Methods
Michael Atkinson

Key Concepts in Tourism Research
David Botterill and Vincent Platenkamp

Key Concepts in Leadership
Jonathan Gosling, Ian Sutherland and Stephanie Jones with Joost Dijkstra

Key Concepts in Sociology
Peter Braham

The SAGE Key Concepts series provides students with accessible and authoritative knowledge of the essential topics in a variety of disciplines. Cross-referenced throughout, the format encourages critical evaluation through understanding. Written by experienced and respected academics, the books are indispensable study aids and guides to comprehension.

KATE CREGAN

Key Concepts in
Body and Society

Los Angeles | London | New Delhi
Singapore | Washington DC

Los Angeles | London | New Delhi
Singapore | Washington DC

SAGE Publications Ltd
1 Oliver's Yard
55 City Road
London EC1Y 1SP

SAGE Publications Inc.
2455 Teller Road
Thousand Oaks, California 91320

SAGE Publications India Pvt Ltd
B 1/I 1 Mohan Cooperative Industrial Area
Mathura Road
New Delhi 110 044

SAGE Publications Asia-Pacific Pte Ltd
3 Church Street
#10-04 Samsung Hub
Singapore 049483

Editor: Chris Rojek
Editorial assistant: Martine Jonsrud
Production editor: Katherine Haw
Copyeditor: Rosemary Campbell
Proofreader: Helen Fairlie
Marketing manager: Michael Ainsley
Cover design: Wendy Scott
Typeset by: C&M Digitals (P) Ltd, Chennai, India
Printed by: Replika Press Pvt. Ltd, India

Library of Congress Control Number: 2011938975

British Library Cataloguing in Publication data

A catalogue record for this book is available from the British Library

ISBN 978-1-84787-543-3
ISBN 978-1-84787-544-0 (pbk)

contents

About the Author   vii

Introduction   1

Ageing and Childhood   5

Anorexia/Bulimia/Obesity   10

Appearance and Beauty   16

Civilizing Processes   21

Class/Caste   25

Clothing   29

Colonialism/Post-colonialism   34

Consumption   39

Cyborgs   44

Death and Dying   48

Difference   56

Disability/Ability   60

Discourse   64

Dualism   68

Emotion   74

Feminism   79

Food and Eating   84

Gender/Sex   89

Genetics   94

Gesture and Habits   98

Habitus   102

contents

v

Health and Illness 107

Identity 112

Media and Representation 116

Medicine and Science 119

Modification/Dysmorphias 124

Nature/Culture 128

Pain 131

Performativity 135

Phenomenology 138

Power 142

Private and Public 145

Psychoanalysis 149

Queer 152

Race/Ethnicity 156

Religion 159

Reproduction 164

Sexuality 169

Sport 173

Technology 180

Violence 183

Work 187

Youth and Children 192

Glossary 195

Bibliography 200

key concepts in
body and society

about the author

Kate Cregan is the author of *Sociology of the Body: Mapping the Abstraction of Embodiment* (2006) and *The Theatre of the Body: Staging Death and Embodying Life in Early Modern London* (2009). The majority of her writing and research is based around understandings of embodiment across time, space and culture – with particular reference to medical interpretations of the body, medical technologies, and the representation of the body in images. Two of her allied interests are ethics (human, social and research) and writing pedagogies, in particular how becoming a writer informs the process of becoming a researcher. She has extensive experience teaching and researching in the humanities and social sciences. Recently, she has co-ordinated the teaching of ethics to medical students across the five years of a medical degree and lectured in sociology at Monash University. Currently, she is co-ordinator and senior lecturer of the interdisciplinary Graduate Researchers in Print writing programme in the Faculty of Arts, Monash University, Melbourne.

introduction

The sociology of the body has, over the past two or three decades, become a recognized disciplinary sub-field within the social sciences. It influences, and is influenced by, parallel work being undertaken not only in other areas of sociology but also in cultural studies, literary studies, anthropology, politics, drama and theatre studies, nursing and allied health studies (to name but a few). This book, like the other publications in the Key Concepts series, is intended to function as a conceptual map, enabling the reader to gain a broad overview of the field, in this case the body in society. That reader is assumed, in the first instance, to be an undergraduate or postgraduate student in any of the disciplines named above. However, the book is written in a style intended to be approachable and accessible to any interested reader.

My approach to the concepts included in this book has been based on a broad survey of the field of research into the body in society. At times that means the entries may be firmly embedded in sociological traditions but they may also stray into the areas that have influenced the sociology of the body, by including a cultural and historical contextualization on given topics. The concepts covered are a combination of abstract theoretical approaches (e.g. Habitus, Discourse, Ethnicity, Feminism, etc.) and key concepts encompassed in the socially embodied effects that are underpinned by those abstract concepts (Ability/ Disability, Beauty/Appearance, Clothing, Death, Gesture, etc.). There are 43 individual entries, as outlined in the table of contents, with a number of these covering paired or collocated concepts. Each entry begins with a definition of the term under discussion. This is followed by an explanatory essay that sets the term in a wider analytical and social context. Finally, a short paragraph recommending some examples of further reading, with a list of references, is supplied at the end of each essay for those interested in delving further into a given concept or issue.

What should be said from the outset is that the sociology of the body, and other studies of the body in society, is also one of the outcomes of a historical moment in social, political and cultural theory. While it appears in many theoretically informed robes, it can be shown to have roots in prior social theories. Those prehensile roots of the sociology of the body are sometimes referred to as an absent or 'implicit presence of the body in ... classical sociology' (Shilling, 1993: 9), in the work of Marx, Weber and Durkheim. Similarly, there is an early and suggestive essay by Marcel Mauss on body techniques in which he prefigured much of the work on the sociology and anthropology of the body (Mauss, 1979). Nevertheless, the greater part of what has become the study of the body in society is in many ways the result of the interplay of a number of post-modern projects

The term post-modern appears explicitly in a number of entries (for example, see **Feminism, Queer**) but I have chosen to describe the importance of it here, rather than provide a separate entry, because it is interwoven in so many ways in the generation of the concepts covered in this book. In the discussion of a number of the specific theoretical approaches to the body in society below, reference has been made to the major shifts in thinking that began post-World War II. One of those approaches was structuralism, which was based in the anthropological theories of Claude Lévi-Strauss. This is a theoretical framework based around the formation of meaning within language, in which terms of binary opposition (see **Gender/Sex**) are said to be a central part of meaning creation across cultures. This tendency to universalism was contested, and followed by post-structuralism, which is more associated with literary criticism and Derrida's work on deconstruction. Derrida showed that individual words can contain binary oppositions that are in fact co-dependent and hierarchizing, using the example of *pharmakon*, which in Ancient Greek meant both medicating 'drug' and dangerous 'poison'. While not a sociological theory, post-structuralism and post-modern deconstruction have influenced areas of sociological study, particularly in relation to the body (see **Colonialism/Post-colonialism**, **Nature/Culture**). This kind of destabilization of meaning, boundaries and certainties is related to post-modern approaches to social inquiry, which in turn underpin many of the categories here. There have been several major trends in social theory that have given risen to the study of the body in society that are dealt with in detail throughout this book which are indebted to post-modern approaches (see **Cyborgs, Discourse, Feminism, Habitus, Performativity, Phenomenology, Queer**, etc.). However, for our purposes, we are concerned with how that has been reflected within the development of key concepts in the social sciences. Foucault, for example, has been identified as a post-structuralist and his work has in turn been co-opted to post-modern projects, such as Donna Haraway's (**Cyborg**) and Judith Butler's (**Performativity**).

Key thinkers in the body in society, like Bourdieu (**Habitus**) and Foucault (**Discourse**) were conducting their early research in the 1950s and the early 1960s but were not known in English until the 1970s. Nor were Ariès (**Ageing and Childhood**) and Elias (**Civilizing Processes**), although the latter in fact wrote his first major work in the 1930s. The explicit study and theorization of the body in society did not begin to take place in the social sciences until the mid-1960s and did not emerge as a recognized field of study until the late 1970s and early 1980s. The 1960s and 1970s was a period when feminism gained its second wind, gay liberation arose, civil rights movements gained prominence and deeply *embodied* issues became prominent social and political issues. Each of those movements challenged the social and political structures that allowed the proliferation of sexism, hetero-sexism and racism, respectively. The intellectual legitimation of a proliferation of world views – which is a post-modern project – made space for the re-thinking and re-theorization of a plethora of taken-for-granted social objects: one of those objects was the human body. So, while there are many ways of approaching the study of the body in society, and there are many who study the body who would reject post-modern theorizations, understanding what we might know about (the epistemology of) the human body as being contingent upon historical, social, political and cultural contexts is at least in part the outcome of the post-modern breaking down of hardened, positivist definitions.

My aim in writing this book has been to cover all the dominant, relevant themes that run through and inform the varied work around the body in society. My allied aim has been to structure the content of the book to assist the inspired reader to search out further answers, if there are any gaps I may have overlooked. All of the entries in this book relate to one or more of the other entries. To assist the reader, those inter-relationships are clearly identified using in-text cross-references within the flow of the essays, and supplementary definitions of a number of the more commonly used theoretical-conceptual terms (e.g. embodiment) are provided in the Glossary at the end of the book. Therefore, a reader who wants to gain insight into the whole field may read each entry in sequence, but the book functions equally well as a text that can be dipped into to give a clear overview on a selected topic from which the reader can move directly to one or more related entries.

Lastly, I would like to thank several cohorts of students I have taught over the past four years for helping to shape my thoughts on the content of the book and for helping me to find the most appropriate means of expressing the ideas covered here. In particular, at Swinburne University I would like to thank the students in the *Sociology of the Body* and *Genetics and Society* in 2007–2008, and at Monash University, the students in *Global Childhoods*, the *Qualitative Research Strategies* honours class, and the *Graduate Researchers in Print* participants. My particular thanks go to Dilinie Herbert, Amber Moore, John Waugh, Denise Cuthbert and (my son) Camille Robinson for their direct input on the manuscript in its final stages.

REFERENCES

Mauss, Marcel (1979) *Sociology and Psychology: Essays*, trans. B. Brewster. London: Routledge & Kegan Paul.
Shilling, Chris (1993) *The Body and Social Theory*. London: Sage.

Definition Childhood is stage of life that can be said to be a period of growth and physical maturation. The United Nations (UN) defines childhood as the period from birth to 18 years of age (see especially the UN Convention on the Rights of the Child (1989)). This is a very broad and sometimes unworkable span of time: it doesn't necessarily fit with the lived realities of people across all social and cultural differences. The UN's intention is to protect the rights of young people who might be seen to be vulnerable because of their age, and who may not enjoy full rights under the law within a society (see also **Youth and Children**). In contrast, ageing is the process of growing older – which might occur at any stage of life although, in practice, it generally refers to the later stages of life. It is often described in terms of bodily decline (see **Death and Dying**) but it can also be seen in terms of 'positive ageing', which focuses on prolongation of the individual's physical activity and social productivity. Both the very young and the ageing or aged are implicitly, and sometimes explicitly, contrasted with the normative adult (generally a white, ablebodied male) and frequently found to be deficient in this comparison.

French social historian Philippe Ariès is famous for being the first to claim, in *Centuries of Childhood*, that childhood as we think of it in contemporary modern societies is a social and cultural invention. He argues that the concept of childhood has gradually taken shape over the past five centuries and most particularly in the past two or three. Ariès' basic argument on childhood is that, in its current form, it is a construct of bourgeois sentimentality that arose as part of the identity formation of the rising middle classes of Europe. He claims that childhood and the differentiation we would understand between infant, child, adolescent, youth, adult and aged infirmity only came into being in the seventeenth and eighteenth centuries. On the basis of representations in art and in educational manuals, Ariès argues that this evolution of childhood is observable through shifts in the positioning of games, clothing and education that are in turn related to age and social strata. So, the evolution of the idea of childhood took hold through bodily techniques: age-specific

5

clothing such as skirts for small boys before they could wear breeches (knee length pants); sports intended to train up a body to a specific physique and ideal of health; and education that entailed physical requirements (sitting still) and that involved physical correction when its requirements were not met (corporal punishment). The intertwining of these techniques marked out, using Bourdieu's terms, the habitus of childhood (see **Habitus**). Foucault, in *Discipline and Punish*, also placed a great emphasis on the controlling nature of education in bringing young bodies into docile agreement with the forces that work through educational institutions, although the focus of his study was on the effects of diffuse power (see **Power**) and its endpoint in adulthood rather than infancy and childhood. Nevertheless, both Foucault and Ariès saw the training up of the young by physical means – whether through sport, manners, or classroom discipline – as being of central importance.

Using medieval and early modern illustrations in support of his thesis, Ariès argues that the major physical differentiations between life-stages are respectively between the infant in the cradle and the neophyte-adult; and the aged and the bed-ridden (imbecilic) infirm who have returned to an infant-like state. The illustrations he provides track life-stages through embodied changes but do not include a period that is recognizable as 'childhood'. First came infancy, followed by a remarkably extended youth or the prime of life, and eventually old age. As he describes it, the idea of adolescence – a period in which one became a social being – did not exist. Rather, '[t]he idea of childhood was bound up with the idea of dependence: the words "sons", "varlets" and "boys" were also words in the vocabulary of feudal subordination' (1962: 26). So, conversely, a 'lad' or 'boy' could be in his twenties. (We can see that the latter term of subordination continued to be used well into the twentieth century, as applied pejoratively to adult African-American males.) Small children, Ariès argues, were considered unimportant because they were likely to die: recognition only came with the likelihood of survival. The shift towards the invention of a sentimentalized childhood is evident in the inclusion of infants in funerary monuments and family portraiture in the seventeenth century (1962: 46–7).

Subsequent historians have criticized Ariès' evidence for his claims and it is quite true that what appears in art or an educational manual is not necessarily good evidence of lived realities. Representations almost always serve other purposes than simply to reflect reality (see **Media and Representation**), and educational manuals might be said to hold up an ideal rather than be sound evidence of the actual behaviour of children. It is also demonstrably untrue that infants were considered unimportant, both from the evidence of literary sources (memorial poetry) and from legal statutes for the prosecution of crimes such as infanticide. However, few deny his general thesis that our understanding of childhood has changed over time, as has our expectation of what is and isn't appropriate in the treatment of children. Up until at least the seventeenth century, seven was considered the age of rational thought in Western Europe and it was from this age onwards that children might be sent into other households as apprentices, or indentured servants, or, when a little older, into the military forces such as the navy.

Indeed, what Ariès started has flowed outward to many other disciplines and is particularly important in understanding the cultural specificity of ideas of childhood, such as those upheld in the United Nations (UN) Convention on the Rights of the Child (1989) and in the International Labour Organization's (ILO) *Convention on the Worst Forms of Child Labour* (1999). In such documents the UN explicitly and implicitly promotes an idea of childhood as a time of innocence and vulnerability, which is a historically and culturally contingent construction that is not necessarily appropriate or helpful in situations where people under the age of 18 can be shown to be agents in control of their lives. The young in Europe were once considered to have the ability to take all that life offered or required of them from a much earlier age than we are inclined to think of now, much as children in developing countries might be active and productive contributors to the family economy today. However, the UN and ILO have shown some understanding of the ability (and need) of children in developing contexts to combine forms of employment with gaining education. (See also **Youth and Children**)

The body in society is not static; it changes over time and can be perceived differently in different contexts (cultural, spatial and experiential). The body is interpreted or experienced at either an individual or social level. This becomes clear in discussions in many of the sections in the current book (for example, **Appearance and Beauty**, **Difference**, **Queer**). When we consider childhood and ageing, these life-stages each bring up particular ways in which power is exerted, autonomy is questioned and control is sought over the body at these times in our lives. Childhood and ageing are the periods in our lives when our bodily capacities are generally considered to be less competent than the 'normative body' that is expected of the life-stages in between: although the 'normative body' is a fiction that quickly falls apart in relation to many of the concepts discussed in other sections of this book (see **Colonialism/ Post-colonialism, Difference, Disability/Ability**).

Both childhood and ageing are embodied *processes*. In ageing, at an individual level that process may involve loss of embodied capacities and competencies, either physical or mental, to a greater or lesser degree. Ageing is generally recognized by and through the physical changes that happen to the human body over time such as changes to the quality of the skin and hair, the diminishing capacity to maintain a desired body shape and the gradual degeneration of the major systems of the body (vascular, muscular, skeletal and nervous). Ageing, as understood at a social level, is subject to a range of discourses on ageing (see **Discourse**) that become part of the shaping of an ageing person's identity (Hepworth, 2000). In the developed world those discourses are largely concerned with aesthetics (Twigg, 2006), medical implications and government responsibilities.

In the developed world, these physical signs of ageing are often seen as something to avoid or overcome (Blaikie, 1999; Featherstone and Wernick, 1995). At the simplest level that might involve using sunscreen and make-up or dying one's hair, and at the more interventionist end it might involve complicated cosmetic surgeries. The medical implications of ageing across populations, that is, shifts in the demographics as a result of lower birth rates and longer life expectancies, have led to an increasing anxiety about the likelihood of a rise in the numbers of people living with Alzheimer's disease (along with other age-onset diseases) and how they are to be cared for. Public health messages over the past 15–20 years have become far more concentrated on the prevention of diseases that are likely to occur and become chronic in later life. This has, in turn, led to support for increasingly contentious research into treatment options to combat the processes, not just the logical consequences, of ageing itself. This includes therapies such as stem cell therapy, genetic therapies and nanotechnologies – treatments that are still associated with science fiction, that raise concerns as to their sociopolitical and ethical consequences (Cregan, 2005), and that are increasingly being applied in clinical practice.

It should be emphasized that these are largely concerns of developed countries, where life expectancies are higher and these specific implications of ageing are more pressing. In developing countries, there are related concerns with ageing but more in terms of people increasingly developing age-onset diseases related to dietary changes (see **Food and**

Eating) where preventable or treatable conditions may affect the whole population (e.g. malaria, tuberculosis, polio) in circumstances of under-resourced medical care and lower overall life expectancy. There are serious issues of inequity inherent in any discussion of ageing and childhood when looked at from a global perspective.

It should also be said that there are more positive stories to be told about ageing. In many non-Western cultures, the aged continue to be revered and cared for in the home within a family and/or community structure rather than that responsibility and duty being relegated to medicalized professional care in institutions like nursing homes and hostels (see **Death and Dying**). Unlike the public health discourse of 'positive ageing' – the underlying message of which is keeping elderly people active, productive and *independent* – in cultures where independence is less important than group allegiance there are more overtly reciprocal understandings of care. The young who were cared for will, in turn, care for those who cared for them, which inevitably includes the most basic forms of bodily care: washing, dressing, toileting. Within sociology, both childhood and ageing have become major areas of inquiry, in which we can see there are basic concerns of embodiment that are specific to life stages.

FURTHER READING

See also readings under **Youth and Children**.

There have been a number of critical responses to Ariès' (1962) work from within history for which Margaret King's *Renaissance Quarterly* essay (2007) provides a sound contextualization, rehearsing the main debates around Aries' work while acknowledging its enduring worth as well as its shortcomings. There are numerous alternate readings of the history of childhood from feminists such as Pollock (1983) and Luke (1989), through to more recent historians like Heywood (2001). Jenks (1996) and the edited collection by James and Prout (1997) are representative of psycho-social research into contemporary childhoods, that is, underpinned by the modern notion of childhood as conceived within the UN Convention. An early sociological introduction to an embodied approach to ageing in popular culture can be found in Featherstone and Wernick (1995), and in Blaikie (1999) in a more extended form. Arber and Ginn's collection (1995) takes a more concentrated approach to the study of the relationship between gender and ageing, while Hepworth (2000) analyses fictional representations of ageing in relation to identity formation. Twigg (2006) writes of the practical and policy implications with respect to medical care in the UK and includes chapters on both ageing and infancy.

Arber, S. and J. Ginn (1995) *Connecting Gender and Ageing: A Sociological Approach.* Buckingham: Open University Press.

Ariès, Phillipe (1962) *Centuries of Childhood: A Social History of Family Life,* trans. Robert Baldick. New York: Alfred A. Knopf.

Blaikie, A. (1999) *Ageing and Popular Culture.* Cambridge: Cambridge University Press.

Featherstone, M. and A. Wernick (eds) (1995) *Images of Ageing.* London: Routledge.

Hepworth, M. (2000) *Stories of Ageing.* Buckingham: Open University Press.

Heywood, C. (2001) *A History of Childhood: Children and Childhood in the West from Medieval to Modern Times.* Cambridge: Polity.

International Labour Organization (1999) *ILO Convention No. 182 on the Worst Forms of Child Labour.* Available at: http://www.ilo.org/ilolex/cgi-lex/convde.pl?C182 (accessed May 2011).

James, A. and A. Prout (eds) (1997) *Constructing and Reconstructing Childhood: Contemporary Issues in the Sociological Study of Childhood.* London: Falmer Press.

Jenks, C. (1996) *Childhood.* London: Routledge.

King, Margaret L. (2007) 'Concepts of childhood: What we know and where we might go', *Renaissance Quarterly,* 60: 371–407.

Luke, Carmen (1989) *Pedagogy, Printing, and Protestantism: The Discourse on Childhood.* New York: State University of New York Press.

Pollock, Linda (1983) *Forgotten Children: Parent–Child Relations from 1500 to 1900.* Cambridge: Cambridge University Press.

Twigg, J. (2006) *The Body in Health and Social Care.* London: Palgrave Macmillan.

United Nations (1989) UN Convention on the Rights of the Child. Available at: http://www2.ohchr.org/english/law/crc.htm (accessed May 2011).

..... Anorexia/Bulimia/Obesity .....

Definition Anorexia nervosa, bulimia nervosa and obesity are medical diagnostic terms for what are often grouped under the heading of eating disorders.[1] Obesity is more likely to be treated as a physical disorder that is a public health issue with social determinants. Anorexia and bulimia are classified in the Diagnostic and Statistical Manual of Mental Disorders (DSM) and are predominantly treated as psychological or psychiatric conditions. In the simplest terms, anorexia is characterized by a refusal to eat and a perception of oneself as 'fat', despite having a low or very low body weight. Bulimia usually manifests in practices of binging (eating to excess), purging (vomiting, taking laxatives) and/or obsessive exercise, aimed at maintaining an average body weight. Obesity is the term for a body weight that is a medically defined percentage beyond a calculated norm for a given height and frame.

From the medical perspective, the diagnosis of each of these conditions is based on means and norms of ranges of 'healthy' bodyweight. The simplest way of calculating the parameters of what are considered low, median and high body weights is the Body Mass Index (BMI). This is a calculation of weight in relation to height expressed as kilograms per metre squared (kg/m^2) of body mass. However, the BMI can only be taken as indicative not prescriptive, as it does not take into account the variability of the proportions of an individual's fat, muscle and skeletal frame. Despite the WHO maintaining a database on global variability of BMI (http://apps.who.int/bmi/index.jsp) and recommending different category ranges for a variety of body types (WHO, 2004), the predominant scale remains based upon a normative Caucasian body type. So, it is a rationalization of the body into abstract metrics that can affect an individual's perception of themselves – that is, their identity (**Identity**) – both at an individual and a cultural level. The national definitions of the ranges of the BMI scale also vary but in general terms it is grouped into the categories of underweight (below 18.5 kg/m^2), 'normal' (18.5–25 kg/m^2), overweight (25–30 kg/m^2) and obese (over 30 kg/m^2).

From a social perspective, the simplistic medicalization of anorexia and bulimia is highly contentious. The grouping together under the medical heading of 'eating disorders' tends to pathologize the person

---

[1] I have chosen not to name this entry Eating Disorders because it prioritizes the medical categorization for the complexes under discussion, whereas the individual terms are (slightly) less loaded.

with the eating behaviour: that is, people who 'have an eating disorder' are understood to be psychologically unwell. When medicine 'discovered' anorexia, in the late nineteenth century, it did so in terms of female psychopathology: hysteria. Freud's diagnoses of food refusal reflected his wider theories around sexual drives and familial tensions (**Psychoanalysis**). For him, anorexia was a form of hysteria in which an inability to come to terms with sexual impulses resulted in food refusal, that is a rejection of the impulse to eat (and survive). In later psychoanalytic theories this was transmuted into theories of anorexia as a rejection of a mature woman's body in favour of retaining the asexual child's body (Hepworth, 1999). Bulimia is also within the range of hysteria, but the bodily effects – excoriation of the oesophagus and degradation of the teeth due to persistent vomiting – are less obvious as near-normal weight is maintained. We can see, in this, notions that persist in contemporary media representations of anorexia (and bulimia): that is that it is a problem almost exclusively of young females and often put down to poor family dynamics. The public reporting of Princess Diana's bulimia was often cast in terms of her immaturity, or, her lack of control over her life. In each case the categorization as 'suffering from an eating disorder' is cast in gendered terms of irrationality and passivity, which were characteristics widely seen to be a natural part of femininity (**Gender/Sex, Nature/Culture**). The psychoanalytic pathologization of eating behaviours simultaneously robs the sufferer of any legitimate causal relationship in the development of the condition (the patient is 'wrong-headed' by definition) and of any capacity for agency (the patient needs to be treated and cured by the doctor).

Feminists have argued that such passivity is not necessarily an accurate way of describing 'eating disorders'. It is undeniable that the body in society is frequently subject to attempts to shape and control it (see **Ageing and Childhood, Civilizing Processes, Power**), and to ideals and images of bodily perfection that are largely unattainable, but which nevertheless can be internalized (**Appearance and Beauty, Media and Representation**). However, the ingestion of food and its expulsion from the body can also be seen as a means of exerting and displaying control to the world: that is, as a site of agency (Orbach, 1986). Consequently, there are a number of ways of understanding eating disorders in social and cultural contexts that affect the body in society.

An anorexic's obsessive fear of fat may well be related to an unrealistic (psychological) self-image, but at least a part of that image is dependent on external representations of ideal body shapes that exist within a social context (Bordo 1993; Orbach, 1986). Idealized body shapes change over time and according to culture. A quick glance at the portraits of females by Reubens, or Lely's portraits of King Charles II's mistress Nell Gwyn, shows that the attractiveness of the 'fubsy wench' of the sixteenth and seventeenth centuries was unashamedly plump. Hour-glass figures (the result of corsetry) were popular in the nineteenth century, and again in the 1950s. As we shall see below, fuller body shapes for both men and women remain the ideal in some cultures, particularly in the South Pacific. However, a public association of slimness with good health has been a persistent factor since the formation of the health (and eugenics) movements of the late nineteenth century and is closely allied to modern medical views of the human body (**Medicine and Science**).

In recent years, concern over anorexia and bulimia has seen regular popular criticism of the fashion and film industries' desire for models and actresses of a low to very low body weight. There is widespread condemnation of these women as poor examples of a realistic body shape for girls and young women. There are also socially and culturally inflected studies that involve detailed research, including interviews with those who display given eating behaviours – some in relation to their use of pro-anorexia websites (Burke, 2009) – that show a high degree of self-control and self-determination that can be exerted through controlling the ingestion or expulsion of food from the body (Orbach, 1986). That is not to say that anorexia is a laudable political act, but that its bases and expressions are highly complex, that they extend beyond an individual pathology and they deserve detailed contextualization.

At the same time, but at the other end of the spectrum of these medically diagnosed 'eating disorders', is the increasing concern with obesity, which is rapidly coming to constitute a moral panic. The means of attempted social control exerted through public health initiatives aimed at reducing weight pervades primary and secondary schools, popular culture, community campaigns and preventive medicine regimes across many industrialized nations.

Each of these eating patterns can also be seen as a problem of sociopolitical development and prosperity, and each is a relatively modern concern in so far as being understood as pathologies (Hepworth, 1999). For example, in a prior European religio-moral framework, eating to excess and obesity were characterized as one of the seven deadly sins (gluttony), and, conversely, where food was less abundant fat was a bodily marker of prosperity and social status, as it remains in some contemporary societies such as Samoa or Tonga. Currently, obesity is generally linked to abundance and the over-consumption of food – cheap, processed, high in fat and low in nutritional value – in combination with a lack of exercise (Hinde, in Dixon and Broom, 2007). Reality television shows where obese contestants compete in a discourse that reinforces that the fat-self is a false, complacent self (the slim 'I' is the real, motivated 'I'), assist in this process. In a social context, we know from the sociology of health literature that each of these descriptions flattens out just who those most likely to become obese are in the developed, and increasingly in the developing, world: that is, people from low socio-economic (LSE) backgrounds (Friel and Broom, in Dixon and Broom, 2007). It is not simply an abundance of food that may lead to obesity but one of cheap high-calorie food and a lack of availability of affordable low-calorie unprocessed food. This may also be combined with a lack of knowledge, a lack of time and/or a lack of desire to know how to prepare it. In Bourdieu's terms, our habitus informs what we see as appropriate foods, so people eating what may be considered to be a medically inferior diet will not necessarily respond to greater education around food.

Acceptable weight is also culturally determined, so what might be considered obese in developed countries today may in the past have been considered voluptuously desirable, or in contemporary societies with an overall lower access to food may still be seen as a sign of high social status and prosperity. Similarly, in cultural context, anorexia may be an ascetic choice based on a conscious cosmological decision to privilege spiritual attainment over and above physical or material satisfaction. On the diagnostic criteria of the DSM, most Catholic Saints as depicted in medieval and Renaissance paintings would have been diagnosed as anorexic (Hepworth, 1999), as would many gurus or Buddhist monks and nuns be today. In response to the pathologization of consumption behaviours that lead to non-normative body shapes, there have been counter-movements in developed countries, particularly in the US from the 'fat acceptance movement' (Braziel and LeBesco, 2001) and via online anorexia- and bulimia-support websites (Burke, 2009). Less contentiously, there have also been advertising campaigns by a particular soap company based around promoting acceptance of the variable body shapes of 'real women', in which Susie Orbach was personally involved. As conditions affecting bodies in society, none of these 'disorders' exists simply and straightforwardly as a bio-psychosocial medical condition. Apart from the possibility of each of them being exertions of agency, or a conscious expression of difference, as members of the Pro Ana (pro-anorexia) and fat acceptance movements would argue, the conception of these phenomena as medical disorders can be seen to be related to ideals of bodies in society that are historically and culturally specific.

FURTHER READING

Hepworth (1999) has taken a social constructionist approach to the embodied effects of 'eating disorders' in modern society and is an excellent place to start. Orbach (1986) and Bordo (1993) are feminists whose works were amongst the earliest to study the social and cultural causes and effects of such eating patterns, and remain influential to this day (Bordo as a feminist academic, and Orbach as a practising feminist psychoanalyst). Dixon and Broom's (2007) collection encompasses an excellent range of discussions on the social factors involved in the construction of the obesity 'epidemic'. Braziel and LeBesco's (2001) collection comes from a more cultural studies perspective and is in sympathy with the fat acceptance movement. Bronwell and Fairburn's (2002) collection reflects the range of bio-psychosocial classification of, and approaches to, eating disorders with guides to the (current) dominant medical and psychological treatments. Burke (2009) and Fox et al. (2005) each enter into the debates and critical discussions around pro-recovery and pro-anorexia online support groups.

REFERENCES

Bordo, Susan (1993) *Unbearable Weight: Feminism, Western Culture and the Body*. Berkeley: University of California Press.

Braziel, J.E. and K. LeBesco (2001) *Bodies Out of Bounds: Fatness and Trangression*. Berkeley: University of California Press.

Bronwell, K. and C. Fairburn, (eds) (2002) *Eating Disorders and Obesity: A Comprehensive Handbook*, 2nd edn. New York: The Guilford Press.

Burke, E. (2009) 'Pro-anorexia and the internet: A tangled web of representation and (dis)embodiment', *Counselling, Psychotherapy, and Health*, The Use of Technology in Mental Health Special Issue, 5(1): 60–81.

Dixon, J. and D.H. Broom (eds) (2007) *The Seven Deadly Sins of Obesity: How The Modern World is Making Us Fat*. Sydney: UNSW Press.

Fox, N., K. Ward and A. O'Rourke (2005) 'Pro-anorexia, weight-loss drugs and the internet: An "anti-recovery" explanatory model of anorexia', *Sociology of Health and Illness*, 27(7): 944–71.

Hepworth, J. (1999) *The Social Construction of Anorexia Nervosa*. London: Sage.

Orbach, S. (1986) *Fat is a Feminist Issue*. London: Arrow Books.

WHO (n.d.) *Global Database on Body Mass Index*. Available at: http://apps.who.int/bmi/index.jsp (accessed 6 June 2011).

WHO Expert Consultation (2004) 'Appropriate body-mass index for Asian populations and its implications for policy and intervention strategies.' *Lancet*, 363(9403): 157–63.

Appearance and Beauty

Definition Appearance is the way we present ourselves to the world, in other words what we look like. However, appearance is never simply how we look in an unmediated way. It is something that is shaped at the most basic level. We make deliberate choices (whether conscious or not) every day in the way we will enter the world – from basic acts of personal grooming, through to choosing to surgically alter aspects of our appearance. Beauty is a relational term: it is in perception; it is in social norms that interpret a particular form of appearance that is valued; and, it is a factor in influencing people to shape themselves and alter their appearance in order to conform to those norms.

key concepts in body and society

16

American sociologist George Herbert Mead was one of the founding theorists of symbolic interactionism, within which he formulated his notions of identity (1934). These ideas are intimately related to appearance as a projection of the 'self' in society, as expressed in and through the 'me' and the 'I'. The 'I' is our internally understood self and the 'me' is how we perceive others to be seeing us. The 'me' involves a degree of reshaping of our outward behaviour in anticipation of the judgement of others when in society. Erving Goffman's (1963, 1971) notion of face work is a related theoretical explanation of how we shape our appearance, whereby he argued that we alter our outward expression to fit the social situation, sometimes in contradiction to our inner feelings. That tendency to make our bodies conform to meet social expectations can be extended to the physical reshaping of our appearance on the basis of the relative weight we give to the opinions of others. So, we may feel compelled to alter our appearance to meet with external judgements on our appearance that may or may not involve standards of beauty. For example, modifying one's appearance or adopting a particular group-approved fashion does not necessarily accord with wider social markers of standards of beauty or appearance. Nevertheless, peer pressure has readily observable outcomes on the appearance of those who seek to achieve group approval, from EMOs through to Ferrari enthusiasts.

There are several further concepts allied to appearance that are important to the body in society. Two of the more central involve Hochschild's (1983) adaptation of Goffman's ideas around face work into her categories of surface acting and deep acting. Surface acting refers to the way people in industries that require them to appear friendly, helpful and sympathetic to others (hospitality, sales, nursing) may perform face work to modify their appearance to meet that requirement. For example, a sales assistant may smile and be pleasant to a customer when they feel otherwise (they are unwell, having a bad day) and/or when a customer is unpleasant to them (hiding their anger or resentment). This is a basic level of the capacity to mobilize what were once called 'social graces': most of us use face work strategies like this at some time in our daily lives.

Deep acting takes that attempt to suppress our immediate reactions to a deeper level and involves the person not only *appearing* other than they really feel but also internally *altering* the way they feel to make their emotions match their face work. This is a tactic familiar to the teaching of many religions – that is, to feel compassion even (or especially) for those who are unpleasant to us. In Christianity such practices are known as 'turning the other cheek', in Buddhism this is known as 'letting go'. It is also present in theories of method acting (that stem from the work of Russian drama teacher Stanislawski) where actors research and 'inhabit' a character, often to the point of temporarily taking up the imagined lives of the character (as parodied in Robert Downey Jr's character in *Tropic Thunder*). In practice, Hochschild argued, this can lead to unhealthy consequences for those who modify their feelings, with stress and emotional burnout being observed in many professions that require such self-modification. It is not hard to see that these also involved gendered expectations: women in many societies are expected to be more forgiving, compliant, patient and accommodating and so face and body work are seen as their talent or responsibility.

Beauty, as the saying goes, is in the eye of the beholder, but it can also be the apex of a socially approved sense of appearance. It is that wider social approval of a particular expression of beauty which forms the pressure to strive to achieve that norm. Feminist social researchers have had much to say about the pressure on women to conform to standards of appearance that imply notions of beauty (and what is not beautiful) (Gimlin, 2002). Beauty and the reshaping of appearance in its pursuit have been shown by social research to be implicated in eating disorders (**Anorexia/Bulimia/Obesity**) and the lived experiences of gender, ethnicity, difference and disability (**Colonialism/Post-colonialism, Difference, Disability/Ability, Gender/Sex, Race/Ethnicity**). Naomi Wolf argued in *The Beauty Myth* (1990) that women are embedded in the discourse around beauty, adhering to and promulgating stereotypical standards of beauty promoted by cosmetic industries, not only for themselves but for all women. So, those who accede to the socially approved norm are implicated in its spread and its power.

Young men are increasingly affected by the discourses around appearance (Bordo, 1999) that are the mainstay of cosmetics industries. The companies that have been promoting moisturizers and cleansers to women for over a hundred years have begun employing prominent 'rugged' Hollywood actors as spokespeople in their campaigns around men's beauty products. The messages contained within the associated advertising are very different from those presented to women – and stridently hetero-normative – while the products in the jars are virtually indistinguishable from those sold to the feminine market. In the nineteenth century politeness required that 'Horses sweat, men perspire and ladies glow'. Today, women 'moisturize' and 'age-defy' but men who jet-ski, paraglide and work-out 'hydrate' to 'combat dryness' and overcome the appearance of 'fatigue'. (Horses still sweat.)

The number of young men suffering from eating disorders is also becoming increasingly visible and just as 'thin is in' has been the mantra for female models since Twiggy's popularity in the 1960s (Hepworth, 1999), increasingly the ideal in male models is adolescently gaunt. It is ironic that popular observations in the press, during the 1990s, that designers seemed to style for the adolescent male body in their preference for underweight androgynous young women, should now be borne out in the popularity of equally slight, androgynous young men on catwalks. However, there have been ideals of male 'beauty' and appearance for millennia, albeit expressed in quite different terms.

As noted above, appearance and beauty are strongly implicated in gender discourse, but are also central to the definition of all 'others' against an (unspoken) ideal of masculine bodily perfection. As Bakhtin (1984) has argued, the male body has been seen in its perfect form to be muscular, controlled and inviolately 'closed' – like a piece of classical statuary. The female body, in contrast, is soft, uncontrolled and incontinently 'open' – like the carnivalesque female characters in the writings of Rabelais, whose bodies are open runnels of birth and sex, incapable of continence of any kind. Bakhtin's ideal male bodies do not need to be overtly described: they are the silent (white, heterosexual, able-bodied) ideal from which all other bodies are differentiated.

Sander Gilman, in his work in *Difference and Pathology* (1985) shows that this was not only a part of the differentiation of female from male, but also all 'other' males who do not fit the Western heterogeneous and hetero-normative ideal of male (**Difference**). At the level of the individual this can lead, for some, to a 'spoiled identity' and an accession to social and cultural pressures to 'appear' white. The attempts of Michael Jackson to appear as white as possible, both in skin tone and in facial appearance, notoriously led him into multiple cosmetic surgery procedures. For others, like Hobson (2005), it can lead to the reclamation of representations of beauty that challenge Western ideals. As we can see in the example from the men's moisturizer campaigns, Western ideals of masculinity remain within that range of the classical body: the men in the advertisements are muscular and completely in control of their bodies (see also **Gender/Sex, Sexuality**). Over the past 20 years or so, the pressure on men to conform to ideals of masculinity has been recognized, and normative masculinities have been challenged as part of the wider project of gender studies (see **Gender/Sex, Sexuality**) and postcolonial studies (**Colonialism/Post-colonialism**).

FURTHER READING

See also the reading lists for **Anorexia/Bulimia/Obesity**, **Difference**, **Disability/Ability**, **Gender/Sex** and **Media and Representation**.

Mead (1934) and Goffman (1963, 1971) are central to the understandings of the social meaning of bodily appearance for many researchers, both within and beyond sociology, and remain key readings in sociological thinking. Hochschild's (1983) work on emotional labour is a direct intellectual descendent of their theories, and is widely cited in body studies (see also **Emotion**). Wolf's (1990) third wave feminist manifesto popularized the critical analysis of (women and) beauty in the public sphere. Bordo (1999; see also Bordo, 1993) turns her gaze on the increasing effects of image on the male body. Taking a cultural studies approach, Sander Gilman (1985, 1999) is equally influential on studies of the historical construction and the colonialist rhetoric in the creation of norms of beauty, while Gimlin (2002) writes of the female body as a site of oppression, subject to the systems of control inherent in diet, exercise, beauty regimes and cosmetic surgery. Hobson (2005) takes the example of the woman known as the Hottentot Venus and in telling the story of her objectification and sexualization relates that to persistent images of black women into the present.

REFERENCES

Bakhtin, Mikhail (1984) *Rabelais and His World*, trans. Helene Iswolsky. Bloomington: Indiana University Press.

Bordo, Susan (1993) *Unbearable Weight: Feminism, Western Culture and the Body*. Berkeley: University of California Press.

Bordo, S. (1999) *The Male Body: A New Look at Men in Public and in Private*. New York: Farrar, Straus & Giroux.

Gilman, Sander (1985) *Difference and Pathology: Stereotypes of Sexuality, Race and Madness*. London: Cornell University Press.

Gilman, Sander (1999) *Making the Body Beautiful: A Cultural History of Aesthetic Surgery*. Princeton: Princeton University Press.

Gimlin, D. (2002) *Bodywork: Beauty and Self-Image in American Culture*. Berkeley: University of California Press.

Goffman, Erving (1963) *Behaviour in Public Places*. New York: The Free Press.

Goffman, Erving (1971) *The Presentation of Self in Everyday Life*. Harmondsworth: Penguin.

Hobson, J. (2005) *Venus in the Dark: Blackness and Beauty in Popular Culture*. London: Routledge.

Hochschild, A.R. (1983) *The Managed Heart: The Commercialization of Human Feeling*. Berkeley: University of California Press.

Mead, G.H. (1934) *Mind, Self and Society*. Chicago: Chicago University Press.

Wolf, Naomi (1990) *The Beauty Myth*. London: Vintage.

key concepts in
body and society

Civilizing Processes

Definition Civilizing processes – or manners – are the mechanisms by which a given social formation confers approval on certain codes of behaviour and differentiates them from behaviours that are not approved. Social stratification (Class/Caste) is created and supported by such civilizing processes. The term is most closely associated with the work of Norbert Elias, who connected the progressive systemization of manners with the formation of the social and political systems that characterize nation-states.

Civilizing processes and civilization are vexed and contested terms (see **Colonialism/Post-colonialism**). They can carry within them assumptions about the worth of particular cultures over and above other cultures, if they are used without due care. Norbert Elias (1897–1990), the social theorist who wrote *The Civilizing Process* (2000) and with whom the term is most closely associated, grew up in the Austro-Hungarian Empire and witnessed the devastation of World War I first hand, as an ambulance driver. On his return from the war he studied medicine and then turned to sociology instead. Germany experienced a profound depression following the loss of the war, which was shortly after followed by the rise of National Socialism. Elias' use of the term is best understood in that context and more specifically in terms of the construction of civility – that is polite behaviour, or manners, which involve embodied processes.

Although Elias left Germany in early 1933 to continue his academic work – like many Jewish intellectuals – and was living in the UK by 1939, his work did not become known in English until the late 1970s. There is much to be gained from his studies of manners and courtesy in relation to understanding contemporary and historical approaches to bodily habits in social complexes. His most famous contribution to the understanding of the body in society is through a detailed study of the stated and unstated rules and customs agreed upon for acceptable (and unacceptable) social behaviour. His choice of societies was Western European and *The Civilizing Process* spans seven centuries, from the medieval to the modern. It is therefore a very particular understanding of society and manners, based in very particular power relations, which he links overtly to the rise of nation-states.

Elias' study of manners makes clear how focused these codes of behaviour are on bodily practices and bodily habits. Manners set out the rules for how to eat, how to move, how to withhold and when (and where) to expel bodily products. Using textual evidence – specifically, literary sources and courtesy manuals – Elias uses examples from courtly society to support his argument, that the progress of manners and the taking up of the concept of *civilité* are expressions of the progress of (European) civilization. He cites Erasmus' 1530 publication, *De civilitate morum puerilium* [On Civility in Boys], as a turning point in the spreading of those codes. Erasmus was one of a new class of man, in the peculiar position of not being of the courtly classes himself and yet able to comment upon and shape courtly manners. He could be 'detached' from the court, because of his own position, and yet lend credence to and disseminate its values and rules. This eventually helped those manners spread out to the middle-class: '[a]ccordingly, Erasmus did not see his precepts as intended for a particular class. He placed no particular emphasis on social distinctions, if we disregard occasional criticism of peasants and small tradesmen' (Elias, 2000: 65–6). So, he did in fact continue to support class distinctions, although at a different level.

According to Elias, Erasmus shifted the rhetorical strategy. His recommendations did not come in the form of direct command – which was the style of earlier courtesy manuals – they were framed as personal observations or anecdotes, which imply a far greater degree of the internalization of the importance of the opinions of others. That is, the reader was being asked to think of themselves in terms of how they appeared to an observer, in public. Elias links this to three factors: to medieval traditions; to the examples from antiquity that had become accessible in the Renaissance rediscovery of Greek and Latin texts; and to the increase in literacy (67). This internalisation of the importance of the gaze of others extends to one's individual outward appearance, through dress, 'the body of the body' (Elias, 2000: 67). Clothing, gesture and bodily deportment (posture and movement) are signs of inner life that are explicitly linked to mental states.

The longer-term outcome of the success of this change in the passing on of manners was a gradual pressure to conceal, cover, hide or suppress what was increasingly seen as improper. This imperative to conceal becomes more and more successful over time, to the point where what Erasmus could write of directly in the sixteenth century farting, belching, guzzling, slurping, dribbling, pissing, shitting – albeit in far more restrained tones than his predecessors – by the nineteenth century had become unspeakable (see also **Discourse**). Another eventual outcome was that this *civilité* in turn became superseded, or lost its strength, amongst the social elites it had originally been copied from: the term became so current it also became bourgeois (**Class/Caste**). New elite codes took their place.

Elias supports these claims by giving a series of selected examples – predating and postdating Erasmus – from courtesy manuals and other literary sources from the thirteenth through to the eighteenth centuries. His first examples relate to table manners. The fork, in particular, is shown to be an implement that marks one of those turning points in the manners related to eating habits. At a time when soup was a staple, spooned directly out of communal bowls into the mouth and all one required was a platter (or a stout slab of bread) and a knife to cut off your choice of meat from the roasted carcass, forks were initially thought of as pretentious.

In bodily terms, forks enabled a diner to lift food from a communal eating pot, and eventually from individually served plates, without dirtying his or her fingers or having to mix his or her spittle with that of the rest of the diners. 'The fork is nothing other than the embodiment of a specific standard of emotions and a specific level of revulsion … a change in the economy of drives and emotions' (Elias, 2000: 107).

Coming into too close contact with the bodily substances of another person, bar the closest of family members, became a matter of increasing disgust. Further, eating utensils distanced people from each other in more ways than simple proximity. As luxury items they did so hierarchically, and as they eventually made their way 'down' the social scale, they contributed to an increasing distance between individuals of all social strata both in the form and make of the object (wood, pewter, silver) and in the distancing of bodily interactions.

Elias follows this pattern of argument through a variety of other bodily behavioural controls, including the curbing of speech. Again, we have the problem of the shift in styles, making social divisions more obvious and acting as an exclusionary measure: courteous language, if too formal or archaic, made clear the speaker's social position and identified the social climber. However, Elias argues that, despite this, the spread of the civilizing influence flattened out social difference. 'Here, too, as with manners, there was a kind of double movement: a courtization of bourgeois people and a bourgeoisification of courtly people. Or, to put it more precisely: bourgeois people were influenced by the behaviour of courtly people and vice versa' (Elias, 2000: 93–4).

Similarly, there are shifts in the eating and serving of meat, from proud traditions of carving whole beasts to the obfuscation of meat beneath sauces until their animal origin is totally obscured; the shift in the use of knives from personal weapons as well as implements, to the point where it is considered utterly improper to bring a knife to one's mouth (**Food and Eating**). The same pattern is repeated in his treatment of the relocation of peeing and shitting from the courtyard or the street to specific, enclosed spaces. In the process of marking out what is proper and improper, such writings 'had precisely the function of cultivating feelings of shame' (Elias, 2000: 114). Erasmus could write openly about recommending the release of 'wind' in either direction; by the eighteenth century even the mention of holding in wind, which was by then required, has become a matter of delicacy. All these proscriptions are about social boundaries, 'changes in the way people live together, in the structure of society' (Elias, 2000: 135). These changes also extended to the bedroom, where 'the emotional barrier erected by conditioning between one body and another, had grown continuously. To share a bed with people outside the family circle, with strangers, is made more and more embarrassing' (Elias, 2000: 142) (see also **Sexuality**).

Throughout *The Civilizing Process* Elias traces the increasing abstraction of the human body, its distancing from self and other, through the processes of the regulatory regimes that characterize traditional and early modern societies. The outcome is that the body becomes an entity made up of parts that function as a whole. This end product is what Shilling has rightly identified as the triple process of 'individualization', 'rationalization' and 'socialization' underpinning Elias' theories. The influence of Elias' writing on manners has spawned decades of writing and theorization around the control of the body in society that come up in multiple entries across the current book.

FURTHER READING

Elias' *The Civilizing Process* and *The Court Society* are, on the whole, clear and approachable texts and therefore constitute the primary further reading for this concept. For helpful analyses and further related essays, see Goudsblom and Mennell (1998). For discussions of Elias' work, specifically in relation to the body in society, see also Shilling (1993), Turner (1996) and Cregan (2006).

REFERENCES

Cregan, K. (2006) The *Sociology of the Body: Mapping the Abstraction of Embodiment*. London: Sage.

Elias, Norbert (2000) *The Civilizing Process: Sociogenetic and Psychogenetic Investigations* (revised edition), trans. E. Jephcott. E. Dunning, J. Goudsblom and S. Mennell (eds). Oxford: Blackwell Publishers. First published 1936.

Elias, Norbert (1983) *The Court Society*, trans. E. Jephcott. New York: Pantheon.

Goudsblom, Jan and Mennell, Stephen (eds) (1998) *The Norbert Elias Reader*. Oxford: Blackwell.

Shilling, Chris (1993) *The Body and Social Theory*. London: Sage.

Turner, B. (1996) *The Body and Society: Explorations in Social Theory*, 2nd edn. London: Sage. First published 1984.

Class/Caste

Definition Class is a basic sociological category closely linked to work and identity. Different theorists have delineated class categories on a variety of models, but one of the basic processes in the description of class is stratification. Classically, it has been associated with forms of labour undertaken, places of habitation, access to education, levels of prestige, social mobility and the variations in those (and other) categories. There have also been influential arguments for race as class (Gans, 2005). Caste is most closely associated with the Hindu caste system, a system of stratification that involves social ranking, but which is a closed system that entails levels of ritual purity (or impurity) and endogamy (marriage rules) in its stratification.

Class is increasingly difficult to define, particularly in post-modern societies where the traditional markers of class have either dissipated or mass
consumption and an associated intensified individualism has made class
identification and class consciousness less immediately relevant than it
once was. Marx's classes were divided between the propertied and those
without property; Weber included greater differentiation based on skills
and education and the idea of social status in formulating working, middle
and upper classes. With the technologization of many workplaces, including the agricultural sector, it has become increasingly difficult to define
class on the basis of the form of labour involved. It has become more
accurate and meaningful to speak in broader terms of stratification and
socio-economic status (SES) or even in terms of post-modern reflexive
identity (Giddens, 1991). However, particularly in relation to the latter,
for a discussion of the body in society the theories of Bourdieu, which are
intimately related to prior notions of class, remain most applicable.

Caste, like class, is linked to work, wages and social position with the
added marker of heritability and/or physical attributes. Caste in India
has been legally abolished but is socially persistent. It is associated with
forms of identity; is transferred by physical lineage; defines who one may
or may not marry; and is at least partly defined by skin colour. Hindu
caste is much less open to mobility than class. In a wider sense, caste may
also be used to refer to other forms of social stratification that include
endogamous social rules that are not based on religious or ritual value
systems, such as in Hinduism, but rather on the basis of perceived ethnicity. Examples that might fit into this use of the term caste are apartheid in South Africa or segregation in the Deep South of the US. These
were closed systems that structurally restricted access to and mobility
between markets, modes of employment and positions of prestige.

In relation to the body in society, whether we call it class or social strata,
socio-economic factors have a concrete effect on the body, as Bourdieu
(1984) has shown (see also **Habitus**). With a team of research assistants,
he conducted a massive study of the lives of people in Paris in the 1960s.
The study consisted of research with a huge sample of respondents from
across the spectrum of classes of French society at the time. Within the
research, people were surveyed about their daily lives. He found that,
among other factors, the labour which characterized a given class had
direct effects on the physicality of that class. For example, working-class
men developed particular musculature as a result of the work they performed; upper-class women had different body shapes from women who
worked in factories; in each case this could also be related to their respective preferences for and variations in diet and exercise. People of a given

class have, then, varying physical capital. This study found that there were also links between social strata and what people considered appropriate for their bodies: what they ate and drank (which affected their body shape as well as their health); how they moved and held themselves (gesture, gait, sport); where they circulated in space (where they lived, where and how they undertook leisure pursuits), and so on. These groups had preferences in the aspects of social capital they valued (education, art, sport, food, etc.) that also had effects on their bodies, which in turn was interconnected with wider effects on a given group's general ability to make choices about what aspects of social capital were appropriate for them to pursue. Bourdieu came to argue that class is not only a social category it is also an embodied category (**Habitus**). The body has social value, then: it can be both invested with and a bearer of social capital.

The woman who does not have the leisure to exercise and diet but is nevertheless active in the daily work she does, will have her body shaped in particular ways. Her body shape and the clothes she chooses – or can afford – to put on it further define the strata from which she comes. Even if she gains the relevant education and qualification, her embodied attributes may restrict her ability to move out of the work considered appropriate to her strata, as her shape, apparel, gestures and deportment may preclude her from being employed in workplaces that value the presentation of women from a different strata. Unlike caste, she is not restricted from social movement on the basis of customary law. Nevertheless, Bourdieu argues, she will embody her class and others will be able to read that.

We can see in this last point, a connection to Elias' work on civilizing the body (**Civilizing Processes**) as a means to civilizing society. Elias argued that class mobility is a continuous race in which the most privileged will always lead because they set the standards that other classes attempt, but are never entirely able, to emulate. One who has less expertise in demonstrating the elite codes of behaviour will always betray their origins. Although Elias did allow that over time the 'trickle down' effect would also have a complementary outcome, limiting many of the aspects of social difference.

Bourdieu's notion of the embodiment of class has been criticized on the grounds that it does not allow for movement between classes, and it is perhaps this factor that helps us to see how it might be applicable to notions of caste. Caste, as in the habitus of a given class, has aspects that are visible markers of one's background and group association that one cannot escape, as the earlier example of apartheid shows. In apartheid, in segregation practices in the US prior to the Civil Rights movement, and in various examples of Indigenous peoples being excluded from citizenship and/or physically confined to remote encampments (reservations) we have examples of a system of stratification that excludes those categorized as being of a particular grouping. Terms such as 'full-blood', 'half-caste', 'creole' and 'octaroon' – to name only a few – were markers of an unofficial but nevertheless powerful classification system that marked out perceptions of acceptability on the basis of heritage and racial purity. Under many of these systems inter-marriage was socially, and often legally, impossible (endogamy) but sexual relationships were not, as the proliferation of the categories themselves makes clear. Such systems of stratification made possible the Stolen Generations of Australia (forced removal and institutionalization of Indigenous children of 'mixed' parentage) (Australian Human Rights Commission, 1997); and the British Child Migrants (forced removal, emigration and institutionalization of children from single parent or working class families) (House of Commons Select Committee on Health, 1998).

Relatedly, as Gans (2005) has recently argued, race can be seen as a new expression or system of class, specifically in relation to the social position and identity formation in contemporary US society. Gans argues that common perceptions of difference, made on the basis of skin colour and the shape of facial or bodily attributes, reflect the reality of advantage and disadvantage in US society: as he says, the social 'pecking order'. That is, people recognize what were once used as 'scientific' markers of race because they are ingrained in the social imaginary. They also recognize the characteristics of the people who are in positions of affluence and influence. The fact that, by and large, those who are the most affluent are of Anglo-European ancestry and those who are the least affluent are African-American or Latino-American, instantiates the perception of racial markers as also defining categories of class.

Featherstone made a parallel point about ageing, that youthfulness is socially prized and an indicator that is taken into account in the judgement of social success and achievement. The older one becomes, particularly for women, the lower down the 'pecking order' one goes, until, as Elias noted, we are relegated to the status of social outcasts, institutionalized in care facilities.

key concepts in
body and society

FURTHER READING

See also the readings under **Consumption** and **Work**.
Bourdieu's (1984) study of Parisian society in the 1960s gives a good insight into one way of understanding class structures, allegiances, identities and is one of the keenest observations of the embedded social effects of

class on the human body. As noted, Gans gives a compelling account of the concordances between race and class in US society in which he recommends Fields (1990) as influential on his thinking on race and class. The two reports, from the Australian (1997) and British (1998) governments are deeply affecting documents that include testimony from those who were removed from their families regarding the treatment they received under institutionalization, which was inflicted on the basis of their classification by caste and class, respectively.

REFERENCES

Australian Human Rights Commission (1997) *Bringing Them Home: The Report of the National Inquiry into the Separation of Aboriginal and Torres Strait Islander Children from their Families.* Sydney: Human Rights and Equal Opportunity Commission.

Bourdieu, P. (1984) *Distinction: A Social Critique of the Judgment of Taste*, trans. R. Nice. Cambridge, MA: Harvard University Press.

Fields, B.J. (1990) 'Slavery, race and ideology in the United States of America', *New Left Review*, 181: 95–118.

Gans, H.J. (2005) 'Race as class', *Contexts*, 4(4): 17–21.

Giddens, A. (1991) *Modernity and Self-Identity: Self and Society in the Late Modern Age.* Cambridge: Polity Press.

Great Britain, House of Commons, Select Committee on Health (1998) *The Welfare of British Child Migrants.* London: HMG Stationery Office.

Clothing

Definition Clothing is, and is more than, what we use to cover various parts of the body. It can be a means of exerting power, either over others or over oneself. It can be a marker or a statement of social distinction and stratification. Clothing can be used to exert identity in the form of rebellion (clan tartans, punk), individuality and prestige (haute couture), community (ritual adornment or vestments) or conformity (military uniforms). Clothing in all its forms – apparel, adornment, dress and fashion – is always symbolic.

clothing

29

In early modern England, sumptuary (clothing) laws were enacted to prevent anyone who was not of a particular (high) social rank from wearing certain garments (Hollander, 1980). The laws were deliberately aimed at policing social boundaries by ensuring the visibility of markers of stratification: dress codes set apart members of the nobility, members of guilds and colleges, artisans and so on. People who broke these laws could be fined or imprisoned. The objects of these laws in Elizabethan England were many and varied. They included, but were not limited to: the wearing of particular items of clothing (collars); the use of particular fabrics, threads or styles (silks, precious metals); and the degree of titivation involved (jewellery, embroidery). During this period, clothing was the most valuable possession the majority of the population owned, and the increase in regulation was due at least in part to a concern with excessive expenditure, but also the possibility that anyone who amassed money might be able to pretend to rank through their style of dress (Jones and Stallybrass, 2000).

Sumptuary laws, both at this time and in other eras or under other systems of law, can function as an exercise of power over a group and a means of conveying and marking out identity. In the instance of Elizabethan England, power was exerted to maintain distinction and to ensure the visibility of social stratification upon and through the body (Hollander, 1980). The banning of kilts in the Dress Act of 1746 by a later English ruler, King George II, recognized the power of group identity that clothing can convey: that is, wearing the kilt was a statement of clan allegiance and political rebellion, even if the kilt itself was not an original piece of Highland dress (Trevor-Roper, 1983). Foot-binding was a gendered expression of wealth and power (Kunzle, in Barnard, 2007). One does not need to look any further than the laws passed in 2004 in France, banning the wearing of the hijab, in particular in schools, to find contemporary examples of the political sensitivity and power that can be invested in a piece of cloth. Under these laws observant young Muslim women can be expelled from school and thereby denied an education for continuing to wear their headscarves.

Even where it is no longer subject to secular legal regulation, the symbolism of clothing as a bodily marker of rebellion continues to be understood and utilized by youth (for example, the punks of the 1970s and their many successors). Cross-dressing, the wearing of clothing that subverts the gender identity of the body underneath, can be seen as an act of conformity in the context of the Elizabethan stage, when there were female roles but no professional female actors. In contemporary society, it can also be seen as a rebellion against gender norms and stereotypes (Garber, 1992). Clothing can also be used as a conscious assertion of membership, community and conformity. Muslim women who wear clothing that covers them to varying degrees can be seen alternately as subjugated by their religious leaders or as empowered by not having to be subjected to unwelcome male attention – in either case it asserts membership, in this case of a faith. Orthodox Jews, similarly, abide by sumptuary laws as observed in their sects and publicly assert their faith through the embodied symbolism of dress. Mary Douglas has shown the power of the adorned body as a natural symbol across a range of cosmologies (**Religion**). Even in cosmologies where the majority of the faithful are not expected to wear specific clothing, the cleric will be marked off from followers by recognizable, ritual dress or adornment even if that is as small as a symbolic pin. In each of these examples, clothing is used consciously as an exertion of embodied spiritual and community identity.

Uniforms subjugate individual identity in the conscious solidification of a group identity that simultaneously marks out rank (Craik, 2005). Tribal armies assert a group identity through dress but these are not uniforms as such, they are their 'everyday' clothes (for example, the penis gourds or *koteka* of the PNG Highlands). Early modern armies were often funded by and named in honour of noble patrons who attired them in an early form of uniform of the noble's colours, which made for a multi-coloured battlefield. The Parliamentary Army uniforms of the English Civil War are an early instance of a group identity formed as a symbol of the state. In the mid-eighteenth century, Britain's Admiral Anson ordered standardized and ranked uniforms to be designed for naval officers, although the lower seamen continued to wear their own clothes at sea into the nineteenth century.

The intention of a uniform is to put the position one holds before any notion of the individual. Within armed and other forces, uniforms uphold the distinction(s) of rank through the stratified variation that marks out the position within the group of the wearer. As with Elizabethan sumptuary laws, improper wearing of the uniform has potentially serious consequences. Not maintaining one's uniform can lead to disciplinary action; wearing the incorrect uniform (impersonating an officer) can lead to court-martial and imprisonment. In putting on a uniform with particular insignia the soldier or seaman is putting on more than the fabric, s/he is putting on the role embodied in the clothing and its accompanying status and power. Military uniforms also become symbols of nation as well as status within the force. This becomes most present and obvious in celebrations of nation, from the massed soviet parades of USSR May Days gone by, to the annual memorialization of fallen soldiers past, to the flag-draped coffins of the returned dead from recent conflicts. Being found out of uniform in enemy territory is generally considered to be an admission of spying.

Clothing may be used in consciously performing individual embodied identity (**Performativity**) by making a statement about one's cultural allegiance or the health of one's bank account (Davis, 1994). Most of the fashion houses that grew up in an era of haute couture, when only the richest could afford the individually fitted items, now have ready-to-wear lines. Some, like Stella McCartney even produce lines specifically for budget mass markets. Fashion is simultaneously a powerful industry, a process that subjugates pieceworkers in developing countries, and a set of undeclared rules that we adhere to in our daily lives (Küchler and Miller, 2005). Even in rejecting fashion, it is difficult to find clothing truly outside it – as we find out along with Anne Hathaway's character in *The Devil Wears Prada*, when she is lectured by her boss, Meryl Streep, on the temporal progression of a particular shade of blue from high fashion to bargain remainder bin. Appropriating the clothing of other cultures is a fashion, or a style statement, in itself and it can also be a statement of post-colonial 'ownership' of traditional style, as witnessed in the 'ethnic chic' of Pakistani-American designer, Safia Ahmed and others (Paulicelli and Clark, 2009).

Barthes (1983) argued that clothing is a means of communication and representation that can carry meaning (have a semiotics) in the way a sentence carries meaning, so that an outfit can be organized for a particular occasion into a given syntax of the appropriate combination. Within that structure is another set of choices, between what *type* of a particular piece of dress (high heels v. ballet flats, Panama hat v. baseball cap) one will use to form the 'sentence' (Miller, 1982). Davis (1994), on the other hand, has argued that while there is undoubtedly meaning in our choice of clothing it is not as fixed a semiotic system as Barthes would have it. It may be a way to 'say' one thing but how clothing is 'read' is another matter entirely and will depend on the experiences of class, status, aesthetics and culture of the person observing: those choices will be interpreted in ways beyond the control of the person wearing the clothes.

We use dress to say something about ourselves and in the political charge lent to clothing we are also making claims about our power over ourselves and our bodies. Dress is a means of communication, to express erotic desires, identity, power, belonging or outsider status, our ability to consume, our modernity or post-modernity: in short, ourselves.

FURTHER READING

See also readings on **Media and Representation, Identity** and **Religion** for the use and meaning of clothing as bodily adornment.
Jones and Stallybrass (2000) is a fascinating study, specifically concerned with the historical place of clothing in early-modern England. Baclawski's book (1995) is an excellent illustrated encyclopaedia which details specific items of clothing that have been worn across the centuries. Barthes' *Fashion System* (1983) is a somewhat dated but insightful introduction to clothing as language. Hollander's (1980) art and social history text is a frequently cited germinal text, that looks at the ways in which art has depicted understandings of clothing as both shaping and reflecting the (shaped) body. Garber's *Vested Interests* and Gaines and Herzog's *Fabrications* are similarly central texts in analytic approaches to the social and cultural meaning of clothing. Davis (1994) gives historically contextualized, sociological explanations of the popularity of particular forms of dress and its ambivalent effects on identity. Craik's (2005) volume on uniforms is a subtle treatment of the use and meaning of uniforms across time and cultures. And for a comprehensive introduction to the field of fashion theory, which takes a broad view of the history, anthropology, sociology and cultural study of clothing, it is hard to go past Barnard's (2007) reader.

REFERENCES

Baclawski, K. (1995) *The Guide to Historic Costume*. London: B.T. Batsford.
Barnard, M. (ed.) (2007) *Fashion Theory: A Reader*. London: Routledge.
Barthes, R. (1983) *The Fashion System*, trans. M. Ward and R. Howard. New York: Farrar, Straus and Giroux Inc.
Craik, J. (2005) *Uniforms Exposed: From Conformity to Transgression*. Oxford: Berg.
Davis, F. (1994) *Fashion, Culture and Identity*. Chicago: University of Chicago Press.
Gaines, J. and C. Herzog (eds) (1990) *Fabrications: Costume and the Female Body*. New York: Routledge.

clothing

Garber, M. (1992) *Vested Interests: Cross-Dressing and Cultural Anxiety*. London: Routledge.

Hollander, A. (1980) *Seeing Through Clothes*. New York: Avon Books.

Jones, A.R. and P. Stallybrass (2000) *Renaissance Clothing and the Materials of Memory*. Cambridge: Cambridge University Press.

Trevor-Roper, H. (1983) 'The invention of tradition: The Highland tradition of Scotland', in E. Hobsbawm and T. Ranger (eds) *The Invention of Tradition*. Cambridge: Cambridge University Press.

Colonialism/ Post-colonialism

Definition Colonialism refers to the social and political effects of the colonization of one people by another, usually as the result of an imperial expansion. Colonialism, in many instances, resulted in active attempts to wipe out the social, political and cultural values of the colonized society. Even when a population was not obliterated, the 'stories' of the colonized (if they appeared at all) were encapsulated with the colonizing powers' world view. Post-colonialism has its bases in the politics and philosophy of the 1950s and 1960s, most notably in the work of Franz Fanon and Albert Memmi. Post-colonialism came to academic prominence as a literary-theoretical movement that attempted to give voice to those prior 'stories' by re-reading history, literature, art, etc. to include colonized peoples, or from the point of view of the peoples. Post-colonialism is therefore one means of attempting to reclaim the history, culture and values of colonized and/or Indigenous peoples.

Historically, colonialism has generally involved the explorers, traders and settlers from the colonizing states taking for granted that people in other societies were 'savage', 'uncivilized' and therefore in need of the colonizer's values and world view. For example, between the late fifteenth and twentieth centuries many sea-faring Western European sovereign states explored the globe; mapped its outlines and boundaries; laid claim to many lands they mapped; set up trade connections with local rulers; and gradually colonized a multitude of societies in Africa, North and South America, Central and East Asia, Australasia and the Pacific. In doing so, they set up bureaucratic and political structures and exerted power over the peoples in those societies, with little or no regard for the social formations that were already in place. The colonizers believed what they encountered was less civilized and of less worth than the values they brought to the settled. Where they had governing authority, they had the power to shape the discourses around identity, nationality, history, language, art and politics (amongst many other factors), which in practice frequently left out the multiple contradictory voices that can be found in any society. A quick look at the entries in a popular 1930s encyclopaedia of Empire, *The Modern World Encyclopaedia*, swiftly yields dozens of examples of patronizing, racist, oppressive or simply silencing discursive strategies that claim (rightful) dominance for the colonizer and marginality for the colonized – known in post-colonial theory as the 'other'.

The 'other' is a key term in post-colonial theory that implies the lack of voice and a consequent lack of identity in the colonized. The construction of the colonized subject, it is argued, is one of binary opposition in which the colonizer is the dominant term of 'the centre' which is paired with the disempowered and voiceless colonized at 'the margin'. Post-colonial critiques of colonialism have done much to demystify these kinds of discursive strategies. Contemporaries of Foucault, Bourdieu and Derrida, and in a period of widespread decolonization of old empires, Fanon (1961/2004) and Memmi (1965/1991) were born in the French colonies of Martinique and Tunisia respectively, and brought that experience to their respective critiques of the social and political effects of colonization on colonized peoples. Fanon's politics were overtly revolutionary and favoured violence as a tool for change. His stance was informed by the racism he experienced as a descendent of slaves in French colonial Martinique and his observations of Algerian struggles for independence. Memmi, a Tunisian Jew who migrated to France, was no less critical of the effects of colonization in his early writing, but having lived to see decolonization and independence in practice over time (unlike Fanon) his writing has since turned to the analysis of the failings of post-colonial, post-independence governments (*Decolonization and the*

Decolonized, 2006) . Both these theorists were keenly aware of the power of embodiment as a determining factor in one's life, Fanon writing overtly on the effects of racism on identity and Memmi on the difficulty of finding ways for different cultures to coexist.

As noted above, post-colonial theory took hold in academic pursuits as a critical analytical tool in literary theory. That is, it was a project determined to re-read colonial literature to find the missing story of the colonized; to question the veracity of the colonial world view; to put forward counter-views; and, to use the parlance of the discipline, disrupt and destabilize hegemonic colonial 'his'-stories. The theorists most associated with post-colonialism are Edward Said and Gayatri Spivak, both of whom were from colonized states (Palestine and India, respectively) but whose academic careers were spent in the US. Said's *Orientalism* remains a highly influential, if criticized, text in the field that has deconstructed the way in which discourses of exoticism are ultimately disempowering of people. Spivak is best known for her use of the notion of the post-colonial subject as 'subaltern' – in the starkly embodied form of Indian wives who perform *suti* by self-immolating on their husbands' funeral pyres – and questioning whether it is possible for those who have been silenced in colonialism to find an effective voice.

Colonialism and post-colonialism are areas of theorization key to embodiment and to which embodiment is key. Waves of colonialism and globalization, from the Greeks to the present, have exerted bodily controls over those colonized. That exertion of power over a people has frequently involved the physical domination of original populations and the containment and branding of those peoples' bodies. The act of colonization has also supported and depended on the enslavement of third parties, most notably in the trade in enslaved peoples from Africa to support the labour needs of European colonial empires in the Americas, up to the late nineteenth century. Where colonized peoples have not been absolutely enslaved, they have often been denied the rights of citizenship, and their subjugation has still involved them being defined within the colonizers' terms (see also **Discourse**) whereby the colonized gradually absorb those terms and become assimilated into the dominant discourse, accepting the position of 'other'. Scientifically proposed and validated systems of classification such as phrenology, physiognomy and racialization (see also **Race/Ethnicity**) have all been used to define and politically confine colonized peoples. Post-colonial theory is concerned with discrediting the construction of the 'other' via such means.

Because the terms by which colonized peoples are defined frequently rely on bodily aspects (skin colour, body shape, facial features, bodily markings) post-colonial critique has often centred on the representation of the 'other' *as* body (emotional, open, sexual) in binary opposition to the colonizer who is constructed *as* mind (rational, contained, restrained). We can see too that there are associations here with the embodied 'other' and Nature as feminine or feminized, and the colonizer with masculinized Culture. This is obvious even in the early material outcomes of the exploration that enabled colonization; that is, in early cartographic atlases (Lestringant, 1994). The frontispieces of these books are heavily illustrated, with depictions of Nature as female, which was a standard gendered association of the time (see **Nature/ Culture**), but in the context of exploration the new worlds (and the people in them) this also becomes a part of a web of feminizing associations that are attributed not only to the colonized country but also to its people. This is seen in the public exhibition of Saartjie Baartman between 1810 and 1815, known in Europe as the Hottentot Venus (see **Nature/Culture**), whose body was an object of both scientific and sexual fascination. Her body was kept as an exhibit and not repatriated from the Musée de l'Homme in Paris to her homeland in South Africa until 2002 (Hobson, 2005).

As a series of academic debates taking place within literary or cultural studies, post-colonialism steadily exerted influences in other disciplines, including history, anthropology, geography and sociology, amongst others, often in relation to identity. The concrete effects on the body in society became apparent once the debate started to be taken up – and contested – by social researchers and by people who live with the effects of colonization in their everyday lives (Indigenous peoples in particular). For example, post-colonial debate has become central to social research methodologies and methods. Indigenous theorists, like Linda Tuhiwai Smith in New Zealand, are dedicated to finding ways of appropriately including not only Indigenous stories but also promoting Indigenous methodologies and methods in social research practices in ways similar to the feminist methodologies devoted to practices of inclusion (**Feminism**). In Australia, there have been concerted efforts in social research with Indigenous peoples, much of it done around health, to be as collaborative and reflective as possible by entering into research partnerships with Indigenous communities, whereby the communities have a direct input on and ownership of the research process: for example, the SEARCH program of the Sax Institute (http://www.saxinstitute.org.au/index.cfm).

Issues related to post-colonial debate also appear across other entries in this book. We have already seen direct links with the Eurocentric concept of **Nature**. It also arises in the discussion of **Medicine and Science**, **Difference** and particularly in **Sport**. There is symbolic importance in the winning of sports that were introduced as a part of colonial expansion and that were representative of colonial/national ideals – such as cricket – that have been successively dominated by post-colonial teams since decolonization (Bale and Cronin, 2003).

FURTHER READING

Fanon and Memmi have been noted as the key thinkers in the political critique of colonialism. Said (1978) and Spivak (1988) are two of the foundational figures in post-colonial literary and cultural theory and each gives insights into the political strategies that are implicit in the classification, interpretation and exoticization of the body of the 'other' by European colonists. Many subsequent thinkers have come to question and 'problematize' arguments written, as these were, 'at a distance' in the US. By contrast, Tuhiwai Smith writes as an Indigenous (Maori) researcher about changing the nature of thinking about and conducting research with Indigenous peoples, by putting the power of definition and research back into Indigenous hands. Bale and Cronin's book gives a good overview of the importance of sport in relation to post-colonialism or decolonized nations. Anderson (1991), on the other hand, questions what colonial and post-colonial ideas (of any form of community) might mean in the face of the intensification of globalization on the nature of community and identity. Ahmed (2000) and Ahmed and Stacey (2001) offer more complex but important approaches to the body in post-coloniality. As noted under **Appearance and Beauty**, Hobson (2005) relates the sexualization of one South African woman to persistent stereotypes of black women's sexuality into the present.

REFERENCES

Ahmed, S. (2000) *Strange Encounters: Embodied Others in Post-Coloniality*. London: Routledge.

Ahmed, S. and J. Stacey, (eds) (2001) *Thinking Through the Skin*. London: Routledge.

Anderson, B. (1991) *Imagined Communities*. London: Verso.

Bale, J. and M. Cronin (eds) (2003) *Sport and Postcolonialism*. Oxford: Berg.

Fanon, F. (2004) *The Wretched of the Earth*, trans. R. Philcox. New York: Grove Press. First published 1961.

Hobson, J. (2005) *Venus in the Dark: Blackness and Beauty in Popular Culture*. London: Routledge.

Memmi, A. (1991) *The Colonizer and the Colonized*. Boston: Beacon Press. First published 1965.

Memmi, A. (2006) *Decolonization and the Decolonized*, trans. R. Bonnono. Minneapolis: University of Minnesota Press.

Said, Edward (1978) *Orientalism*. New York: Pantheon Books.

Spivak, G.C. (1988) 'Can the Subaltern speak', in C. Nelson (ed.), *Marxism and the Interpretation of Culture*. Chicago: University of Illinois Press. 271–313.

Tuhiwai Smith, Linda (1999) *Decolonizing Methodologies: Research and Indigenous Peoples*. London and New York: Zed Books.

Consumption

Definition In economic terms, consumption is the intended endpoint of production. Within capitalism, goods and services are produced, exchanged and consumed (supply) in response to demand. It has been argued that the body has become another object of consumption: this may refer to what we buy to adorn ourselves (**Clothing**); a particular way of living we may 'buy' into (**Performativity**); or it can refer to the ways in which we may package, present and sell ourselves to the world (**Habitus, Identity**).

Consumption is most often associated with the financial exchange relationships of capitalism. As theories of 'the gift' (Godelier, 1999; Mauss, 1990; Strathern, 1988; Titmuss, 1997) have shown there are and have been exchange relationships that function in less abstracted terms than monetary exchanges, in material exchanges in barter systems and in the symbolic exchange of the *kula* ring of the Trobriand Islands. These prior forms of exchange do not depend on the emptying out of the value and content of the object exchanged, rather they exhibit reciprocity and/or form on-going bonds between the parties involved. Consumption and consumerism in modern developed societies function as abstracted financial exchanges that do not require ongoing relationships between the producer and the consumer. Through consumption people take to themselves material items, products and services – they embody them – and the lifestyles associated with them (Falk, 1994).

It is the last of these terms that relates directly to the effects of the concept of consumption on the body in society. Advertising (see **Media and Representation**) has for decades sold products on the basis of attempting to inspire a desire that goes beyond the product in itself, to the lifestyle or ideology presented as integrally associated with the product. Between the 1960s and the 1980s, one international cola drink was predominantly sold in terms of the representation of an eternal teenage beach holiday and was the drink of choice both amongst those who were part of, or aspiring to, surf culture. There are innumerable examples of successful advertising campaigns with similar dynamics. One of the more prominent over the past three decades has been the drive towards 'green' and/or ethical consumerism in all manner of products, from toilet paper and detergents to solar hot water systems and rainwater tanks. Each sells a lifestyle along with the product. That is, as is seen in relation to Mead and Goffman's notions of outward presentation of the self (**Appearance and Beauty, Identity**) social beings can be seen to be reactive to external opinion. What, and how, one consumes can form a part of that dynamic. In an era of mass consumption that is simultaneously preoccupied with messages of environmental crisis, the push to this kind of ethical consumption, and the discourses around sustainability, are attempts to counter massed consumerism. At the same time there are global shifts in consumption, where the 'luxuries' of developed countries are highly desirable to people in developing countries. Mobile phone technology is becoming ubiquitous in countries where clean drinking water is not available to the majority of the population. Ethical or sustainable products and mobile phones each confer forms of identity on the consumer.

People may, in their choice of consumption, aspire to a particular form of identity – in the prior examples that might be 'surfer', 'environmentalist' or 'technologically connected'. Elias made a point about the middle classes adopting particular manners, habits or language in their aspiration to pass as a higher class that has resonance here. Ownership of the latest 'must have' object can be said to make a similar statement about identity and contemporary aspirations to a look, a lifestyle, or a social milieu. Each also involves a process of abstraction and rationalization, whereby the aspirant re-forms their identity in response to the abstracted act of consumption. A particular form of body modification such as a tattoo or a ritually pierced septum may mark entry into full membership of the social group within the tribe for whom it holds cosmological symbolism (**Modification/Dysmorphias**). However, where such practices are no longer attached to the ritual meaning of the culture from which they have been appropriated, as in a tattoo parlour on the local high street, they become bodily accessorizing and assertions of identity as acts of consumption. They may still be used as a marker of identity associated with some form of group or imagined community, but it is likely to be within the looser bounds of an abstracted postmodern act of self-construction (**Performativity**). The consumption of lifestyle and identity need not be restricted to capitalistic consumption – many ethical consumers would openly reject that paradigm. It is nevertheless an assertion of identity which is related to one's capacity to buy.

Logically, if consumption of what is desired or demanded (whether lifestyle, identity, product or material object) requires considerable funds, only those with sufficient resources are going to be able to do so. This encourages a hardening of the division between those who are affluent and those who are not. In the case of ethical consumption, this is borne out in the incapacity of those on a low income to access high-technology eco-friendly power sources or organic foods that, because they cost more to produce, cost more to the consumer. Relatedly, it can also become easier to enact and to rationalize the exploitation of those who have very little, to meet a given demand. Cheaper goods, including food, are linked to massed and/or exploitative production practices, as is the production of clothing and footwear with which we shape our public identities (**Clothing, Identity**). With respect to the body in society, this can also be related to the proposition that the body and life itself is increasingly commodified.

There are innumerable documented instances of extremely poor people in developing countries selling (or subletting) parts of themselves to people from developed countries who have the funds to pay. This may include people from ethnic minorities in countries like Turkey, people from chronically poor sections of Romania or people living in poverty in India or China (Scheper-Hughes, 2000). Most developed countries forbid financial exchanges in relation to human parts or tissues within their own borders and, where surrogacy arrangements are allowed, they are tightly controlling. The US is a partial exception, in allowing the sale of gametes and payment for blood products. The possibility of allowing financial incentives for organ donation is regularly raised in the bioethics literature, but has yet to find wide support, and in the interim an international trade in organ transplantation, IVF and surrogacy flourishes. Each of these ventures depends on favourable, or non-existent, laws in the country of residence of the person supplying his or her body parts for sale or making her uterus available for gestation.

There are many ethical issues at stake related to the exploitation of the supplier in each of these practices: the capacity to give informed consent; ongoing health problems in nations with poor health systems; the recurrence of financial pressure (most do it to repay debt); the place of agencies and middlemen who facilitate the supply and profit from the transaction; the familial/patriarchal pressure put on women to carry surrogate pregnancies, and so on (Gupta and Richters, 2008). Within all this the body of the supplier and his or her constitutive parts become commodities. In the case of surrogacy, not only is the surrogate's womb commodified, the infant itself is at the centre of a web of financial transactions, and made the ultimate commodity through the labour of the mother who has become the 'perfect' worker (Pande, 2010). Legal proceedings around disputed cases of intra-country surrogacy and international adoption, particularly in the US, only intensify the construction of the infant or child as property: a commodity for which the parents have paid.

FURTHER READING

Featherstone's (1982) early and influential article is a good starting point for further exploration of the body and consumption. Falk's (1994) is an important and sophisticated contribution to the theorization of embodied consumption. For the importance of the different forms of embodied exchanges and their social and symbolic significance, Mauss' (1990) anthropological study of gifts and commodities in tribal Papua New Guinea is *the* key text. This has been subjected to important feminist (Strathern, 1990) and post-modern (Godelier, 1999) anthropological theorization, although the reader should be warned that these two books are highly theoretical in style. Conversely,

Richard Titmuss' (1997) discussion of blood donation as a social gift is clear, straightforward and directly aimed at affecting social policy; as is O'Neill's recent updating (2004) of his meditations of the social status of the body. Furthering the conceptual work done by Titmuss on the body-as-gift in modern societies, Fox and Swazey's (1992) ground-breaking medical anthropological study of organ transplantation in the US explores commodification and abstraction into replaceable parts of the human body. Scheper-Hughes (2000) and Scheper-Hughes and Wacquant (2002) extend that approach into case studies in international contexts, while Gupta and Richters (2008) and Pande (2010) are concerned with the construction of the commercial surrogate mothers in India as, respectively, self-determining individuals and piece-workers extraordinaire.

REFERENCES

Falk, Pasi (1994) *The Consuming Body*. London: Sage.

Featherstone, Michael (1982) 'The body in consumer culture', *Theory, Culture and Society*, 1(2): 18–33.

Fox, Renée and Judith Swazey (1992) *Spare Parts*. New York: Oxford University Press.

Godelier, M. (1999) *The Enigma of the Gift*, trans. N. Scott. Chicago: University of Chicago Press.

Gupta, J.A. and A. Richters (2008) 'Embodied subjects and fragmented objects: Women's bodies, assisted reproduction and the right to self-determination', *Journal of Bioethical Inquiry*, 5(4): 239–49.

Mauss, Marcel (1979) *Sociology and Psychology: Essays*, trans B. Brewster. London: Routledge & Kegan Paul.

Mauss, Marcel (1990) *The Gift: The Forms and Reasons for Exchange in Archaic Societies*, trans. W.D. Halls, foreword by Mary Douglas. New York and London: W.W. Norton and Co.

O'Neill. J. (2004) *Five Bodies: Refiguring Relationships* (revised edn). London: Sage.

Pande, A. (2010) 'Commercial surrogacy in India: Manufacturing a perfect "mother-worker"', *Signs: Journal of Women in Culture and Society*, 35(4): 969–92.

Scheper-Hughes, Nancy (2000) 'The global traffic in human organs', *Current Anthropology*, 41: 191–224.

Scheper-Hughes, N. and L. Wacquant (eds) (2002) *Commodifying Bodies*. London: Sage.

Strathern, M. (1990) *The Gender of the Gift: Problems with Women and Problems with Society in Melanesia*. Berkeley: University of California Press.

Titmuss, R. (1997) *The Gift Relationship: From Human Blood to Social Policy*, eds A. Oakley and J. Ashton. New York: The New Press. First published 1970.

Cyborgs

> **Definition** The term cyborg was first coined in the 1960s in science fiction. A cyborg is a biological organism that has been combined with cybernetics (robotics) to create a cyber-organism: hence, cyborg. This remains a familiar trope in science fiction. For example, the cybermen in Dr Who and the Terminator in the movies of the same name are cyborgs. In terms of the body in society, the cyborg is a term usually associated with the work of Donna Haraway, who used it to describe her theorization of the human body as no longer straightforwardly organic. A cyborg, in Haraway's terms, is any human who has had a technological intervention that is taken into, appended to or an extension of his or her body that forms a part of the body's ongoing functioning.

Newer technological advances, such as the various nano-technological or stem cell therapies may initially come to mind as technologies that would be classified as creating cyborgs when applied. Other obvious but more familiar examples of cyborgs would be people who are living with pacemakers, implantable defibrillators, transplants, cochlear implants, but it can also include those people dependent on wheelchairs, prosthetics and glasses. Less obviously, immunization, which introduces a bio-technologically mutated form of an infection that changes a body's capacity to react to an otherwise potentially overwhelming infection, also makes us cyborgs. So too can our adoption of increasingly sophisticated communication technologies that are becoming extensions of our embodied selves.

Donna Haraway set out her theorization of the effect of the meshing of flesh and machine in 'The Cyborg Manifesto' in 1985 in *Socialist Review*, which was later revised and reprinted amongst a series of essays in the book *Simians, Cyborgs and Women* (1991). Haraway began her academic career as a scientist, moved on to becoming a (Marxist) historian and philosopher of science, which then led into an interest in women's studies. Her immersion in women's studies eventually led her to a critical appraisal of Marxism, Marxist-feminisms and some radical feminisms which she concluded tend to flatten out, or, 'have simultaneously naturalized and denatured the category "woman" and consciousness of the social lives of "women"' (1991: 158). She has (rightly) connected this to the central importance of economic forces (modes of production) in Marxist theory and the implicit reduction of women's lives or women's labour to reproduction in most Marxist theorizations.

Like Butler's notion of performative gender (**Performativity**), this manifesto is deliberately utopian and forthrightly feminist. In the Cyborg Manifesto, Haraway offers a different place for women in the modes of production, one in which the body and labour take an altogether different turn. She argues that technologies, and in particular communications technologies, are a means of remaking 'our bodies, our selves' (1991: 180). 'The cyborg is a kind of disassembled and reassembled, postmodern collective and personal self. This is the self feminists must code' (1991: 163).

She builds this argument by first setting up lists of terms that are differentiated along the lines of societal, political and technological shifts that characterize modern and postmodern life – by which she means pre- and post-World War II life. She sees postmodern communications technologies and coding as the means of taking control of meaning and redefining the world and thereby ourselves. Re-crafting the body – and in particular women's bodies – is a matter of embracing and harnessing technoscience to one's own (feminist) ends.

> Communications technologies and biotechnologies are the crucial tools re-crafting our bodies. These tools embody and enforce new social relations for women world-wide … in which all resistance to instrumental control disappears and all heterogeneity can be submitted to disassembly, reassembly, investment, and exchange. (1991: 164)

Language is the code of the 'software' and the 'operating system' of embodiment. Code is the underpinning logic of communications technologies and biotechnologies. Women can take control of the logic of communications technologies and biotechnologies to their own ends and 'rewrite' embodiment. Computers, the internet and the integration of medical technologies with the human body open the way for women to use each of these to their own ends. Biotechnical, cyborg bodies are bodies beyond patriarchal constraints of sex and gender. They are bodies beyond 'nature' (**Nature/Culture**): 'A cyborg body is not innocent; it was not born in a garden; it does not seek unitary identity and so generate antagonistic dualisms without end (or until the world ends); it takes irony for granted' (Haraway, 1991: 180). (Irony and 'play' are central to post-modernism.)

Haraway uses this linguistic metaphor – cyborg re-coding – and combines it with ideas of 'boundary crossing' or hybridity. Boundary crossing is a term borrowed from anthropologist Mary Douglas (see also **Death and Dying, Religion**), although with some adaptation. For Douglas, there are ways in which the body is permanently 'unfixed', but the body and its products are always symbolic of wider social and political concerns about purity, danger, good and evil. In *Purity and Danger* (1966/2000) Douglas makes clear that it is not only the crossing of bodily boundaries that brings bodily matter under suspicion as potentially polluting, but that by the same token whole bodies are endangered when either their boundaries are breached, they breach the boundaries of others, or they are implicated in the crossing of social boundaries. The moral and ethical aspects of embodiment are inseparable from issues of transgression. Douglas modified this stance somewhat in *Implicit Meanings: Essays in Anthropology* (1975) by admitting her inability to account for the reverence for the (boundary-crossing) pangolin by the Lele people which contrasts so strongly with the Biblical abomination of the pig.

> Foul monster or good saviour, the judgment has little to do with the physical attributes of the being in question and much to do with the prevailing social pattern of rules and meanings which creates anomaly ... Such a response to a mixed category is essentially a gut reaction. (Douglas, 1975: 285)

Boundary-crossing becomes a sign of liminality or indeterminacy, and what is liminal has the potential to confer either sacredness *or* defilement. Douglas situates that judgement firmly in the embodied response: these are 'gut' reactions. Haraway utilizes Douglas' work with respect to bodily boundary crossing being potentially dangerous (which Haraway wants the cyborg to be), but she tends to leave out Douglas' equally important observation that boundary-crossing can be associated with the sacred. That is, boundary-crossing is as much, or more, a force for the status quo rather than revolutionary rewriting.

The body can cross boundaries or have its boundaries crossed. Like Butler, Haraway blurs the line between psychoanalytic theories based around language-formation and culturally embedded ethnographic observations, two domains that do not necessarily sit comfortably together. She also appeals to the arguments of self-creation through language and writing that come from the work of a number of psychoanalytic feminists (see **Psychoanalysis**) such as Kristeva, Irigaray and Wittig. The biotechnological body has also become inextricable from highly sophisticated means of distancing and abstracting the self from intimate relations of life and death. For example, the techno-soldier who is able to wage war without perhaps ever seeing the enemy is distanced, abstracted, from his actions of killing (**Violence**). Cyborg bodies do not reproduce, they regenerate, so there is no need for women to have their labour reduced to the ability to procreate or fulfil a maternal role. Nor need cyborg sex or gender categories be constrained by simple divisions between male and female, masculine and feminine, hence theoretically offering the possibility of rewriting stereotypical and essentialized gender norms.

The essays that follow on from the Manifesto serve to expand upon its basic claims and refine the lists of terms that are divided along the lines of what, in Foucault's terms (**Discourse**), would be called an epistemic shift. For, though she adamantly distances herself from Foucault (1991, 245, n.4), Haraway is telling a story of social construction and historical contextualization. She recognizes this, and it makes her 'nervous'. Haraway is also conscious that relying on metaphors, as she does, can obscure the material relations and material effects of embodied being. Her answer, however, is to try and take control of those metaphors, specifically the metaphorics of vision which so dominates 'objective' scientific endeavours and has done since the seventeenth century. When Haraway writes 'I am arguing for politics and epistemologies of location, positioning, and situating, where partiality and not universality is the condition of being heard to make rational knowledge claims' (1991: 195), she is, I think, arguing that vision is presented as clear and reliable but it too is never objective. Instead, we can be empowered by locating and identifying ourselves with a particular 'point of view' (pov). And in taking control of that metaphorics and becoming 'visionaries', we can use bodily boundaries to our advantage in a techno-poetics of self-construction.

We are rewritable because we are text. And other texts – such as science fiction and science fantasy – become tools at the service of this rewriting. Haraway offers the narratives of science fiction as utopian alternatives to current lived conceptions of sex, gender, embodiment, society and politics. Rewriting the female body as a replicator – linked in to the creative potential of the internet and reproductive technologies – not as a reproducer, is part of this freeing us all from the bonds of a science that pretends it is 'natural'.

The primary reading on cyborgs is, of course, Haraway both in her initial conception of the Cyborg Manifesto (1991) and in her subsequent elaboration on the theme of the liberatory power of technology (1997). Balsamo (1996) extends Haraway's ideas into the meaning of gender in technology, and is particularly concerned with women's self-construction within aesthetic surgery, bodybuilding, reproductive technologies and virtual realities. For a greater understanding of Haraway's use of Mary Douglas' work on dangerous bodies in her anthropological research, see Douglas' original works (1966/2006; 1970/1996; 1975) which are engaging and very approachable reading.

REFERENCES

Balsamo, A. (1996) *Technologies of Gendered Bodies: Reading Cyborg Women*. Durham, NC and London: Duke University Press.

Douglas, Mary (1975) *Implicit Meanings: Essays in Anthropology*. London and Boston: Routledge and Kegan Paul.

Douglas, Mary (1996) *Natural Symbols: Explorations in Cosmology* (with a new Introduction). London: Routledge. First published 1970.

Douglas, Mary (2000) *Purity and Danger: An Analysis of Concept of Pollution and Taboo*. London: Routledge. First published 1966.

Haraway, Donna (1991) *Simians, Cyborgs and Women: The Reinvention of Nature*. London: Free Association Books.

Haraway, Donna (1997) *Modest_Witness@Second_Millennium.FemaleMan©_Meets_ OncoMouse™: Feminism and Technoscience*. New York and London: Routledge.

key concepts in
body and society

48

Death and Dying

Definition In the most straightforward terms, death is the cessation of life and dying is the process which culminates in death. However, in the developed world, since the 1960s, a body may continue to experience blood circulation, respiration and bodily excretion and yet be considered no longer to be 'alive' due to the lack of discernible higher-cognitive function. This is due to the development of life-supporting respiratory technology and, as a direct consequence of this technology, the formulation of the ancillary diagnosis of 'brain death'. Conversely, in the developing world, millions die of preventable diseases and treatable conditions.

Death and dying are complex, social processes. Funerary ritual marks the moment of a community's acknowledgement of the loss of a community member. This may happen in the context of family, kin group, village or national loss and mourning. In whatever context, the dead body is the object of the proceedings and there will be ceremonies and practices associated with appropriately dealing with the body. Burial (by land or at sea) was once considered the only appropriate means of disposing of Christian remains. However, in the latter 40 years of the twentieth century this has been overtaken as the dominant practice by cremation in the UK (Jupp, 2006) – and other Commonwealth countries such as Canada, Australia and New Zealand – rising steeply from World War II onwards, to 34.7 per cent in 1960 and 73.3 per cent in 2009 (http://www.srgw.demon.co.uk/CremSoc4/Stats/National/ProgressF. html). Cremation is common to many cultures, one of the most famous examples being the open Hindu pyres beside the Ganges in Varanasi, India. Some groups of Indigenous peoples (North American, Australian, Melanesian) traditionally leave their dead in the branches of trees to decay for months or years, after which the bones may be cleaned and placed in a sacred place. In medieval and early modern Europe the tradition of storing bones (ossuaries) was also common, particularly amongst some orders of monks, and is still practised in parts of Greece. Mummification is well known to have been practised in Ancient Egypt, Iceland and areas of South America. Funeral rituals and funerary practices vary enormously around the world, across time and between cultures, but cultural practices of marking the death of a community member and tending to their bodily remains are universal. Conversely, one who is outside the bounds of the community, for example 'paupers' or criminals, might be accorded only the most basic rites. Death, then, relates to a specific moment and the attendant observances performed with respect to the body. Dying is an experiential and relative *process*. One person may consider themselves to be dying from the moment an unfavourable diagnosis is presented;

another person may consider themselves to be very much alive up until their final breath.

As can be seen under **Religion** that Mary Douglas, in her discussion of the sacred and profane, has argued that what is considered abominable can also become revered. Douglas, referring to the Lele tribe's cult around the pangolin, relates this to the ultimate bodily act or attribute that is inseparable from physical corruption, and therefore implicit pollution: death.

> Just as the focus of all pollution symbolism is the body, the final problem to which the perspective of pollution leads is bodily disintegration. Death presents a challenge to any metaphysical system, but the challenge need not be squarely met. (2000; 174)

Death is abject and horrifying, awe-inspiring and revered: sacred and profane. In some cultures it is welcomed and for many individuals it is feared. Whether accounted for positively or negatively, it is universally respected and attended by ritual practices: 'we find corruption enshrined in sacred places and times' (2000; 180). In the same contradictory counterpoint that Douglas used to balance extreme pollution and its re-absorption, the ultimate form of corruption affirms life and in this we are again 'all the same'.

The discussion of death and dying in what follows is largely a dilemma of developed countries, where the means of both prolonging life and of being able to make decisions about medically-assisted death are available. As noted in the example from Papua New Guinea related under **Health and Illness**, a diagnosis of breast cancer or a brain tumour that would be treatable and even 'curable' in a country with a functioning health system becomes a death sentence because of near complete lack of primary facilities and treatments, let alone radiotherapy and chemotherapy. A quick glance at any of the World Health Organization's statistics on mortality and morbidity in developing countries shows that the experiences of death and dying in countries with poor sanitation, poor access to water, dysfunctional health systems, endemic poverty and pandemic diseases (malaria, HIV/AIDS, tuberculosis and polio to name a few) appears to be little different from that experienced in early modern Europe. Approximately one million deaths a year, mostly of children in Africa, are attributable to malaria, which is both a preventable and treatable parasitic infection (http://www.who.int/mediacentre/factsheets/fs094/en/). While lifespans are increasing across the board, the disparity between life expectancies in the poorest and the richest countries remains stark. In developing countries, death remains more present and more likely, and dying is a process undergone largely in the care of family or community members.

In the developed world, death and dying are much less open and visible than has been the case in the past or may remain the case in other cultures. Death has moved firmly into the hands of professionals; doctors, nurses, funeral directors, palliative care specialists, etc. This was not always the case. Various waves of the (Bubonic) Plague occurred across Europe between the mid-fourteenth and the late-seventeenth century, which led to open transportation of bodies and massed communal burials taking place (see *The Diary of Samuel Pepys* for a contemporary account).[2] This emphasized the public nature of death. However, up to at least the nineteenth century, one was far more likely to die at home in bed, even under a doctor's care, than in a hospital or hospice (Ariès, 1981; Elias, 1985). In Europe, only the workhouse poor or those without relatives had to rely on strangers to witness their death and see to their burial. Death and dead bodies, then, were not unfamiliar, and with higher mortality rates mourning was a more familiar experience (though, despite Ariès' thesis (1981), not necessarily a less grieved one) than most people in developed countries are accustomed to.

In the *Loneliness of the Dying* (1985) Norbert Elias set the tone for a range of studies into the shifting practices in relation to the dying and the increasing institutionalization and professionalization of the final days (or months, or years) of life in the West. While he does not openly discuss the body, much as in the discussion of embodied manners in *The Civilizing Process*, the body is not theorized upon specifically, yet it is clearly implicit in Elias' speaking of the physicality of dying, death and decay. He is interested in the sociality of death, in the 'repression' of death from social consciousness: the receding from public/attended deaths and a movement towards contemporary habits of private/hidden, and at times extraordinarily lonely, death. He contrasts this with the open physicality of death of former times, using as examples the open celebration of breasts and lips in death, of worms and corruption. It is true that the seventeenth-century English poets John Donne or Andrew Marvell could, and frequently did, link death and sexual delights. They did so in meditation on the transience of earthly pleasures, in ways that

---

[2]The disease has not disappeared, but it is now treatable. Later waves affected the Middle East and, into the twentieth century, China.

are manifestly different from recent artistic fetishizations of dissected bodies, as in the work of Damien Hirst who has set butchered animals in perspex and exhibited photographs of himself smiling beside a severed head in a morgue. But then, when Marvell or Donne wrote of rotting flesh, they had first-hand experience of it in their everyday lives, thanks in no small part to the Plague. They were warning their audience to enjoy the warmth of life while it is available: death and Judgement Day will come soon enough. The more recent repression of the social function of death and dying that Elias writes of extends to the care of the deceased and their resting places. In the West, the care of graves, and of bodies, is now the province of specialists rather than family members. With this particularization and professionalization of death processes, combined with longer life spans, death has become more remote both for the individual and for society except in circumstances where the physical realities of massed death cannot be avoided, as in war (Elias, 1985: 50–1) (**Violence**). The necessity to adjust to the greater frequency and visibility of death is observable in the similar realities evident in massive natural disasters, such as the 2004 Boxing Day Tsunami that killed over 200,000 people in total, leaving tens of thousands of bodies to be cremated, and thousands more who were buried under debris, never to be recovered. In this instance, although those killed were overwhelmingly from the developing countries which were inundated, several of those countries are tourist destinations popular around the globe and the graphic reporting of the deaths was felt worldwide.[3]

As a result of this process of individualization, and the hiding away of even the approach of death in hospitals and nursing homes, the embodied experiences of the dying – and particularly the aged dying – are treated differently within society. That is, they are predominantly valued or understood only by those most directly involved in their daily care: close family members and nursing staff. Ageing bodies have gradually shifted from being cared for within village life/family groups, to industrialized, specialized, institutionalized 'care' facilities for the ageing and dying – which 'means not only the final severing of old affective ties, but also means living together with people with whom the individual has no positive affective relationships' (Elias, 1985: 74) (see also **Ageing and Childhood**). Elias closes this brief but important book with the observation that our increasing concentration on the fragmented body

---

[3]The politically troubled and non-tourist areas of Aceh and the (Tamil) east coast of Sri Lanka were two of the worst affected, but drew the least reporting.

(**Consumption** and **Medicine and Science**) is at the cost of the whole person: 'It is perhaps not yet quite superfluous to say that care for people sometimes lags behind the care for their organs' (Elias, 1985: 91).

The approach and experience of death is now far more likely to take place in a hospital or a nursing home in developed countries, no matter what the cause. Even those people who might otherwise have simply died at home – for example, from a catastrophic stroke – are more likely to be transported to hospital for death to be pronounced officially by a doctor, and from there, if the condition was known, to be taken to funeral parlour, or if unknown, more likely to a coroner's office. All sorts of complications can arise when people do not die under the observing eye of a clinician where there is a functional and watchful health system.

Conversely, the representation of both prosthetic and actual dead bodies has become more graphic in popular culture. There is a plethora of television dramas based around autopsies, in which lurid, model body parts are salaciously displayed; and where broadcasters may be shy of showing images on free-to-air news programmes, such images are uploaded by news agencies, governments and perpetrators in graphic footage of war, murder and dismemberment online. The hanging of Saddam Hussein is one such example, where the officially released footage of his death stopped at the placing of the noose around his neck, but mobile phone footage of his death by hanging quickly surfaced on the internet. Various major national and international news agencies played the official version in their free-to-air reporting, in some instances criticizing the practice while at the same time providing information on where the full footage could be found. Further, the study of bodies postmortem, the meaning and ritual surrounding the deceased across cultures, and the treatment of the dying are all important to the study of the body in society. Cemeteries can also be sites of community, with traditions persisting of family members tending graves on a regular basis in diasporic Greek Orthodox, Islamic and Roman Catholic communities in the midst of more abstracted and non-observant societies (**Race/Ethnicity, Religion**).

The discussion of death and dying also entails a discussion of the meaning and importance of suicide. From a psychological standpoint, suicide is generally assumed to be an irrational act, one that requires treatment for the underlying pathology that has provoked the desire. Durkheim, famously, saw this issue from a rather different, social perspective and argued that suicide was a social rather than an individual problem due to the individual feeling socially alienated, which could be averted through improved social integration. Suicide in the context of a terminal illness can be seen as an ultimate act of liberal individualism and is more likely to be spoken of in terms of euthanasia, although the same issues of rationality (**Dualism**) and coercion are regularly raised in objection. If one's identity is bound to a notion of autonomy, in which the mind retains precedence over the material body, an informed rational decision to want to choose the moment of ending personal suffering is in keeping with that identity.

Some of the earlier discussion related to sophisticated medical practices that enable the prolongation of life become relevant here. As the ability to extend life increases through more sophisticated medical treatments and the medical technologies that brought about the formulation of the concept of brain death in the first place, the notion of 'quality of life' becomes an issue. Euthanasia – an ultimate act of bodily control – is frequently argued for on the grounds of rights (mental social facts) but they are at the same time strongly linked to what level of bodily, existential and experiential discomfort or dissatisfaction one is prepared to put up with (**Phenomenology**). Dualistic understandings of the body put cognitive decisions at the forefront of controlling bodily processes. So, in modern medical practice informed consent for the commencement or cessation of treatment, based on rational decision-making capacities of the individual, is legally required. Conversely, a person's rational capacity to consent is put into question if they request the cessation of treatment, and particularly if they ask for assistance to die. This is not the case in all developed countries, for example in the Netherlands and Switzerland medically assisted euthanasia is possible and legal. And even in conservative societies the doctrine of 'double-effect' – that is, administering potentially lethal medication with the *intention* of alleviating suffering with the predictable outcome that it will also shorten life – is practised. However, the decision to do so is in the hands of the medical practitioner, not the patient. This has led to considerable ethical and legal debate, particularly in the case of euthanasia 'tourism' to Dignitas clinics in Switzerland where medically assisted suicide is legal.

FURTHER READING

As with childhood, a great deal of argument and research has flowed from the writings of Ariès (1974, 1981, 1985). I have not gone into his writing on death in detail here as it is based on a very selective study of funerary monuments that is not supported by wider historical research into death and dying. However, his work is worth reading alongside writers such as Elias (1985), who gives a more socially textured meditation on the experiences of dying and death under more contemporary conditions, and Douglas (1966/2000, 1970/1996) who introduces different cultural and symbolic nuances around death and dying. Gittings (1984) takes a socio-historical approach to death and individuality as understood in a specific (early modern) period, but in relying on a greater breadth of documentary evidence she introduces a textured specificity that Ariès does not. Hallam et al. (1999), by contrast, are interested in contemporary understandings and social trends in dying and death practices. Other areas that the reader might like to look into are social studies of palliative care, and the allied foundational psychological text in that area, Elisabeth Kübler-Ross's *On Death and Dying*. For the statistical facts of death around the world, see the WHO websites, which are regularly updated.

REFERENCES

Ariès, Phillipe (1974) *Western Attitudes to Death from the Middle Ages to the Present*. Baltimore: Johns Hopkins University Press.

Ariès, Phillipe (1981) *The Hour of Our Death*, trans. H. Weaver. London: Allen Lane.

Ariès, Phillipe (1985) *Images of Man and Death*, trans. J. Lloyd. Cambridge, MA: Harvard University Press.

Douglas, M. (1996) *Natural Symbols: Explorations in Cosmology* (with a new Introduction). London: Routledge. First published 1970.

Douglas, M. (2000) *Purity and Danger: An Analysis of Concept of Pollution and Taboo*. London: Routledge. First published 1966.

Durkheim, E. (1952) *Suicide*. London: Routledge & Kegan Paul. First published 1897.

Elias, Norbert (1985) *The Loneliness of the Dying*, trans. E. Jephcott. London: Continuum.

Elias, Norbert (2000) *The Civilizing Process: Sociogenetic and Psychogenetic Investigations* (revised edition), trans. E. Jephcott., E. Dunning, J. Goudsblom and S. Mennell (eds). Oxford: Blackwell Publishers. First published 1936.

Gittings, Clare (1984) *Death, Burial and the Individual in Early Modern England*. London: Croom Helm.

Hallam, E., J. Hockey and G. Howarth (1999) *Beyond the Body: Death and Social Identity*. London: Routledge.

Jupp, P. (2006) *From Dust to Ashes: Cremation and the British Way of Death*. Basingstoke: Palgrave Macmillan.

Kübler-Ross, E. (1997) *On Death and Dying*. New York: Scribner.

World Health Organization, Data and Statistics http://www.who.int/research/en/index.html

death and dying

Definition Difference is an extremely broad concept. Difference is tied to the practices of defining and excluding the 'self' from the 'other', and the 'other' from a perceived social 'norm'. Difference is relational: it frequently implies binary oppositions between the category defined and the (unspoken) category from which differentiation is made. This process is accompanied by value judgement(s) which position the differentiated as the 'low' category and the unspoken norm as the 'high' category. In relation to the body in society, categories of difference are frequently formed on the basis of bodily characteristics, the most basic of which is the differentiation between male and female.

In social terms, difference is implicated in many (if not all) of the terms covered in other sections in this book. The most obvious examples occur within the social definitions of **Ageing and Childhood, Appearance and Beauty, Class/Caste, Colonialism/Post-colonialism, Disability/Ability, Gender/Sex, Identity** and **Race/Ethnicity**. Each of these categories has some basis in the construction and/or perception of bodily attributes which are then coded with social and cultural meaning that carries with it judgements of what is and is not valued. Difference, then, is inextricably mingled with the social construction of embodied markers – that is, in the interpretation of materiality.

The sex/gender distinction, as dominantly understood in terms of male/masculine and female/feminine, is probably the most basic of differences employed in relation to the body in society. Under **Gender/Sex** there is a broader discussion of the challenges to that narrow conception of gender, but here we will look at its development and its power. In modern medical discourse (**Medicine and Science**) the standard, and historically idealized, human body is that of the male. From the first illustrated anatomical manuals to appear in Europe in the fourteenth century, it is the male body that is used as a model for understanding the structure and the treatment of the body. In Renaissance art and architectural principles, the male body was the model of perfect godly proportions underpinning aesthetic theories. In both anatomical illustrations and in medical texts discussing ailments and cures, the female body only appeared in terms of generation; that is, in discussions of the female reproductive capacities. All other systems of the body were presented as male (Cregan, 2009). Females were defined in terms of their *difference* from the male norm. And in that construction, they were imperfect. That differentiation is at the base of a wealth of associations which have had concrete effects on the embodied lives of women (Gatens, 1996) and can still be found in assumptions around treatments and dosage rates of drugs. The recent promotion of a Viagra-like medication for women is an example of such an assumption that ignores the different sexual physiologies and erotic psychologies of men and women.

The construction of difference as founded in sexual difference has formed a site of a great deal of debate in feminism (**Feminism**). It underpins the discourses around social and political equality (rejecting difference) and also debates around rights based in difference, for example maternity leave. It is also at the heart of a great deal of French feminist thought, particularly in psychoanalytic feminisms. The theories of Kristeva, Cixous and Irigaray all turn on a recognition and celebration of the differences of women from men and staking out a feminine 'space', often in relation to the formation and uses of language (**Feminism**). Nor, it should be remembered, is 'woman' a homogenous category, any more than 'man' is.

If one looks at the paired categories we began with, it is easy to see how each holds a sense of binary oppositional difference within it: that is, difference that implies a normative, approved and/or idealized term that is asymmetrically related to an excessive, deficient or non-normative 'other'. We often know what is valued or reviled because of what it is *not*. Disability is a category from which the boundaries of an unspoken, able-bodied norm are marked out. The (fictional) category of race is almost inextricable from notions of scientifically verifiable purity in the 'self' and immutable, embodied inferiority in the 'other'. Ethnicity defines people as belonging to various linguistic or social groups in terms of their difference from a dominant group whose ethnicity is rarely enunciated, notwithstanding whether it is used to oppress or empower. Children and youth are defined as *not* being adults, most often in terms that accord with the UN Convention on the Rights of the Child, in which adults possess power and the non-adult has the status of one incapable of agency and who is in need of 'care'. Colonial power actively defines the differences between the

difference

settler and the settled/Indigenous peoples, rhetorically and politically subordinating the latter. Class and caste are not so much binary category systems, based as they are on multiple levels of differentiation between classes or castes, but they nevertheless express levels of distinction between (and over) a range of social categories based on bodily traits.

Of all of the terms mentioned at the beginning, the concept of identity is probably the most open to association with all manner of what might be called differences after **Gender/Sex**. Identity is a concept that most clearly makes a claim to an 'essence' – that is, that a person's identity is a basic category of self and being. (This is challenged by understandings such as performativity, in which identity is seen as a changing and unstable process rather than as having an immutable and original source.) Identity is a conscious demarcation of self (same) and other (different). Sander Gilman (1985) has argued that constituting self and differentiating the other can lead to the pathologization of the latter. That is, difference can become a categorization that implies physical or mental illness in the 'other'. He gives the examples of the stereotypes that associate physical and mental illness with people who were considered very much 'other' in the eighteenth and nineteenth centuries. African women were stereotyped as hyper-sexualized and were the objects of anatomical prurience (**Colonialism/Post-colonialism, Nature/Culture**); European prostitutes were contemporaneously stereotyped as diseased; and all manner of 'others' were stereotyped as fundamentally prone to irrationality or 'madness' (African men, Jews, artists …). So, difference is not just a means of categorization it is also the vector for discrimination against the other.

From these examples it is clear that the work of difference is, in each case, based on an embodied divergence from what is considered 'normal' and socially acceptable, that has been framed through processes of value-judgement as 'aberrance'. For example, artists like Van Gogh or Toulouse-Lautrec did not fit the middle- and upper-class expectations of their families and a great deal of how they were understood in their own time centred on the pathologies and/or disabilities attributed to them. Indeed, these matters continue to flow through into the interpretation of their art today. Van Gogh's paintings of the night sky are seen as symptomatic of hallucinatory mania and his self-portrait in which his ear is bandaged cannot be mentioned without being glossed as an example of suicidal self-harm.

Similarly, the assumption that prostitutes are diseased, which has been rife for centuries, persists into the present. This is despite the simple logic that any infection that a sex-worker might contract is highly likely to have been passed on to them by a client. Indeed, those sex-workers employed in licensed brothels are far more likely to be subject to regular checks for STDs and are therefore much less likely to pass on disease to their clientele than the brothel patrons are to infect the sex-workers. The ascription of irrationality on the basis of difference may vary over time, but a quick survey of the action cinema of the past 20 years provides evidence of sufficient 'mad' terrorists of a number of national or ethnic backgrounds to carry the point; as does any review of the reporting of political uprisings, particularly in post-colonial states (**Violence**).

On the other hand, difference can also involve agency. Much of the politico-social activism of the past 40 years – under the radicalizing influence of post-structuralism, post-modernism, feminisms and deconstruction – has been based on taking terms of oppression or positions of subjection and recasting them as terms and positions of empowerment. Within this dynamic of making (what the dominant paradigm marks out as) a vice into a virtue, embodiment has been key. To overturn the dominant understanding in each instance, 'owning' embodied states, rewriting pejorative meanings ascribed to them and making them socially visible has led to social change (see **Colonialism/Postcolonialism, Disability/Ability, Feminism, Gender/Sex, Gesture and Habits, Queer**, etc.).

FURTHER READING

See also the reading lists for **Disability/Ability, Colonialism/Postcolonialism, Gender/Sex, Nature/Culture, Queer** and **Sexuality**.

There are innumerable writings on bodily difference. A good starting point is Sherry Ortner's (1974) essay on gender and bodily difference, and Gatens' (1995) related monograph that questions the ethics and practical effects of the construction of embodied gender differences. Gilman's books (1985, 1988) trace the cultural construction of difference through medical discourses both in the past and into contemporary cultures. Cregan (2009) examines the historical construction of sex and gender in popular sixteenth- and seventeenth-century anatomical texts in connection with art and architectural theory.

difference

REFERENCES

Cregan, K. (2009) *The Theatre of the Body: Embodying Life and Staging Death in Early-Modern London.* Turnhout: Brepols Publishers.

Gatens, M. (1995) *Imaginary Bodies: Ethics, Power and Corporeality.* London: Routledge.

Gilman, S. (1985) *Difference and Pathology: Stereotypes of Sexuality, Race and Madness.* Ithaca, NY: Cornell University Press.

Gilman, S. (1988) *Disease and Representation: Images of Illness from Madness to AIDS.* Ithaca, NY: Cornell University Press.

Ortner, S (1974) 'Is female to male as nature is to culture?', pp. 67–87 in M.Z. Rosaldo and L. Lamphere (eds) *Woman, Culture and Society.* Stanford, CA: Stanford University Press.

Disability/Ability

Definition Ability and disability are bio-psychosocial categories as much as they are markers of the capacities of bodies and/or minds. The medical diagnosis of particular physical and mental conditions leads to people being socially judged as 'disabled'. Disability is used as a blanket term to distinguish people as not 'able-bodied'. Ability is a normative term that assumes certain physical and cognitive capacities in the general population, despite the fact that those capacities are widely variable in any population.

key concepts in body and society

60

Into the 1960s in the developed world, those people who had received a medical diagnosis that put them into the category of what might now be labelled 'disabled' were frequently institutionalized. At the time, the terms used – often as playground weapons of insult – were more likely to be 'crippled', 'retarded', 'feeble-minded' or 'spastic'. It is only as a result of decades of change in practices and the progressive neutralization in the terminology that these earlier definitions have receded. People with cognitive diagnoses were the most likely to be put 'into care' and many babies with early outward signs of either physical or mental conditions (for example Down's Syndrome, cerebral palsy, blindness), were often institutionalized shortly after birth.

Disability can also be acquired, through acute illness or injury (paralysis, brain injury) in which physical and/or cognitive impairment occurs. There are also conditions, like schizophrenia, which typically do not manifest until early adulthood. People with acquired injuries were less likely to be institutionalized but even if they were not, the services and facilities to enable them to lead independent lives simply did not exist on any scale before the 1970s. Disability was both defined in bodily terms and implied a state of bodily dependence.

Like many of the battles fought under the banner of feminism, disability activists have had such an impact on public policy since that time that it can sometimes be difficult for anyone born after 1990 to comprehend the degree of change that has occurred since the 1960s. Before disability activism, people labelled as disabled were out of the public eye and little consideration was given to basic amenities that make independent living possible. The disabled body was neither literally nor figuratively visible to the general public. Thanks to disability activists, matters like adequate wheelchair access are acknowledged in building codes, council bylaws and public transport regulations, even if these are not implemented everywhere they could be (see Gleeson and Gathorne-Hardy in Butler and Parr, 1999). The political activism around disabilities that arose in the 1970s was in response to the institutionalization and unequal treatment of people of different abilities. Disability activists were central to the de-institutionalization of hundreds of thousands of people who had been deemed to be inappropriate members of society. So, ability and disability are the social recognition and categorization of embodied properties, with very real socio-political consequences for those so categorized (Oliver, 2009).

Following on from early activism, disability has become a huge area of academic research, particularly in the social sciences. As a bodily key concept, disability and ability rely on bodily evidence for the diagnosis which leads to the social and political effects – whether liberatory or oppressive. Aspects of disability studies have focused very clearly on the bodily effects of specific bodily and psychological conditions, whether congenital, developed or acquired. These have included studies of the lived experience of disabilities, often from phenomenological perspectives (**Phenomenology**), such as Seymour's *Remaking the Body* in which people in wheelchairs, from various backgrounds, were interviewed in-depth about their lives. Jean-Dominique Bauby's autobiographical novella *The Diving Bell and the Butterfly* (1997), made into a film of the same name, is a personal narrative of 'locked-in syndrome' that is a confronting testament to the capacity to enjoy a quality of life even in the experience of complete paralysis. The political effects of disabilities and breaking down persistent attitudes to mental conditions within medicine and broader society, as unremittingly negative, has been a core project of the study into disabilities (Jenkins, 1998).

The importance of physical environments, as noted above, in the form of adapting space to take into account a wider variety of needs both in social and work places is another key area of activism and research (Butler and Parr, 1999). Finally, disability studies are at the border between theoretical research and political advocacy, and as a result there has been an enormous amount of work done on making independent living not only conceivable but possible in practice (Imrie in Shakespeare, 1998; O'Brien and Sullivan, 2005; Oliver, 2009). That can include taking into account the range of differences apparent not only in the kinds of conditions encompassed in the term 'disability', but also the differences apparent in wider society that also occur within any population of people living with disability, such as gender, ethnicity and sexuality.

Let me introduce an anecdote from Papua New Guinea (PNG). I was visiting a government department and there was a conference at which PNG disability activists were in attendance. Port Moresby is still something of a 'frontier' town in a country of great natural resources but where 95 per cent of the population subsists outside any formal economy that might provide the most basic infrastructure (Cregan, 2008). So facilities are poor and disabled access pretty much non-existent. These local activists were very angry that they could not enter parliament because there was no wheelchair access and were lobbying, as many disability activists in the developed world would lobby, government departments to introduce equal access to government buildings. This is important work and if PNG is to fulfil its view of inclusivity of all groups – generally understood in terms of the panoply of clans – it should certainly form a part of that inclusivity. At the same time, I could not help contrasting it with a very personal experience of being in a remote island village a few weeks earlier where there were people with disabilities, both mental and physical. One young man had received a brain injury at birth; there was a young woman that a doctor might say was in the grip of psychosis; and there was a man in his thirties who had received a spinal injury in his teens that had left him paraplegic, but who had since married and fathered at least five children. The young man was clearly loved and looked after by the whole village, including the children. The young woman was not acknowledged – she was believed to be possessed and eye contact was considered dangerous – but she was allowed to take whatever food she needed from various cooking pots or clothes from washing lines and to sleep where she chose. The man with spinal injury lived much of his day in a hut that had holes cut into the woven matting walls to allow him as much of a view of the village as possible. He was visited throughout the day, tended to by his wife and children, and was carried when he needed to move elsewhere. He had had a wheelchair but it proved utterly impractical in sandy soil and a wet climate. What struck me at the time was that, despite the real need for activism in the urban centre, there was much that was positive in what the people of this impoverished country were already doing on the basis of traditional values. There is little doubt that each of these people would benefit from some assistance – nutritional, medical or structural – but they were not being labelled or ostracized: they were members of the village community. What I mean to do by giving such a long anecdotal example is to point up just how socially variable (and determined) a category like disability can be.

FURTHER READING

Oliver's revised book (2009), like Shakespeare's reader (1998), is informed by disability activism and each is probably a good place to start in appreciating the field of disability studies. Shakespeare's more recent book both reviews the field and challenges disability orthodoxies that, in his words, have since 'stagnated' (2006). For a personal narrative of acquired brain injury, see either the book (1997) or the film (2007) of Jean-Dominique Bauby's account of his year of life after a catastrophic stroke. Seymour's (1998) study of men and women with acquired para- and quadriplegia, gives a phenomenological account of people living with disabilities. Jenkins' edited collection (1998) provides analyses of the social construction of intellectual disabilities through a series of cross-cultural studies. Butler and Parr's collection (1999) is from the perspective of human or critical geography and provides a range of essays on aspects of disabled bodies in space. O'Brien and

Sullivan (2005) is more directed at care providers and policy makers, with the intention of promoting partnership and support rather than top down 'service'.

REFERENCES

Bauby, J-D. (1997) *The Diving Bell and the Butterfly*. London: Harper Perennial.

Butler, R. and H. Parr (eds) (1999) *Mind and Body Spaces: Geographies of Illness, Impairment and Disability*. London: Routledge.

Cregan, Kate (2008) 'The informal sector', in P. James, Y. Nadarajah, K. Haive and K. Cregan, *Community Sustainability, Community Livelihoods: Learning for Wellbeing, Resilience and Sustainability in Papua New Guinea*. Ministerial Report for the Department For Community Development, Papua New Guinea.

Jenkins, Richard (ed.) (1998) *Questions of Competence: Culture, Classification and Intellectual Disability*. Cambridge: Cambridge University Press.

O'Brien, P. and M. Sullivan (2005) *Allies in Emancipation: Shifting from Providing Service to Being of Support*. Melbourne: Dunmore Press.

Oliver, M. (2009) *Understanding Disability: From Theory to Practice*, 2nd edn. London: Macmillan.

Seymour, Wendy (1998) *Remaking the Body: Rehabilitation and Change*. Sydney: Allen & Unwin.

Shakespeare, Tom (ed.) (1998) *The Disability Studies Reader: Social Science Perspectives*. London: Cassell.

Shakespeare, Tom (2006) *Disability Rights and Wrongs*. London: Routledge.

key concepts in
body and society

Discourse

Definition There are several definitions of discourse, the most prominent of which relate to semiotics (Saussure) and to linguistics (Peirce). In its broadest sense, discourse relates to the flow of language between speakers. In the more specialized sense widely used in sociological research, discourse relates to the nature of the meaning and production of knowledges as they are created in and constructed through language.

Discourse in the latter sense is intimately related to post-structuralism, a wave of theorization that grew in strength in the late 1950s and early 1960s. Post-structuralists, like Roland Barthes, took as a basis the theories of Ferdinand Saussure and used language to explore the disconnection between the materiality (reality) of objects in the world and the symbolic representation of those objects. Saussure used the terms 'the signifier' and 'the signified' to differentiate between a word or symbol and what that symbol was intended to convey. For example, the word 'pear' is a representation (signifier) that bears no resemblance to the materiality of the fruit (what is signified) except in so far as, when we say 'pear' it is understood what is meant. In other words, the ways in which we understand the world – knowledge(s) – are dependent on a process of agreed meaning rather than any necessary objective connection between the signifier and what is signified. In language, we agree that the representation stands in for the material object. This stream of argument is based on a philosophical idea about how we perceive and construct knowledge about reality, that goes back at least as far as Plato's *Republic* and the allegory of the 'cave'.

When talking about embodiment, discourse (or discursive construction) is a term most often associated with the writing of Michel Foucault, and refers to his particular explanations of the way language is used in the production of knowledge(s) (see also **Power**). Much of the writing on discourse and the body in society flows from Foucault's ideas. Discourse in this sense refers not so much to the way people talk as to the way that 'we' authorize particular groups of people to have the right to define and control a particular area of knowledge (episteme), and the language which they use to retain and exert that power (discourse). This is not a power that resides in the control of any one person. Rather, it is the sum total of the power of discourses to influence, shape and control knowledge formation (*The Archaeology of Knowledge*, 1994). Foucault was particularly interested in the way the intersection of power and knowledge is enacted on and through the body.

For instance, doctors use a vocabulary not accessible to most of us when diagnosing illness. That serves not only to help them make diagnoses but it also bestows on them an expertise which entails excluding others from access to that vocabulary. Doctors have control over the discourse of medicine, of the ways of speaking about disease, because they are *recognized* as having the authority and expertise in that sphere: they are the 'authorities of delimitation' (Foucault, 1994). So, it's not just a matter of technical capacity or qualification – some doctors may have access to the discourse but be very poor clinicians – it relies on the inter-play of the power *and* knowledge. Foucault uses the term discourse to describe the language used, and 'episteme' to describe the body of knowledge to which it is related (epistemology being the science or phi-losophy of knowledge). Another important facet of discourse in this sense is that, like language, it is not static. Meanings of individual words can gradually change over time; so too can a discourse and an episteme. This process of discursive change is often referred to as an 'epistemic shift'. A great deal of Foucault's work was engaged in mapping such changes in discourse. The two clearest examples of the body being sub-jected to discourses of power that have shifted over time relate to illness and to sex.

To expand on the example of medicine given above, in the middle of the seventeenth century in Western Europe there was a major shift in the understanding of the world, as the dominant social formations moved from traditional to (early) modern social structures. A part of that shift took a particular form in the understanding and treatment of illness. Where once illness had been largely a domestic and/or spiritual matter, treated on the basis of community knowledge (folk remedy) or by scholastic dogma (physic), it increasingly became the professional-ized business of artisans (surgeons) and university educated secular men (physicians). In Foucault's *The Birth of the Clinic* (1975) we see that by the eighteenth century, illness in the body came into a new kind of exist-ence. Doctors imagined living processes on the basis of anatomical learn-ing from dead bodies and listened to internal sounds. Through the abstracted visualization of and listening to the symptoms, the bounda-ries and the depths and cavities, the body came to be understood through an expert discourse that relied very heavily on metaphors of vision. What we would now call a 'clinical history' as a means of diag-nosis is an outcome of this process where the patient is observed and deductions made from those observations. That visualized knowledge formation and its consequent discourse abstract embodied disease expe-riences into the hands, eyes, ears and mouth of the physician (Foucault: 1975: 119). The symptoms and the experience of disease are abstracted away from the body in which it is housed. It becomes an entity in itself under the medical *gaze* of the physician, over which 'he' has the power of defining. Medical discourses on the body have been the dominant understanding of the human body in Western society ever since, and are taught to small children from the first years of education. (It is also the understanding of the body which underpins medical aid programmes aimed at disease prevention in developing countries, and which, through such mechanisms, I would argue, is increasingly over-writing other understandings of the body.)

In relation to the body as a sexual object, Foucault describes the connections between shifts in discourse and straightforward shifts in language behaviours as much more closely allied (*History of Sexuality, Volume 1*, 1990). Foucault argues, in what has become known as the 'repressive hypothesis', that in the eighteenth century speaking about sexual acts or sexuality moved away from being a permissible topic of public conversation (and theatrical depiction) to a private, pathological, judgemental and incessant discourse. This comes out of the twinned effects of shifts in religious and medical epistemologies. The spiritual confessional is one site of this endless chatter – confessing lewd thoughts and actions – the other is the medico-psychological consulting room where sex became a prime subject of the 'talking cure' (**Psychoanalysis**). Sex became a site of power and control on and through the body, within the descriptive and defining powers of religion and medicine.

> beneath the surface of the sins [discourse] would lay bare the unbroken nervure of the flesh. Under the authority of language that had been carefully expurgated so that it was no longer directly named, sex was taken charge of, tracked down as it were, by a discourse that aimed to allow it no obscurity, no respite. (Foucault, 1990: 20)

That authority was effected through self-regulation and self-control mechanisms, in much the same way as the body is trained within the criminal justice system (**Power**). Diffuse mechanisms of power – under the authority of the Church, the medical establishment, and in law – have led to the repression of sex through the paradoxically repressive 'discourse' *on* sex. It was a discourse that did 'not derive from morality alone but from rationality as well' (Foucault, 1990: 24). This, of course, had obvious effects on the way the body functions in society. If sex is a matter of guilt and endless verbal rehearsal, whole regimens of self-control and self-restraint around sexuality come into play.

This way of describing power, discourse and change over time is one of the most influential concepts within body and society, whether as a template to follow or a concept to refute. It has spawned shifts in ways of talking about many of the other categories within this book – **Difference, Disability/Ability** and **Sexuality**, amongst others.

discourse

FURTHER READING

As noted at the beginning of this section, discourse as discussed here is intimately associated with the writing of Foucault. It is a term that can be found in most of his writing, which is on the whole engaging and clear enough not to require a secondary interpretation, with the exception perhaps of the *Archaeology of Knowledge* (1994) which is one of the more abstract and least historically contextualized of his writings. The fields Foucault discusses in relation to discourse include medicine (1975), psychology and psychiatry (1988a), criminality and criminology (1991), sexuality (1990) and governmental power (1988b).

REFERENCES

Foucault, Michel (1975) *The Birth of the Clinic: An Archaeology of Medical Perception,* trans. A.M. Sheridan Smith. New York: Random House.

Foucault, Michel (1988a) *Madness and Civilization: A History of Insanity in the Age of Reason,* trans. R. Howard. New York: Vintage Books.

Foucault, Michel (1988b) *Politics, Philosophy, Culture: Interviews and Other Writings, 1977–1984,* trans. A. Sheridan and others, L.D. Kritzman (ed.). New York: Routledge.

Foucault, Michel (1990) *The History of Sexuality, Volume 1,* trans. R. Hurley. Harmondsworth: Penguin.

Foucault, Michel (1991) *Discipline and Punish: The Birth of the Prison,* trans. A. Sheridan. London: Penguin.

Foucault, Michel (1994) *The Archaeology of Knowledge,* trans. A.M. Sheridan Smith. London: Routledge.

Dualism

Definition The term dualism refers to a philosophical differentiation between the body and the mind (or spirit). That differentiation is characterized as an inseparable pairing of terms, in which the reasoning mind is privileged over the material body: which are paired in binary opposition

(**Difference**). Although the differentiation between the spirit/mind and the body has been a philosophical and cosmological concept for millennia, this understanding of dualism is most commonly attributed to the seventeenth-century French philosopher, mathematician and anatomical experimenter, René Descartes. The mind is Descartes' 'thinking thing', that is, the functioning of the brain which is characteristic of consciousness. Cognition is the multiplicity of thinking processes that the mind/brain complex performs, which includes the capacity for 'rational' thought. In this materialist explanation, the brain along with the spinal cord is the mechanistic housing of the mind, and forms the central nervous system, which sends and receives neurochemical messages that regulate body processes. These are implicated in the regulation of autonomic bodily processes (e.g. breathing) and the processing of signals sent back from the peripheral nervous system as bodily sensations.

When we talk about dualism today we are generally referring to the ingrained modern understanding of the body that constructs the flesh as a material, mechanical entity which is consciously directed by the mind. Descartes' term *cogito ergo sum* (generally translated as 'I think, therefore I am'), puts the capacity to think in a place of dominance over matter: that is, the mind over the body (1980). Descartes came to this conclusion through meditating on the capacity of humans to think, arguing that the sensations of the material body provided inherently unreliable evidence and that it was the mind that ultimately interpreted the world through the filtering effects of 'Man's' ability to reason (Nature/Culture). The world can only be known through the observational and interpretive abilities of human consciousness. Descartes is often credited as the progenitor of the discipline of psychology, largely on the basis of this particular way of understanding the 'body as machine' which valorizes cognition.

This dualistic understanding of the body is central to the bio-psychosocial understanding of the body that permeates medical discourse (**Cyborgs, Discourse, Medicine and Science**). Descartes was a part of the intellectual revolution that resulted in the slow and uneven shift towards science as the dominant means of understanding phenomena. Scientific method is based on the premise that underlying truths about the world exist, that they can be observed and that reliable knowledge can be built as a result of objectively collecting empirical observations

dualism

69

that test our hypotheses about reality. The 'facts will speak for them-selves' when properly collected. Any student of social science method-ologies and methods should recognize these ideas as positivist and empiricist. So, embedded in the notion that the body can be seen into and diagnosed, is the implication that not only is the mind superior to the body but also the interpretation of the body as a mechanistic entity.

It is dualism that makes it possible to think of the body as an entity made up of individual parts that can be replaced and that it is possible to mend, supplement or improve. A brief survey of the terminology around organ transplantation is illustrative. Organs for transplantation are 'retrieved' from 'donors' as 'spare parts' for people who have an organ that is 'worn out'. Referring to organs as spare parts or worn out clearly contains the idea that the body is just a complicated machine that requires the attention of the bodily mechanic, the transplant sur-geon. To say an organ is retrieved implies that it is being saved (brought back) and that not doing so is a loss or a waste (a common idea in pub-lic appeals for organ donors). The allied term, organ harvesting, suggests the ultimate purpose of the organ is to be removed for productive use elsewhere. In all this organs, and other transplantable tissues, are under-stood as interchangeable parts between malfunctioning bodies. The patient has a body which simply requires a replacement part, like a malfunctioning car, as long as a compatible part can be sourced. The 'donor' – a brain-dead human being who is on life support to maintain the functionality of the spare part until it can be removed – and the processes of what is required for that part to be donated tend to disap-pear in the discourse of mechanical materiality (see Hogle, 1999). This tends to underplay the importance of the inter-related systems in the body and the multitude of balancing acts that must be done, particularly in relation to tissue typing and rejection.

Another similar example can be found in the discourse around other forms of surgery, such as cosmetic surgery and gender reassignment surgery. The body in cosmetic surgery is a project, a material object that can be reshaped, rearranged and augmented to suit the *preferences* (the domain of the mind) of the individual (Elliott, 2008). Elective cosmetic surgery explicitly privileges the mind over the body. Similarly, gender reassignment surgery reconstructs the gendered/genital matter of the individual to match the individual's *beliefs* about their true identity. In the latter case, psychological testing and counselling is mandatory in many countries before such surgery can be performed specifically to test the rationality of the individual in requesting the procedure (Hines and Sanger, 2010). If the mind is deemed rational, the surgery is possible, exemplifying the power granted to the mind over and above the body.

As noted at the beginning of this entry, the effects of dualism on the body in society are a product of the dominance of science in Western European thought, and thus are subject to the same sorts of criticism that have been levelled at what is a very specific way of understanding the world when viewed in its historical context. Dualism is Eurocentric. As part of the complex of European thought taken out with colonists in their exploration, conquest and settlement of other societies, it was a mindset that did not mesh with other ways of viewing and understanding the world and the body.

To take the example of organ transplantation, Margaret Lockwood (2002) conducted an anthropological study of organ donation/transplantation in Japan. She found that there is a comparatively low level of organ donation in Japan, much lower than in other developed countries, and in her study concluded that this was largely because the body as a holistic entity retains a greater social meaning than is generally found in societies that accept dualism. In Japan it is not socially acceptable to put the needs of one individual above those of another individual, or the community, even if that person may be pronounced brain dead. This is at least partly based on the medical fact that the brain dead body has not ceased to function, nor can it be allowed to do so if the organs are to be used for transplanting.

As we can see from the definition, the brain is a biological entity firmly within medical (scientific) understandings of the body. The mind is also a product of science but it is not an observable organ like the brain. Within dualism the brain is the controlling mechanism – the microprocessor – thanks to which the bodily machine is animated. Medical and scientific researchers deduce that there is material evidence of cognition – that is, the working of the mind – in the electrical patterns emitted in the brain during thought. It has been argued that this is evidence that memory 'lives' in and across brain cells, but there is no tangible material entity that can be called 'the mind' – which is the sum of all our thinking processes and, from a sociological point of view, our socio-political lived experiences. The brain can continue its most basic (autonomic) functions with no evidence of the mind performing cognition, for a limited time, and albeit with intensive assistance to maintain life in a body that cannot sustain itself. This state of fragile bodily life without evidence of mental function constitutes the basis of a diagnosis of brain death (**Death and Dying**). Science fiction aside, the human mind cannot function without the brain.

Issues around agency or determinism within the brain–mind complex continue to be key questions in the discipline of psychology, which frequently jar with approaches that are concerned with the body in society. Agency is a key concept in sociology, and remains important to discussions of the body as a social object. For example, there are researchers in psychology and psychiatry who are focused on determining the qualities and capacities of 'male' and 'female' brains respectively. An analysis of the terms used to discuss these phenomena within this research quickly yields deeply embedded social assumptions about these aspects of the material body. Scientific discourses are as embedded in discourses as any other knowledge, and at that level perpetuate what is considered to be 'male' (related to 'masculine' traits), and 'female' (related to 'feminine' traits) (Martin, 1991). To a social constructionist researcher who is dedicated to appreciating all the factors that come together in identity, particularly the social determinants in the formation of an individual's gender, such studies may appear faintly absurd. Other examples, such as the studies into the 'gay' brain are similarly informed by prior sociopolitical understandings of what it is to be gay.

While body studies is a disciplinary field often understood as a reactionary response to dualism, aimed at redressing the long predominance of the mind over the body in intellectual endeavour, the brain and cognition are still, respectively, an organ and a function of the body and so are a part of that project. Indeed, the study of the body is itself experiencing something of a reactionary response, with a resurgence of interest in the mind and the mind–body complex in 'new' studies such as neuroethics. What this goes to show is that dualism remains a potent epistemological force. There are ongoing disputes between positivist, scientific interpretations of embodiment that privilege notions of straightforward materiality and social constructivist or post-modern understandings of the importance of the body in society that investigate the value-laden assumptions that inform taken-for-granted materiality.

Brain, mind and cognition – three terms that encompass consciousness – all rest on dualistic, biologistic assumptions about the body. Yet, they each have concrete social aspects to them. Brain injury, whether congenital or acquired, leads to very real social consequences for those whose lives are affected by such conditions (**Disability/Ability**). Further, the brain holds a particular social and cultural aura. In medieval and Renaissance Christianity it was the part of the body closest to God and its shape was the pattern for architectural structures such as cathedral domes (Edgerton, 1985). Even amongst the rational scientists who have studied the brain in the twentieth century there is a degree of awe attached to particular brains. Einstein's brain is preserved as much as an icon of his intellect as an object of scientific research. It is only slightly larger than the average brain and the cognitive functions it processed became inaccessible with his death. For one Papua New Guinean tribe the brain held a similarly iconic function. The consumption of the brain of an enemy in the practice of *kuru* was considered a means of ceremonially transferring to oneself the defeated warrior's power, and only began to drop out of practice when medical researchers realized it also transferred a terminal neuro-degenerative condition similar in effect to Creutzfeldt-Jakob Disease (Spark, 2005). It is in the study of brain injuries that we see the ephemeral nature of any such division in the phenomenological experiences of those whose embodiment fundamentally questions the primacy of one term over the other.

FURTHER READING

To appreciate dualism in context, it is best to return to Descartes' original in any of its many translations. I have included here several key sociological and anthropological writings around organ transplantation, which is an area that is intimately connected with dualistic approaches to the body (see also **Consumption**). Fox and Swazey historically contextualize the normalization of transplantation. Lockwood, as mentioned, gives cross-cultural insights on the meaning of the body, as does Dickenson (2002) in relation to the ethics of international applications. Hogle's book (1999) is a detailed study of the meaning and change in bodily understanding in Germany across the twentieth century based on witnessing organ transplantation practices, while Youngner et al.'s (1996) collection includes essays on a range of histories and cultural concepts of transplantation. Most general texts on the sociology of the body include a discussion of dualism (for example see Howson, 2004; Shildrick, 1997; Shilling, 1993; Turner, 1984 in the Bibliography) as will many texts concerned with specific debates around the body, and the following reading lists will prove useful: **Colonialism/Post-colonialism**, **Gender/Sex**, **Medicine and Science**, **Performativity**. Martin's essay (1991) is a clear and succinct

dualism

feminist criticism of the unacknowledged gendered and social construction of scientific knowledge. Edgerton (1985) is concerned with the intersection of artistic, legal and medical power as played out through the human body, before dualism. Spark (2005) presents a finely nuanced account of the cultural complexity of medical research around *kuru* and its place in the culture of the Fore of Papua New Guinea.

REFERENCES

Descartes, René (1980) *Discourses on Method*. Harmondsworth: Penguin.

Dickenson, Donna (2002) 'Commodification of human tissue: Implications for feminist and development ethics', *Developing World Bioethics*, Volume 2(1): 55–63.

Edgerton, S.Y. Jr. (1985) *Pictures and Punishment: Art and Criminal Prosecution During the Florentine Renaissance*. Ithaca, NY: Cornell University Press.

Fox, Renée and Judith Swazey (1992) *Spare Parts*. New York: Oxford University Press.

Hogle, L. (1999) *Recovering the Nation's Body: Cultural Memory, Medicine and the Politics of Redemption*. New Brunswick: Rutgers University Press.

Lockwood, M. (2002) *Twice Dead: Organ Transplants and the Reinvention of Death*. Berkeley: University of California Press.

Martin, Emily (1991) 'The egg and the sperm: How science has constructed a romance based on stereotypical male–female roles', *Signs: Journal of Women in Culture and Society*, 16: 485–501.

Spark, C. (2005) 'Learning from the locals: Gajdusek, Kuru and cross-cultural interaction in Papua New Guinea', *Health and History*, 7(2): 80–100.

Youngner, S.J., R. Fox and L. O'Connell (1996) *Organ Transplantation: Meanings and Realities*. Madison: University of Wisconsin Press.

key concepts in
body and society

.... Emotion ....

Definition The physical characteristics of emotion can be described in terms of biochemical or hormonal flows. For example, an autonomic reaction such as a 'fight or flight' response involves the release of hormones from the adrenal glands. They might also be understood in psychological terms as 'affects', that is, outward expressions of diagnostic mental states. However, our more intuitive and common understanding of emotions, and the one we are concerned with here, is as embodied phenomena at a social rather than a biological or biomedical level. So when we are faced with someone experiencing a fight or flight response we are unlikely to think, 'that person is producing excess cortisol', and much more likely to intuit on the basis of their facial expression, tone of voice and bodily motions that they are feeling the emotions of aggression or fear, respectively. Emotions are cross-cultural phenomena but, like humour, there is cultural variability in how they are interpreted and understood.

It is important for us to be able to recognize and learn the embodied emotional responses in others of fear, anger, happiness and sadness – amongst the wide range and subtlety of human emotional display – in order to get along in the world as social beings. 'Like languages, emotions result from a merger of an unlearned and a learned process' (Elias, 1991: 116), from a mix of biological propensities and the cultural norms of given social formations (**Nature/Culture**). Failure to respond appropriately to emotions can lead to loss of social status in some instances, or what in East Asian societies is known as a 'loss of face'. In Bourdieu's terms (**Habitus**), to respond inappropriately is to lack sufficient expertise in the 'rules' of a 'field of play', those being the factors and social skills that determine the ability of an individual to succeed in his or her social grouping. In more recent pop-scientific terms, to misunderstand embodied emotional responses it is to lack Emotional Intelligence (EI), a psychological index that claims poor performance (as scored on EI tests) will affect life chances.

If we look at the discussion under **Dualism** (see also **Gender/Sex** and **Nature/Culture**) we can see that there is a direct link between the increasing valorization of everything 'rational' (masculine) over and above the 'emotional' (feminine) during the seventeenth and eighteenth centuries (see Schiebinger 1993). In scientific method and philosophy, objectivity is applauded primarily because it is constructed as a *rational, pure and truthful* means of acquiring knowledge. This is in direct opposition to subjectivity, which is characterized as an *unreliable, emotional and impure* means of acquiring knowledge (Lloyd, 1993). This positivist privileging of dispassionate detached inquiry is, of course, far from being value-free. Purity and truth in method – so defined – was and is socially, culturally and politically situated in ways that privilege those people who possess expertise in, and access to, that method: privileged men. Emotionality is constructed as indicative of incompletely acquired civility or civilization (**Civilizing Processes**) and, historically, became absorbed into understandings of all kinds of 'others' (**Difference**): children, women, people of other cultures and different abilities were understood to be less civilized, irrational and emotional. Emotions are to be distrusted because they are, in this logic, disconnected from the rational, controlling thought processes of the mind.

Civilizing processes teach the *control of bodily responses*, overt displays of emotion are part of what leads to the ascription of irrationality. Part of that controlling process involved the internalization of rules on the basis of avoiding a particular emotional response. In the discussion of **Civilizing Processes**, we can see that a range of bodily practices became the object of greater control over a number of centuries in Western culture. Those bodily practices included toileting, eating and sleeping, amongst others. The motivating mechanism that spurred the adoption of the approved behaviours, and the relegation of those that were disapproved of, was the emotion of shame. The feeling of being embarrassed or shamed in front of one's peers and 'betters' for behaving in an inappropriate manner, Elias argued, was sufficient to perpetuate the civilizing process. Where burping was once acceptable (even applauded) during a meal it gradually became a sign of coarseness. Similarly, rules around the (proper) use of implements at table were social markers that embarrassed the person who displayed their in-expertise. The dynamic of shame – which is an unpleasant emotion, if one is capable of feeling it – remains, but the markers which we find shameful shift. One who does not feel shame, or is not capable of emulating it when required, will not be able to attain a higher status.

This also has cross-cultural ramifications. If one is not versed in the emotional range of a culture one will also have trouble succeeding or adjusting and therefore succeeding socially. The open expression of emotions is considered inappropriate in many cultures. This can lead to the misunderstanding of emotional states both at a simple social level– misreading a smile of politeness for one of agreement – and at more complex levels – when the cultural expression of a mental state is radically different from a Western medical model of a given 'affect', leading to misdiagnoses of psychological conditions. This is closely allied to the cultural differences in gestures and habits (**Gesture and Habits**). It is also a factor that has arisen in qualitative social research methodologies aimed at cross-cultural studies, where it might be easy to misread the emotional cues of participants in interview situations. In qualitative research, the ability to perceive emotions can be an important factor, particularly in relation to observational techniques

Emotions are embodied responses with embodied social effects and social expression. Arlie Hochschild (1983), in her study of people working in service industries, was one of the first sociologists to conduct research on the meaning and effect of emotions in the production of social life. Hochschild's study was an extension and rewriting of Goffman's notion of body work, from the perspective of the gendered nature of emotional work (**Appearance and Beauty, Identity**). Her central research subjects were in service industries, predominantly as (female) flight attendants and also in a comparative sample of (male) debt collectors. Hochschild demonstrated that the conscious attempts of the flight attendants to cover up emotions through face work (for example, smiling when angry) and the internalized attempts to manipulate emotions such as anger into compassion when in stressful situations (deep acting), which were an expected part of their labour, had physical and emotional consequences for those who employed these strategies in the workplace. She also showed that women were more likely both in expectation and in practice to undertake this kind of emotional labour. As noted under **Appearance and Beauty**, these embodied/emotional strategies are social coping mechanisms that may take a particular form in the modern commercial workplace but they have also been embedded in spiritual teachings and had gendered associations for millennia.

There are approaches to the study of the body in society which are particularly amenable to the sociology of emotions. Phenomenological research is concerned to comprehend the full range of embodied experience (**Phenomenology**). Part of that programme is to account for sensations, which we know include not only the physical signals of external stimuli returned from nerve endings but which also comprehend the feelings of emotions. Phenomenological techniques are particularly popular in the sociology of health and illness and the focus on experiential embodied research means that the inclusion of emotions is highly appropriate to such studies. As Williams and Bendelow note (1998: 148) there has been a turn in health and illness research and practice to notions of 'holistic health' that are connected to emotional work. This manifests in a turn to both talking through emotions – the ubiquity of counselling as a structural response to any kind of distress – and ideas of emotions as being tied in to disease states. This can lead to conflicting messages. On the one hand, people can feel empowered that they can mentally affect a disease state, by taking control of their emotional response and using positive thinking as much as healthy eating in responding to disease. On the other hand, people can blame themselves and ascribe responsibility to their emotional responses for particular disease states: for example, women expressing the belief they have given themselves breast cancer because they are worriers (Panjari et al., 2011) or taking on responsibility for the management of their endometriosis (Seear, 2009).

As we can see from Hochschild's example, the sociology of emotions is closely linked to issues of gender. This gendered aspect of emotions extends into debates around the 'democratization' of emotions, specifically in terms of the separation of sex from emotional attachment to be found in post-1960s discourses of guilt-free sexuality (**Sexuality**). It is notable that in the period when emotions first became devalued as irrational and un-scientific in Western culture, in the late seventeenth century, Libertines (Rakes) who promoted sex free from emotion became visible in social life and on stage: in that construction sensation is masculine, emotion is feminine. Lawrence Stone (1977) has famously argued that Romantic love is an invention of nineteenth-century bourgeois sentimentality as expressed through marriage and a particular construction of 'family', which is the forebear of the contemporary nuclear family unit.

FURTHER READING

As noted above, Hochschild (1983, 1998) was one of the earliest researchers in the field of the sociology of emotions, and is highly influential in the field. Elias' discussion of the effect of emotions runs throughout *The Civilizing Process* but is perhaps most succinctly expressed in his 1991 essay in Featherstone et al.'s collection. Barbalet (1998) places emotions in social context, arguing that they are integral to socio-political structure and processes rather than just spontaneous expressions that are described as happening at moments of change. Bendelow and Williams' edited collection (1997) and their co-authored book (1998) similarly, re-read the meaning of emotions in social life, each providing a broad overview of the field. Other essays that are of interest are Panjari et al. (2011) and Seear (2009) in the emotional response to illness, and Duncombe and Marsden (1993) on the gendering of emotional labour in relationships. Stone (1977) is a key text in the history of the family but his thesis on affectivity in nineteenth-century bourgeois relationships is highly relevant here. Lloyd's book (1993) shows how the gendering of emotion is implicit in the construction of philosophical rationality.

REFERENCES

Barbalet, J. (1998) *Emotion, Social Theory and Social Structure: A Macrosociological Approach*. Cambridge: Cambridge University Press.

Bendelow, G. and S. Williams (eds) (1997) *Emotions in Social Life*. London: Routledge.

Duncombe, J. and D. Marsden. (1993) 'Love and intimacy: The gender division of emotion and "emotion work"', *Sociology*, 27: 221–42.

Elias, N. (1991) 'Human beings and their emotions', in M. Featherstone, M. Hepworth and B. Turner (eds) *The Body: Social Process and Cultural Theory*. London: Sage.

Hochschild, A.R. (1983) *The Managed Heart: The Commercialisation of Human Feeling*. Berkeley: University of California Press.

Hochschild, A.R. (1998) 'The sociology of emotion as a way of seeing', in G. Bendelow and S. Williams (eds) *Emotions in Social Life: Critical Themes and Contemporary Issues*. London: Routledge.

Lloyd, G. (1993) *The Man of Reason: Male and Female in Western Philosophy*. London: Routledge.

Panjari, M., S. Davis, P. Fradkin and R. Bell. (2011) Breast cancer survivors' beliefs about the causes of breast cancer. *Psycho-Oncology*, DOI: 10.1002/pon.1949.

Seear, K. (2009) '"Nobody really knows what it is or how to treat it": Why women with endometriosis do not comply with healthcare advice', *Health, Risk and Society*, 11(4): 367–85.

Stone, L. (1977) *The Family, Sex and Marriage in England: 1500–1800*. Harmondsworth: Penguin Books.

Williams, Simon and Gillian Bendelow (1998) *The Lived Body: Sociological Themes, Embodied Issues*. London: Routledge.

Feminism

Definition Feminism, or more properly feminisms, all have a basic concern to analyse (and overturn) the unequal distribution of social and political power, as experienced by women. Such gendered inequity has

(continued)

(continued)

generally been based on the construction of specific characteristics and abilities as belonging to either males or females, based on their bodily differences. Feminism is therefore a concept and a political movement that is fundamentally embodied, both in theory and in action.

Feminism is generally thought of as a movement of the twentieth century, but in centuries of battles fought over social and political exclusion, there have been female voices. Women like Mary Astell argued publicly for equitable education for girls in the seventeenth century, on the basis that girls were as able at learning as boys. In 1792 Mary Wollstonecraft, the mother of *Frankenstein* author Mary Shelley, entered into the political debates of the late eighteenth century to argue for *A Vindication of the Rights of Woman* as others were arguing for the rights of men. Militant Suffragettes in Britain fighting for the right to vote put their bodies on the line, chaining themselves to public buildings, hunger striking when imprisoned and in one famous incident walking in front of racing horses at the 1913 Epsom Derby to gain public (and regal) attention for the cause. It is these publically militant women who sought legal, political and reproductive rights between 1900 to World War II who are generally taken to constitute the first wave of feminism.

Feminist ideals and thought, then, go back much further than the twenty-first century, but when we talk of feminism as a key concept in body and society we are more often referring to the second and third waves of feminism that arose in the early 1960s and the 1990s, respectively. What is known as second wave feminism is associated with the publication of books such as Betty Friedan's chronicle of the discontented lives of college-educated housewives in *The Feminine Mystique* (1963); literary scholars Kate Millett's *Sexual Politics* and Germaine Greer's *The Female Eunuch* (1970); the translation of Simone de Beauvoir's *The Second Sex* (1972) and sociologist Ann Oakley's study of domestic labour in *Sex, Gender and Society* (1972) (see **Gender/Sex**), to name just a few. Each of these books is concerned with the effects of patriarchy (male power structures) on the lives of women, but particularly on the oppression of women based on embodied differences (**Difference**).

From the Suffragettes' prison hunger strikes in the early 1900s in quest of the right to vote; through to the marches against patriarchal oppression in the 1960s; and encouraging women to know their own bodies in the 1970s, feminism has always been an embodied project. Feminisms have been concerned to redress social and political imbalances that have been based on the socio-political perceptions of bodily differences: that is, socially constructed gendered associations of what women are, but more often are *not*, capable of doing. And in that quest, both first and second wave feminist theory and writings have been criticized on the grounds that they assume sameness across the needs and concerns of all women. That blindness was understandable in one sense, in that those feminists were most immediately concerned with rejecting the construction of femininity in terms of dominant (patriarchal) norms that did not differentiate between women (or indeed between men). The suffragettes were upper and middle class women campaigning for the right to vote and equality before the law – particularly those laws that most affected women (e.g. divorce, child custody) – and subsequently, the right to lead public lives in the workforces of their male peers. However, women of the lower social classes in general could not afford to access the law and had never had the option of choosing to work; even when they had children they often had to find work, send their daughters into factories or service, and manage both public and private realms.

Similarly, the women who led women's liberation movements in the 1960s and 1970s were largely from well-educated, if not entirely middle-class, backgrounds and often assumed in their writing that the causes they were speaking to affected all women, and that they would share common experiences on the basis of their being women. The multiple possibilities for identity formation beyond the category of gender – class, cultural, national, sexual, religious, and so on – for many women are at least as important as their status as women. At both the group and the individual level, women will not necessarily have concerns in common. Indeed, post-colonial feminists have pointed to outright conflicts between white Global Northern feminist agendas and local feminisms. These kinds of criticisms came as part of what is known as the third wave of feminist theorization, from the 1990s to the present, which has taken issue with the difference-blindness of second-wave feminisms.

What women do have in common is their social, political and embodied differentiation from a male norm in which their experience is treated as homogeneous. This commonality has formed the basis of several waves of debate around difference (**Difference**) that have been important to feminist agendas. The waves of feminism over the past

50 years have consistently made central an engagement with embodied experience and they have also been at the forefront of raising many key issues that are of importance to the study of the body in society. For example, feminists have been key to analysing the perpetuation of particular body images in the media that, until relatively recently, have been focused almost exclusively on women's bodies. Susan Bordo (1993) is one of the earlier and best known writers on the relationship between idealized body images in popular culture and the development of unhealthy eating patterns in women (**Anorexia/Bulimia/Obesity**). Naomi Wolf (1990) is also widely known for her writing on the effect women have on each other in relation to the public presentation of themselves and the cultivation of their appearance (**Appearance and Beauty**).

Feminism is one of the main theoretical approaches, and socio-political forces, that has actively sought to engage in the study of the body in society. As we know from debates around nature and culture the female body and feminine attributes have for millennia been on the 'low' side of the logic of binary opposition (**Nature/Culture**). The body as a category has been cast as emotional and feminized in opposition to the masculinized rational mind. It is logical, then, that a great deal of this research has been undertaken in areas that are of most concern to women; for example, in the sociology of health and illness. For example, the power of medical discourse (**Discourse**) lies in its gaze into the human body. As we can see in relation to reproduction, one of the sites where the gaze is at its most powerful in medical discourse is in the gynaecological clinic. From the time that barber-surgeons first attempted to wrest control of birthing from midwives in the early seventeenth century, gestation gradually became dominated by male professionalism within Western medicine. A process that is neither a disease nor a pathological condition has become one of the most controlling of the medical specialties. Pregnancy in developed countries is monitored, scanned, tested, and the phenomenological experience of carrying a child reflected back to women as something in which they are inexpert. Feminists researchers, like Oakley (1981) have gone into the clinic with the express intention of giving voices back to women's experience of the medicalization of their bodies by conducting collaborative research that uses the interview process closer in quality to the mutual experience of conversation than a researcher/researched dynamic.

Feminists have also been at the forefront of debates around the ongoing assumptions about the biological determinism of maleness and femaleness and the sexual objectification of the human body. Genevieve

Lloyd (1993) has shown how gender associations are embedded in philosophical discourse around rationality and emotionality, which for centuries have assisted in perpetuating understandings of women as irrational and emotional (**Emotion**). Emily Martin (1991) has taken a similar approach to scientific discourse around reproduction, showing how the language used in supposedly rational and objective scientific research is filled with gendered metaphors that attribute traits of masculinity to sperm and femininity to ova (**Gender/Sex**). Finally, Judith Butler (1990) completely undoes any notion of stability in gender categories and argues for gender as a performative act that takes place in the moment and can shift at will (**Performativity**).

Feminist sociologists have been important not only in researching and analysing the effects of patriarchy on women's lives but also in developing new methodologies and methods for gathering research data. Ann Oakley (1972) is credited with being one of the first to bring the questioning of the unquestioned allying of sex with gender into sociological inquiry (**Gender/Sex**). We saw in the discussion of emotion that Arlie Hochschild (1983, 1998) contributed to the opening out of a new field of enquiry into emotions in social life, based on an analysis of the heavier burden women are expected to carry in this respect (**Emotion**). In addition, there have been programmatic efforts in feminist social research methodologies to take women-centred approaches and, based around qualitative research methods, to propose more appropriate ways of researching women's lives than prior masculinist scientific models of research. These are many and varied, taking in non-positivist, non-empiricist, interview-based, flexible, highly reflexive, openly subjective and emotional, and collaborative research methods. One of the most effective of these, that is politically committed to opening out spaces for Indigenous voices, is Maori researcher Linda Tuhiwai Smith (1999) (**Colonialism/Post-colonialism**).

FURTHER READING

There are numerous compilations of feminist thought and histories of feminisms in print that will give an overview of the field; of which, Pilcher and Whelehan's (2004) volume in the *Key Concepts* series is an excellent introduction; and, Freedmans' (2007) compilation of original sources is remarkable in its historical and cultural breadth. Oakley's (1981) research methodology has formed the basis for many later attempts at creating feminist research methods and remains a touchstone

feminism

in the field. For a closer appreciation of the concerns of very early feminists, in full, see Astell (1694) and Wollstonecraft (1792). Some of the key texts in second and third wave feminisms have been mentioned above and the details listed in the Bibliography. More recent feminist theorists can be found under individual sections with appropriate readings, for example, Butler under **Performativity**, Haraway under **Cyborgs**, Harding under **Technology**, and many of the authors under **Gender/Sex**.

REFERENCES

Astell, M. (1694) *A Serious Proposal to the Ladies for the Advancement of their True and Greatest Interest*. London: R. Wilkin.

Freedman, E. (ed.) (2007) *The Essential Feminist Reader*. New York: Random House.

Oakley, A. (1981) 'Interviewing Women: A contradiction in terms' in H. Roberts (ed.) *Doing Feminist Research*. London: Routledge & Kegan Paul, pp. 30–61.

Pilcher, J. and I. Whelehan (2004) *50 Key Concepts in Gender Studies*. London: Sage.

Wollstonecraft, M. (1792) *A Vindication of the Rights of Woman: With Strictures on Political and Moral Subjects*. London.

Food and Eating

Definition At its simplest, food is what we ingest to sustain life. Eating is the embodied act of consuming food. Of course, food and eating also have far more complex associations and hold socio-politically and symbolically significant meaning across societies and cultures. Food can be used for ceremonial purposes; eating is one of the basic communal acts human beings can enter into; and the cultivation, adaptation, exchange and consumption of foods is one of the capacities used to define humans as distinct from other animal species. Food and food practices are used to define cultures and are also a part of the greater globalization of culture: food and eating are political.

Most children in English-speaking countries are taught, in their primary education, that it was food in the form of the cultivation of crops and the domestication of herd animals that began the processes of 'civilization'. The evidence of early agriculture along the Euphrates is evidence of what is said to have made the difference between humans pursuing nomadic social formations and the growth of settled and literate cultures. The capacity to regulate food production and consumption, in one place, is said to have given people the time to develop writing: hence, the logic goes that cultivation led to culture (**Civilizing Processes, Colonialism/Post-colonialism**). This is, of course, a rather Eurocentric view and we know that cultures formed in other ways on other continents, as did settled agricultural practices arise in the absence of literacy. Nevertheless, it is fair to say that the kinds of food production available to a social grouping are interlinked with the way given social formations function.

Mary Douglas has argued that food and food practices are natural symbols the importance of which cannot be underestimated (Douglas, 1970/1996). Food and eating are instances of what Douglas calls 'boundary crossing': that is, food can prove to be both sacred and dangerous because it crosses bodily boundaries in being taken into the human body. Douglas looked at food in its symbolic significance, starting with her own cosmological realm, in the Catholic Eucharist. The body and blood of Christ are transubstantiated into the wafer and wine; only the faithful can take part in communal eating of this and any remainder must be consumed by the priest. She argues that similar ceremonies of sacred food, symbolizing the taking into oneself of, or obeisance before, divinity, can be found across cosmologies. She has also written on the less spiritual, but no less symbolic or meaningful, place of food across societies in its capacity to express hospitality or to inspire community and social involvement (Douglas, 1984).

While there may be radically different meanings attached, there are many ceremonial and spiritual uses of food and eating that entail embodying spirituality in the practitioner. Most cosmologies practice ritual offerings, sacrifices, or ingestion of food in one form or another; for example, two of the largest spiritual communities to do so are Buddhists in the ceremonial presentation of food to their ancestors (and the Buddha), and Hindus in ritual food offerings to their deities. Many faiths also set out rules for what may or may not be eaten on a daily basis by the faithful, or how food should (or should not) be prepared: again, the most well-known examples being Islamic Halal practices and Jewish kosher practices. Ritual food practices can occasionally have disastrous consequences (see the discussion of *kuru* under **Dualism**). It is clear that across cosmologies the bodily act of eating food becomes a socio-political marker and a symbolic statement about who is a member of a given grouping.

Norbert Elias' description of civilizing processes uses as one key example the changing nature of food habits in European society as reflective (and constitutive) of the changing nature of social formations. In European pre-modern social formations food was communally pre-pared and shared and bodies intermixed in its consumption. For exam-ple, in a feudal eating hall all members of the household took food directly from shared platters and vessels. An individual's distance along the table from the food and their technological capacity to take part (whether they owned a knife to cut off and spear meat or spoon to retrieve soup) was a reflection of their status, and determined how well one ate (**Civilizing Processes**). Food also became a byword for that social position: salt was rare and expensive, so the phrase 'below the salt' indicated that one had a lower position on the social scale. As food tech-nologies (cutlery and crockery) became more sophisticated and more available humans' embodied interactions both with the food on the table and with the bodies of their tablemates grew more distant. At the same time, the complexity and variability of practices diversified and food became meaningful in different ways. The use of particular foods to mark specific occasions – such as a christening, wedding or wake – was an expression of community allied to the spiritual realm but at the secular level. A bride cake, groaning cake or funeral biscuit are not for the glory of God, they are for the community celebrating the marriage, birth and funeral, respectively (Mason, 2002). Grand eating, on the other hand, was a statement of a far more restricted community and often a matter of proclaiming social status and instantiating political power (Strong, 2003).

It should be acknowledged that the kind of distancing from the com-munal pot that Elias speaks of is culturally and socio-politically specific to Western European culture. Many cultures continue to eat from shared platters and there are clear skills and manners involved in the eater's ability to perform appropriately and politely in these circum-stances. That said, food and the eating thereof has also become part of the aspirational desires of people in many developing countries. In a country like Papua New Guinea, where what one eats is largely dependent on one's ability to grow it, many people aspire to be able to drink popular cola drinks and eat imported fried snack foods. Rice is an extremely expensive import product and yet people will spend a large proportion of their income on this imported, white, polished luxury rather than yam, a traditional staple food that is widely available and considerably more nutritious, because rice consumption is a statement of sophistication and a capacity to consume. Cola products are gaining an increasing market in Africa, in part due to joint ventures on HIV/AIDS and social sustainability education (http://www.tccaf.org/). Despite the lack of nutritional benefit for populations that may struggle with procuring or producing an adequate dietary intake, health workers are aware of the aspirational desirability of the drink and that the association between the two aims is likely to reach a wider audience: and at the same time the cola producers gain an increased market. There are also well known examples of multi-national dried milk producers marketing their lines into developing countries in Africa, South-East Asia and the Pacific, which are taken up as 'improvements' – to the very real detriment of mothers and babies.

In each case, the foods being marketed have direct bodily effects. Cola drinks are 'empty' foods that offer high caloric and sugar content with no nutritional benefit, which in turn are implicated in the development of obesity and diabetes. Polished rice consumption is well known to be a risk factor for developing Beri-Beri in the absence of other sources of Thiamin in the diet, but in replacing traditional foods (such as taro or yam) which have strong ceremonial and gendered associations it also threatens aspects of the socio-political structure of a society (Kahn in Counihan and Kaplan, 1998; personal observation). In the final example, breast milk is known to be the best possible nutrition for at least the first six months of life; bottle feeding products are expensive and there is little access to clean water to make up the powdered formula or effective sterilization of the bottles, and bottle-feeding is therefore directly implicated in infant mortality. Concern over this kind of inappropriate marketing of food products has led to campaigns in the developing world against particular companies and this has generally made people more conscious of issues such as fair trade practices with developing countries.

In developed countries concern with fair trade practices can be said to be one of a complex of approaches to food that has arisen since the mid-1980s in reaction to the ubiquity of processed foods. The most familiar of these is the Slow Food movement that began in Italy (http://

slowfood.com/). The developed world's relationship with food changed post-World War II: the *Turn Back Time on the High St* (BBC, 2010) documentary series made clear how the availability and forms of food changed in Britain between the 1890s and the 1980s. As processed 'convenience' foods became cheaper and more widely available, chain supermarkets overwhelmed most individual grocers, butchers and bakers, and it became cheaper to buy rather than grow vegetables in one's garden, the nature of food and eating changed. This is a pattern repeated across developed nations. To someone who grew up in an era and an area where most suburban gardens had a vegetable patch and at least one fruit tree – the produce of which would be made into jam or bottled – there are aspects of 'the slow food movement' that would seem better called 'the food movement'. While 'slow food' grew out of dissatisfaction with the incursion of multinational 'fast foods' and the turning away from European locally-produced food – with an interest in trade protection in some instances – one of its main aims is the worldwide preservation of 'heritage' or local foods in opposition to the homogenization of food products (and cuisines).[4]

Food, then, has many embodied aspects to it that extend beyond our need of it to simply support life. Food is a natural symbol that has both cosmological and community meaning; it is the means of forging bonds between embodied individuals and the means of exerting statements of status and power; it is a fuel the constituents of which need to be in balance to ensure our on-going health; it is a primary object of consumption; and it has become an object of political dispute at the local, national and global levels.

FURTHER READING

For a discussion of the cosmological and anthropological significance of foods, see Douglas (1984, 1996). Both Mason (2002) and Strong (2003) are interesting and easy to read historical accounts of food practices in Europe. Counihan and Kaplan's collection (1998), like Douglas, is anthropological in approach and gives a series of examples of the meaning of

---

[4]In practice, there can be some irony in this objective. I have witnessed an aid organizer's effect on local people's diet in Papua New Guinea by showing them how to boost *taste* rather than nutrition by the use of locally available foods that would not usually be used in the same way or in the same quantity – by producing coconut milk and cream. In doing so, she was contributing to the replacement of local cuisine and increasing fat consumption.

food in a range of cultures. Lupton (1996) and Mennell (1991, 1996) each approach food as an aspect of social processes, in the spirit of Elias, and in Lupton's case Bourdieu and psychoanalytic feminists. Mennell's work is on the increasing sophistication of food preparation and presentation in Western Europe (rather than the tastes of food as suggested by the title). Lupton is concerned to uncover the emotional aspects of food in society.

REFERENCES

Counihan, C. and S. Kaplan (eds) (1998) *Food and Gender: Identity and Power*. Amsterdam: Harwood Academic Publishers.

Douglas, M. (ed.) (1984) *Food in the Social Order: Studies of Food and Festivities in Three American Communities*. New York: Russell Sage Foundation.

Douglas, M. (1996) *Natural Symbols: Explorations in Cosmology* (with a new Introduction). London: Routledge. First published 1970.

Lupton, D. (1996) *Food, the Body and the Self*. London: Sage.

Mason, L. (ed.) (2002) *Food and the Rites of Passage*. Totnes: Prospect Books.

Mennell, Stephen (1991) 'On the Civilising of Appetite', in M. Featherstone, M. Hepworth and B. Turner (eds), *The Body: Social Process and Cultural Theory*. London: Sage, 126–56.

Mennell, Stephen (1996) *All Manners of Food: Eating and Taste in England and France from the Middle Ages to the Present*, 2nd edn. Urbana: University of Illinois Press.

Strong, R. (2003) *Feast: A History of Grand Eating*. London: Pimlico.

Gender/Sex

Definition Gender is a social category of differentiation applied to the human body that relates to socially understood sets of behaviours, generally divided into two main categories of femininity and masculinity. Sex is the term used for the biological definition of maleness and femaleness. Just what behaviours are considered appropriate to gender categories has changed over time and varies across cultures. This is often termed 'the sex/gender distinction'.

Ann Oakley (1972) is generally credited as the first sociologist to argue for the sex/gender distinction (see also **Nature/Culture**). While the dominant hetero-normative expectation is that men will be masculine and women will be feminine, there is a vast range of variability in expressions of gendered characteristics. One may be biologically male and display behaviours or characteristics that are socially understood to be feminine. Conversely, one may be biologically female and display characteristics that are perceived to be masculine. This variation between sex and gender need have nothing to do with sexuality (one's desires), although stereotypical hetero-normative expectations commonly result in assumptions that it does.

To complicate matters further, despite the common social assumption that biological sex is invariable, this is not necessarily the case. There are a number of genetic and hormonal conditions that can lead to sexual/biological ambiguity either at birth or later in life. Some infants are born 'intersex', that is, with indeterminate genital organs or, in very rare cases, with both sets of genital organs (see the discussion of Caster Semenya under **Sport**). This condition is treated – in developed countries with the medical systems to support – it by what is (confusingly) termed 'gender reassignment'. This consists of the determination of the appearance of a sex for the infant, most often by the removal of an incompletely developed penis. Some infants are born with the outward appearance of a single sex but with a variation in their chromosomal make-up (for example, XYY or XXY instead of XY). This and other hormonal conditions can lead to bodily changes at puberty that differ from the assumed sex of the baby at birth (**Genetics**).

Gender is a basic category in body studies precisely because it is a property often believed to be immutable, which is in fact socially constructed. The variability of gender – what is deemed appropriate to males and females – across societies is clear evidence that it is a socially and culturally determined phenomenon. However, it has concrete effects on the lives of males and females at the most basic level because of the persistence of social beliefs around gender. While much has changed since Oakley first wrote of gender, there are still expectations of what men and women should and shouldn't do, and should and shouldn't be, based on gender categories.

Historically, access to education and work opportunities were determined on the basis of assumptions, in which sex and gender were conflated, about what were appropriate life roles for males and females. The most common of these was that women *belonged* in the home *because* domestic labour was 'women's work' (**Feminism**). For example, women were expected to return to home-making after World War II on the basis of gender appropriateness, even though they had been working in factories, flying planes and doing all manner of 'men's work' throughout the war. In some cases women were considered ineligible for certain types of employment (such as teaching) if they were married and the dominant social expectation was that (most) women would cease employment on marriage. In this respect, class also mattered, for women were working in factories well before World War II. The more menial the position, the more likely a woman was to be able to gain it and to continue working in it whether married or not; for example as cleaners or in unskilled factory labour (Roberts, 1984).

The assumption that certain characteristics and abilities are natural to women and men goes back much further than the twentieth century – patriarchal (male-dominated) societies, which have existed for millennia, function on the basis of such assumptions. However, gender and sex were seen as being less concretely allied before the seventeenth century because bodies were seen as less absolutely fixed, even in medical theories (Laqueur, 1992). We can see this in the words of Elizabeth I of England, a consummate politician who frequently played with the expectations of gender-appropriate behaviour of her as a female and the gender-destabilizing fact of her absolute sovereignty, a generally masculine office. In her 1588 speech at Tilbury, she claimed the capacities of both male and female, masculine and feminine: 'I have the body of a weak and feeble woman but I have the stomach of a King, and King of England too' (cited in Jankowski, 1992).

Religious dogma was one of the main ways in which gender categories were maintained up to this time in moralizing discourses on appropriate and inappropriate actions and behaviours. There was a constant connection being made between virtues/sins and gender that regulated the habitus of men and women. With the rise in the dominance of scientific and dualistic ideas of the body, this religious overlay of gender gradually became naturalized into male and female bodies as natural facts (Sawday 1995). The scientific or dualistic body is a medicalized body (**Discourse, Medicine and Science**), and within medicine diseases and complexes specific to male and female reproductive organs came to be infiltrated by gendered notions, particularly in relation to women. The condition of hysteria is linked by direct association to the uterus (*hustera* in Greek), pathologizing both the organ and women in general. Socially, women are expected to be emotional and at the same time they are medically condemned for excessive emotionality. Similar associations are made to this day in relation to PMS. That is, women are at the mercy of their moods because of their biology. This is a timeworn gendered association – male/masculine = rational, female/feminine = emotional – which has been naturalized into understandings of the female body (Schiebinger, 1993; Lloyd, 1993).

Men's hormonal levels and moods regularly change too, but they are rarely pathologized as a result. However, they can be pathologized if they do not meet the dominant gender expectations of masculinity. Many men do not identify or feel comfortable with versions of masculinity based in muscularity, sportiness, aggression or rationality that comes at the cost of emotion. A failure to meet masculine norms has historically been conflated with effeminacy and/or homosexuality but this also does a disservice to gay masculinities. Just as feminists have come to appreciate the range of expressions of womanhood, there is an increasing understanding of the range of masculinities available to men (Connell, 1995; Mosse, 1996). Gender stereotypes oppress both men and women. Gender, then, is a political category on which social inequalities can be built and maintained thanks to the solidification of the nature/culture division.

Much of the discussion so far has focused on the norms and history of the Global North. It was noted at the beginning of this section that gender varies across cultures. There are a number of well-known examples of accepted gender indeterminacy in other cultures. The most common examples are males who take on female personas and they can be found amongst the Native American *berdache* or 'Two Spirit'; the *hijra* of India; *kathoeys* or ladyboys of Thailand and the *fa'afafines* of Samoa. These people take on the appropriate gestures, clothes, actions, etc. for femininity. So gender of itself is wider than the two dominant sexes (Fausto-Sterling, 1993).

Men have lived as women and women have lived as men in the Global North over the centuries but not in these kinds of culturally recognized and accepted groups. They have more often done so by 'passing', successfully living cross-gender lives where the crossing remains unrecognized. More recently, with the rise of Gay Liberation in the 1970s and the subsequent waves of critical reflection on gender categories, playing with gender has gained a greater public profile (**Queer**). Cross-dressing has been known in theatrical performance for millennia (Garber, 1992) but as drag it has become both a fetishization and high parody of the stereotypical gender-norms of femininity. Since the early 1960s, it has been possible for cross-gender living to be taken beyond external appearance (clothes, gestures, etc.) by the success of adult gender reassignment surgery (see also **Modification/Dysmorphias**). Transgender surgery has become an adult medical specialty and is performed on people who want the outward bodily signs of biological sex realigned to match the gender they believe to be correct, that is, modifying the body to fit a social category. All these practices 'play' with gender (**Performativity**) at the level of the individual and test the limits of the social construction of gender categories and the physical limits of biological sex.

FURTHER READING

For classic feminist critiques of the scientific characterizations of the distinctions made between sex and gender, see Gatens (1983, 1995), Martin (1991) and Diprose (1994). For more post-modern approaches to a more mobile (performative) notion of gender, Butler (1990) is a key text, as is Connell (1995) on the social constructions of masculinity and Howson (2005) on psychoanalysis and the materiality of the body. Laqueur (1992) was a touchstone in the history of gender in medicine, although the accuracy of his examples has since been deservedly criticized. Garber (1992) and Orgel (1996) also put gender into historical context, through the study of the outward appearance of gender as interpreted on stage and through clothing, respectively, as does Blackwood (2002) in a non-Eurocentric example. Connell (1995) and Mosse (1996) each question the dominant notion of masculinity.

REFERENCES

Blackwood, E. (2002) 'Sexuality and gender in certain native American tribes: The case of cross-gender females', in C.L. Williams and A. Stein (eds), *Sexuality and Gender*. Oxford: Blackwell.

Butler, Judith (1990) *Gender Trouble: Feminism and the Subversion of Identity*. New York: Routledge.

Connell, R.W. (1995) *Masculinities*. Cambridge: Polity.

Diprose, R. (1994) *The Bodies of Women: Ethics, Embodiment and Sexual Difference*. London: Routledge.

Fausto-Sterling, A. (1993) 'The five sexes: Why male and female are not enough', *The Sciences*, May/April: 20–25.

gender/sex

Garber, M. (1992) *Vested Interests: Cross-Dressing and Cultural Anxiety*. London: Routledge.

Gatens, M. (1983) 'Critique of the sex/gender distinction', in J. Allen and P. Patton (eds), *Interventions after Marx*. Sydney: Intervention.

Gatens, M. (1995) *Imaginary Bodies: Ethics, Power and Corporeality*. London: Routledge.

Howson, A. (2005) *Embodying Gender*. London: Sage.

Jankowski, T. (1992) *Women in Power in the Early Modern Drama*. Chicago: University of Illinois Press.

Laqueur, Thomas (1992) *Making Sex: Body and Gender from the Greeks to Freud*. Cambridge, MA: Harvard University Press.

Martin, E. (1991) 'The egg and the sperm: How science has constructed a romance based on stereotypical male-female roles', *Signs: Journal of Women in Culture and Society*, 16: 485–501.

Mosse, G.L. (1996) *The Image of Man: The Creation of Modern Masculinity*. Oxford: Oxford University Press.

Oakley, Ann (1972) *Sex, Gender and Society*. London: Temple Smith.

Orgel, Stephen (1996) *Impersonations: the Performance of Gender in Shakespeare's England*. Cambridge: Cambridge University Press.

Roberts, E. (1984) *A Woman's Place: An Oral History of Working-Class Women, 1890–1940*. Oxford: Basil Blackwell.

key concepts in
body and society

.... Genetics ....

94

Definition Genetics is the study of the chromosomes and the DNA of living organisms. Human beings have 23 pairs of chromosomes and half of each pair is contributed by each of our parents. Each half of the pairs is contained in the respective reproductive gametes (egg, sperm), one pairing of which determines whether we develop as male or female. Since the discovery of DNA there has been great interest in trying to map not only genomes (the genetic characteristics of populations) but also to identify the sections of DNA that may determine various characteristics or diseases. There are social consequences in this mapping, both for how we see ourselves as embodied individuals and how we see ourselves as members of groups.

To begin with the issue of genetically determined sex alluded to above, as we saw under **Gender/Sex**, chromosomal determination of sex is not absolute. There are various intersex conditions that lead to physical indeterminacy of sex, or at least, the incomplete development of male sex organs at birth. Such children are often surgically re-assigned in infancy and early childhood (in a process of multiple operations) with the intention that they will live as girls. This can only be maintained if the child is given supplementary hormones at the onset of puberty, to mimic female development. Both males and females have levels of what are often thought to be male (testosterone) and female (oestrogen) hormones, but they circulate in different proportions and variably over the lifespan. Hormones in themselves are neither male nor female (Oudshoorn, 1994), but in different combinations can bring about bodily changes that are associated with masculinity and femininity. If that balance of hormones is not adjusted at puberty, the re-assignment of the external appearance of sex comes undone as the underlying genes cue hormonal balances that contribute to the development of masculinizing changes. The stability of the notion of an immutable biological sex is, then, rendered something of a chimera both at the genetic and the hormonal level, and genetics become less deterministic than is generally thought.

Genetic testing, as a part of medicine, has effects at the individual, social and societal level (Turner, 1995). The following is a good example of how genetics and genetic heritage can have quite powerful social (and personal) ramifications on our phenomenological or embodied experience. On *Faces of America*, a PBS television programme first aired in 2010, a dozen well-known Americans had their family backgrounds researched and then presented to them by historian Henry Louis Gates Jr. All were framed within an aspect of the history of the United States. Each of these people had a sense of identity that shifted, to varying degrees, on finding out more about their ancestors from historical evidence. The presenter and all but one of the participants also agreed to have their genetic material mapped. In the final episode, they were each presented with their 'genetic heritage'. The techniques used allowed the genetic mappers to make educated guesses about the likelihood of genetic links between the participants going back over the past three or four hundred years: several participants turned out to have such distant links with each other. Using further techniques, aimed at classifying much more distant geographic origins related to the continental migration of peoples many thousands of years ago, they were also told what percentage of their DNA came from particular genomic groups (Caucasian, African, Asian, etc.). Several people, who had very clear senses of themselves as having a particular individual and group identity (**Race/Ethnicity**), were quite confounded to find they were genetically no more than 25 per cent of that background. This abstracted reading of bodily matter on the part of a scientific expert had, in a sense, rewritten their sense of identity, affecting their sense of themselves as individuals and as members of a social group.

The one participant who declined to contribute her DNA for testing was of Native American heritage. This new information on micro-bodily make-up had challenged identity, ethnicity and politics for all of these people to some degree. The woman who identified as Native American made a conscious political decision not to take the test. The strength of the social aspect of her identity made any such testing irrelevant. Genetic testing belongs to a biomedical understanding of the body that is irrelevant in systems of clan or kinship attachment. Other classificatory techniques can and have been used to disempower Indigenous peoples (**Colonialism/Post-colonialism**). Similarly quantitative categorizations of heritage in the nineteenth and twentieth centuries led directly to practices such as the removal of Australian Indigenous children from their 'full blood' birth mothers and to the related practices of describing many Indigenous peoples as 'dying out' (*Bringing Them Home*: Australian Human Rights Commission, 1997). Indeed, there are many parallels between colonialism and the colonization of the genome amongst vulnerable and genetically interesting populations.

Another aspect of genetics which is important to the body in society is in the proliferation of genetic tests that are becoming available. Particularly in the developed world, we are encouraged to undertake genetic testing to screen for a range of conditions. In some instances, that encouragement can be highly emotionally charged, particularly in relation to tests that may be recommended to identify potential consequences for, or conditions in, future children. Even when we willingly undertake diagnostic and/or predictive genetic testing to identify a given condition in our individual DNA, this carries with it ethical dilemmas that spread far wider than the individual. A positive test result in one member of a family has implications for those genetically linked to the individual: whether that involves a possible minor risk of developing a condition at some point in the future; the probable passing on of a treatable condition to others; or, in some instances, the very high likelihood of developing and passing on a terminal condition (Huntington's

Chorea). A person who has a parent with Huntington's Chorea (an incurable neuro-muscular degenerative disease) has a 50 per cent chance of having the condition, and there is the same chance of them passing on the condition to any child if they do carry the gene. Does that person then get tested? Does he or she get tested if they intend to have children? What does the individual 'do' with the information if they do choose to be tested? Added to this, where genetic counselling is offered, which is on the basis of scientific knowledge and 'risks' rather than psychological support, its strong tendency to be directive (recommending further testing and action) is recognized as a problematic issue (Pilnick, 2002).

The individual possesses information that, depending on the condition, may have predictable outcomes for other family members beyond their direct descendants. By investigating their own bodily matter they may have unintentionally breached the privacy of another person to whom they are genetically linked. Similar dilemmas arise with less easily heritable conditions or those with less dire consequences. Such testing can also be used to avoid having children with known heritable conditions: either through pre-implantation genetic screening of embryos in vitro to avoid implanting affected embryos; or through the termination of pregnancies when the foetus tests positive for a condition (Ettorre, 2002). Understandably, disability activists have found the termination or avoidance of pregnancies for genetic conditions highly offensive as this raises serious questions about the value of the life of disabled or differently abled individuals (**Disability/Ability**). The identification of a gene is rarely predictive of a definitive outcome: the expression of a gene (the degree to which it manifests) can vary widely, so some people with the genetic evidence of Down's Syndrome, for example, will be intensely affected and require assistance throughout life while others will be capable of achieving a university degree. All, irrespective of ability, may be capable of rich and rewarding lives and of making contributions to their families and communities.

Privacy in relation to genetic testing also extends beyond the knowledge which an individual may hold, that has potential ramifications for their relatives. The results of a genetic test may be used by an insurance company to deny or restrict a policy, or may constitute grounds for invalidating a policy if the results are not disclosed. From a social or a societal perspective then, there are concerns that the more widespread genetic testing becomes the more likely it is that a genetic 'underclass' will be formed of people who are unable to access services on the basis of predictive testing. Such testing may also affect people's ability to find and retain employment (Pilnick, 2002). We are learning to see our bodies through the lens of biomedical science in increasingly techno-logical ways. We are being sold an increasingly particularized under-standing of embodiment (see **Medicine and Science**) that encourages us to see ourselves in a 'sick role' (Parsons, 1937), through genetic screen-ing, that fatalistically inflates a sense that genetics are deterministic, and solidifies discourses of risk and personal responsibility for disease states.

FURTHER READING

One of the clearest and broadest introductions to the implications of genetics on society is Pilnick's (2002) introductory reader with an empha-sis on the place of genetic counselling. Ettore (2002) offers a similarly detailed inquiry into reproductive genetics, and in particular pre-natal screening, in an accessible text. Relatedly, Oudshoorn (1994) deconstructs the relationship between the derivation and scientific construction of sex hormones and gender categories as naturalized within the human body.

REFERENCES

Ettore, E. (2002) *Reproductive Genetics, Gender and the Body*. London: Routledge.
Oudshoorn, N. (1994) *Beyond the Natural Body: An Archaeology of Sex Hormones*. London: Routledge.
Pilnick, A. (2002) *Genetics and Society: An Introduction*. Buckingham: Open University Press.

Gesture and Habits

Definition Gestures and Habits are means of bodily expression at both an individual and a social level. Gestures are body movements that have socially, culturally or contextually 'readable' meanings. They may be sacred or profane. Habits are the embodied (and gestural) actions an individual characteristically employs in daily life and in social action. Habits are, to a large extent, self-regulated although within a social context. For example, personal grooming can be described as a series of regularly performed bodily habits that have social meaning. Habits can include gestures and some gestures will be habitual (for example, in religious rituals and observances).

Bodily gestures are one of the first means of communication a human infant is capable of replicating. A baby can mirror the poking out of a tongue from approximately three weeks of age, before they have control of their limbs and long before they can shape the most basic word. Most infants can wave (or kick) hello or goodbye before they can verbalize a greeting. Small children are quickly made aware of socio-culturally appropriate, and inappropriate, gestures and revel in challenging the boundaries of acceptability. Small children are also habituated to various bodily acts (Shilling, 2008): walking, toilet training, beginning to play an instrument, learning the rules of a game or sport, learning to read and write. They are often equally delighted to find they can challenge authority by practising (bad) habits: for example, nose-picking. Much of development can be described as the result of acquiring embodied habits and learning gestures that become so embedded in our range of actions that they become unconscious; that is, unless they are disrupted, have to be re-learned, or are entirely lost (**Disability/Ability**). Any form of bodily impairment interferes with our capacity to successfully express ourselves in gestures or habituated movements.

Body language is a contemporary way of speaking about our ability to read gestures. However, a semiotics or set of coded meanings associated with bodily gestures are a fundamental aspect of human knowledge that can be found in a variety of forms across time and social formations, as is evident from the frozen moments in cave paintings to avatars in cyberspace. Gestures are also overlain with considerations of gender appropriateness (a man in trousers sitting with knees spread) or inappropriateness (a woman sitting knees spread in a skirt); they may be religious (a sign of blessing) or profane (giving 'the finger'); and they may be distinctively associated with social or cultural background (different forms of prayer).

To give a historical example of gendered gestures, in the early modern period for a woman to dance, or simply to stand, with her elbows pointing outwards with her hands on her hips (akimbo) was considered both lower-class and sexually suggestive. A respectable, upper-class woman kept her arms close to her body and her hands turned in and contained. An upper-class man, by contrast, was admired for his open armed stance, his broad gestures and his liveliness as a dancer (Bryson, 1990). Tastes in gestures change across time but gender differences can be found in most cultures (Feher, 1989–95). In many cultures, girls are encouraged to be more generally contained in their movements than boys from a very early age.

Common religious gestures include crossing oneself in a number of Christian religions and embodying a sign of respect (such as bowing or kneeling) before a sacred object in many religions. Religious observance becomes habituated into the body in such gestures as well as performing a (natural) symbolic function identifying the individual's association with that faith (Douglas, 1996). Gestures can also denote mood or emotion – such as making a fist in anger or hugging a team-mate in exultation on scoring a goal. And, as noted under **Emotion**, such displays can have specific cultural expressions that may be misunderstood.

Gestures can be used to communicate when no common verbal language exists, whether in the non-formalized attempt of a tourist to barter in a market or in one of the recognizable inter-cultural gestural language systems of Indigenous peoples (for example, Walpiri). Gestures are also integral to the vast number of regularized and idiosyncratic sign languages that have developed for communication between and with the hearing impaired. In these latter examples, which are explicit languages that at the same time consist of signifiers dependent on cultural context, we can see that embodied gestures can be both embodied and habitual.

From these examples it is also possible to see that gesture is a key part of Bourdieu's habitus (**Habitus**). We saw that in the manners that characterized early modern dancing (**Civilizing Processes**), upper-class contained and controlled individuals were less likely to employ crude (and profane) gestures than individuals of the lower classes. It was a public display of their status. Bourdieu found in his study of 1960s Parisians that class was embodied in movement as well as bodily structure. Modern dance movements, sporting techniques and musical performance all involve gestures and also require ingrained bodily habits. To be able to play a piano or to touch type, fine motor skills and particular movements have to become unconscious and habituated in order for the technique to be mastered. Each of these skills has social and class associations, even if these are not insurmountable barriers to gaining the embodied skills – but the finer the motor skill involved and the higher the expertise gained, the less likely one is to perform manual labour. Conversely, the longer one spends in an office at a computer screen touch typing, the less likely one is to develop and habituate the gross motor skills to be a successful footballer.

Gestures are also comprehended in Goffman's (1971) notion of the presentation of the social self as a dramaturgical performance. We learn to present ourselves in particular ways for a given audience, shaping our gestures and bodily deportment to the occasion as much as we shape our presentation of ourselves verbally and intellectually. For example, to enter a job interview and appear overly relaxed (hands clasped behind the head, legs outstretched) would not be appropriate in the majority of cases and the gestures would have an effect on the inter- viewer's perception of the applicant no matter what s/he said or how well s/he presented the knowledge required for the employment. Similarly, we recognize (and judge) people whose gestures are 'out of the ordinary', particularly in public places. When hands-free mobile phones first became available it appeared as if there was a sudden out- break of psychoses, not only because people appeared to be talking to themselves but also because conversations are often accompanied by expressive gestures, which in the absence of a listener was easily misread as delusional.

Each of the issues dealt with here is closely interlinked with discus- sions of **Emotion**, **Civilizing Processes** and **Habitus** and the reader should consult those sections in combination with this entry.

FURTHER READING

See also the categories of and readings for **Civilizing Processes, Emotion** and **Habitus**.

Shilling (2008) is the best place to start in reading further on the topic of ingrained bodily habits as he gives an excellent overview using an original and stimulating approach. Mauss' suggestive essay on body techniques is also a useful source, on which later theorists have built (Mauss, 1979). Bremmer and Roodenberg (1992), Bryson (1990) and individual essays in Feher's multi-volume collection (1989–95) each cover examples of the social meaning of gestures in different historical, and in some instances cultural, spaces. Goffman and Douglas are noted under other key readings.

REFERENCES

Bremmer, Jan and Herman Roodenburg (eds) (1992) *A Cultural History of Gesture*. Ithaca, NY: Cornell University Press.

Bryson, Anna (1990) 'The rhetoric of status: Gesture demeanour and the image of the gentleman in sixteenth and seventeenth-century England', in L. Gent and N. Llewellyn (eds), *Renaissance Bodies: The Human Figure in English Culture c.1540–1660*. London: Reaktion Books, pp. 136–53.

Feher, Michael (ed.) (1989-95) *Fragments for a History of the Human Body, Part 1–3*. New York: Zone Books.

Goffman, E. (1971) *The Presentation of Self in Everyday Life*. Harmondsworth: Penguin.

Mauss, Marcel (1979) *Sociology and Psychology: Essays*, trans. B. Brewster. London: Routledge & Kegan Paul.

Shilling, C. (2008) *Changing Bodies: Habit, Crisis and Creativity*. London: Sage.

Habitus

key concepts in body and society

Definition Habitus is the interpenetration of our social, cultural and physical environment – the faces, places and spaces – that we as social beings inhabit, through which we know ourselves and by which others identify us. Embodiment, or bodily hexis, is the political expression of all the factors that make up one's habitus, which are embodied or embedded in our physical being. So we wear our socio-political being and our background (habitus) on and through our bodies (hexis).

Sociologist and social theorist Pierre Bourdieu formulated his notions of habitus and embodiment (or bodily hexis) as part of his rejection of the supposedly objective, scientific anthropology and sociology that were dominant at the time he began writing. He believed sociological and anthropological method needed to be 'reflexive' and subject itself to 'objective' scrutiny (Bourdieu, 1977: 72); in other words, to take a good hard look at itself. He also wanted to find a way of talking about the complications that are inevitable in lived actions in the moment (praxis). His aim was to create a social theory or methodology – a 'theory of practice' – that is based on a new objectivism that embraces the subjective positioning of the researcher in the research process, and at the same time recognizes the agency of the people being researched, their capacity to act in their given fields of social action or interaction rather than simply being passive research subjects.

The idea of habitus is central to that theory of practice. In his words (translated into English), he aims

> to construct the theory of practice, or, more precisely, the theory of the mode of generation of practices, which is the precondition for establishing an experimental science of *the dialectic of internalization of externality and the externalization of internality*, or, more simply, of incorporation and objectification. (Bourdieu, 1977: 72; the phrases in italics are sometimes termed the subject/object distinction)

Basically, he is arguing that each of us absorbs into our lived experiences given social knowledge and behaviours. At the same time, in an ongoing back and forth movement, we re-present that knowledge and those behaviours in society as an object or identity: 'me in the world'. We all modify our behaviour to suit given contexts; Bourdieu is just saying that there really isn't any time when we aren't doing this, and that includes social theorists or social researchers while they are conducting their research. Most students undertaking social research methods now would be familiar with this kind of scepticism about objectivism. They owe that familiarity to Bourdieu and his contemporaries.

The social behaviours and acquired knowledge that one absorbs in daily life are characteristic of our particular social environment – for Bourdieu this overwhelmingly means one's class (**Class/Caste**) but need not be restricted to that definition. Education, sport, food, fashion, manners and religion are just some of those kinds of knowledges and behaviours (**Civilizing Processes, Clothing, Food and Eating, Gesture and Habits, Religion, Sport**). In addition, a given person may be more or less 'expert' in any of these knowledges, in other words well-educated or school drop-out, fashionista or sloppy dresser, devout or agnostic. Each of these areas in which one may be more or less an expert is known as a 'field of practice'. Individuals who inhabit different environments have expertise in different 'fields of practice' or different levels of expertise in the same field. The sum total of the 'fields of practice' in a given environment 'produce habitus, systems of durable, transposable *dispositions*' (Bourdieu, 1977: 72). And fields of practice have unstated rules. It is the ability to understand and work within (or around) these rules that makes one more or less expert in a field.

These structures are not just restricted to ritual practices; they are integral to a person's relation to the space they inhabit and the relation of their physical bodies to – and the physical movement and placement thereof within – that space. It is through our bodies that we experience the world. Through them we learn to train, restrict, dispose and quarantine our bodily actions in ways that express and make material/ political consequences (**Gesture and Habits**). Through our bodies we live out the social and political effects of all the fields of practice in which we are involved. We embody our habitus through the way we walk; the way we conduct ourselves with others and in different spaces; the way we are disposed to particular ways of dress and our rejection of others; the places we do and don't go; the way we regulate our behaviour in certain areas of our homes and in different public spaces; the way we act depending on whether we are adults or children, male or female, young or old, etc., etc. These are the structures and behaviours we learn and reproduce from the moment we are born and they are deeply political: 'concessions of *politeness* always contain *political concessions*' (Bourdieu, 1977: 95).

Thus our habitus is the social, cultural and physical environment that we as social beings inhabit, through which we know ourselves and others identify us. The factors that constitute a habitus are complex, detailed and interpenetrating. They are all the kinds of social connections, achievements, attainments and attachments one acquires from birth, whether by formal or informal means. These include, but are not limited to, the level of education one has reached, the kind of work one does, the sort of entertainments one enjoys, the places one goes, the cultural pursuits one takes part in or values, the class one identifies with, and so on.

In embodying the habitus in which we are steeped, we each in our way embody the political content of that space and its associations. Bourdieu calls this materialization of habitus within individuals 'embodiment', or 'hexis'. This is the political expression of all the factors that make up one's habitus – embodied or embedded in our physical being. Put more simply, the sorts of sports one does or doesn't play, the kinds of food one eats, the clothes one wears, the distribution of muscles from manual labour or concerted exercise (or their absence), all play out one's habitus in and on one's body. We quite literally embody the social and political spaces we inhabit and/or identify with. The possession of expertise in any such field of practice, Bourdieu has termed cultural capital. The more 'expert' one is in a field of practice, the greater is one's cultural capital in that field, and the more cultural capital one has, the greater one's room to manoeuvre within or to manipulate that field.

There are several serious criticisms that have been levelled at Bourdieu's method, the most damning of which is that it is utterly static (Robbins, 2000), that is, that if we are so bound by our habitus and hexis there is no 'real' agency in the world. We are always enclosed within a set of boundaries. There is room for manoeuvre, but that room remains bounded by the given habitus. This becomes even more problematic in his work on his own culture (Bourdieu 1984), in relation to class habitus. There would seem to be no way of accounting for upward or downward social mobility in the French society he describes.

In his later works Bourdieu (1990b, 1998) refuted criticisms that his theory is static by introducing the notion of 'interest'. Interest is both the attachment one has for a field of practice and also implies the degree of expertise one has in that field. It is not quite in the sense of a 'vested interest' – Bourdieu utterly rejects any idea that this notion of interest implies either conscious actions or a desire for personal gain (financial or otherwise). It is more in the sense of an unconscious allegiance, something that one cannot help but feel involved in because of one's habitus and hexis. When he characterizes expertise or interest in a given field as having a 'feel for the game', he is appealing to unconscious aptitude, an ingrained understanding of how to do well that is influenced by the degree of cultural capital one has. Having a feel for and doing well at 'the game' can sometimes consist in doing 'poorly' – by conducting oneself in a way that to someone outside the game may appear 'disinterestedly' or generously. But the practical outcome of playing against the grain in such a way can end in advantage in the long term.

It is hard to see, however, how this refutes the counter-claim that all actions are thereby being reduced to a more base form of *self*-interest. Acting unconsciously is not the same as acting unselfishly. Nor is it clear how this idea of interest really transcends the criticism that we are prisoners of our habitus and hexis. It does show how some people are able to 'win' but not how anyone gets away from, or outside of, the game. It is also striking in these major works that Bourdieu does not distinguish between cultures – implicitly, all fields of practice are analogous.

habitus

105

Clearly while Bourdieu is, like Elias (see **Civilizing Processes**), correct that the nouveaux riches are social pariahs amongst the elites they aspire to, it is also true that over generations people do move between and become assimilated into higher or lower social groupings. Shilling is quite right that in comparison with Elias, while 'synchronically dynamic, Bourdieu's work is diachronically underdeveloped' (1993: 146). Elias is less detailed but offers a diachronic answer. Between the two of them we have a fine way of explaining social structures and the shifting place and significance of the body within them. What would seem difficult to incorporate into Bourdieu's theory of practice, however, is the inability of disabled people to fully access the embodied life or cultural capital of any or at any level of society, and how this is one means by which prejudice succeeds (Jenkins, 1998). Nor does he attend to the subjective experience of the ethical or moral consequences of breaking the rules of a game.

The idea of habitus and bodily hexis do, however, signify a major turn away from much of the philosophical work from the time of Descartes (**Dualism**). Bourdieu is quite right that scientific objectivism privileges the intellect and the intellectually perceived, constituting it as a field of play viewed from an enlightened perspective. Descartes' observing or thinking thing deliberately forgot its body, or at least consciously distanced itself from it. As a result, as this became the dominant and legitimized form for perceiving knowledge, the body and embodied relations became reformulated and recognized only from a cognitive point of view. An action becomes a given, and is thereby reduced to a symbolic representation, a playing out of a series of actions and reactions. In 'revivifying' the body, Bourdieu opens the way for a much more textured and deeply layered understanding of social knowledge(s).

FURTHER READING

See also the readings for **Civilizing Processes** and **Class/Caste**. While habitus is mentioned in passing by Elias and predates Bourdieu's conceptions, it is Bourdieu's theories that are referred to when speaking of habitus and the body, so it is to his writings that the reader should go for further elaboration (1977, 1984, 1990a, 1990b, 1998). That said, there are a number of explanatory texts that will be extremely helpful in navigating Bourdieu's writing, which is complex and dense. Two of the best explicators of Bourdieu are Robbins (2000) and, particularly in relation to the body, Shilling (2003), to which can be added the writers in the Calhoun et al. (1993) volume and Chapter 6 of Crossley (2001).

For an instance of the application of habitus to historical space, Sennett's *Flesh and Stone* (1994) is an excellent example.

REFERENCES

Bourdieu, Pierre (1977) *Outline of a Theory of Practice*, trans. Richard Nice. Cambridge: Cambridge University Press. First published 1972.

Bourdieu, Pierre (1984) *Distinction: A Social Critique of the Judgement of Taste*, trans. Richard Nice. Cambridge, MA: Harvard University Press. First published 1979.

Bourdieu, Pierre (1990a) *The Logic of Practice*, trans. Richard Nice. Stanford: Stanford University Press. First published 1980.

Bourdieu, Pierre (1990b) *In Other Words: Essays Towards a Reflexive Sociology*, trans. M. Adamson. Cambridge: Polity Press.

Bourdieu, Pierre (1998) 'Is a disinterested act possible?', in *Practical Reason: On the Theory of Action*. Cambridge: Polity Press, pp. 75–91.

Calhoun, C., E. LiPuma and M. Postone (eds) (1993) *Bourdieu: Critical Perspectives*. London: Polity Press.

Crossley, N. (2001) *The Social Body: Habit, Identity, Desire*. London: Sage.

Robbins, D. (2000) *Bourdieu and Culture*. London: Sage.

Sennett, Richard (1994) *Flesh and Stone: The Body and the City in Western Civilization*. New York: W. W. Norton & Company.

Shilling, C. (2003) *The Body and Social Theory*. London: Sage. First published 1993.

Health and Illness

Definition Health and illness are phenomenological or experiential states of embodiment. They are closely related to medical understandings of the body (**Medicine and Science**) and tend to imply – though not exclusively – the patients' rather than the practitioners' point of view. The WHO defines health as 'a state of complete physical, mental and social wellbeing and not merely the absence of disease' (WHO, 1948). Illness is the embodied occurrence of a disease or a medical condition which nevertheless exists in a cultural context. This section then is centrally focused on health and illness as lived, phenomenological experiences.

Health generally refers to a state of wellness combined with wellbeing – the *experience* of being healthy – from which value-judgements may also be construed concerning that which is unhealthy, either for individuals or for the greater public (hence, public health). Health can be a major determinant in an individual's capacity to access opportunities or services in life. The likely health effects of being in a particular stratum or class of society (based on wealth, ethnicity, distance, etc.) are quite concrete. Many studies have shown the clear connections between low socio-economic (LSE) status and a number of health risk factors, such as increased risk of heart disease, particular cancers, diabetes, etc. People of LSE backgrounds are more likely to smoke; more likely to have inadequate nutrition; less likely to be able to access medical care; and are therefore more likely to succumb to the chronic diseases that are the long-term consequence of such factors. They may also be disproportionately reflective of ethnic minorities in a given society (Nazroo, 2001). An overweening message of many public health campaigns is to take responsibility for one's own health. The reverse subtext of many of those messages, when framed in terms of personal responsibility, is that those who come down with the related diseases are seen as having brought it on themselves.

We feel physically different during illness from the way we feel when we are well and bodily changes are generally how we come to conclude we are unwell: illness is an embodied phenomenological experience. This may be transient and recovered from, it may be chronic and lived with, or it may be terminal. Each of these illness experiences has ramifications for the body in society. Transient illness is often infectious, which brings up issues of both public health and moral panics around particular conditions (HIV/AIDS, Avian Flu, Swine Flu). So, illness can be the object of networks of control and surveillance. Chronic illness – which may be congenital, developed or acquired – is, or becomes, an integral part of that person's life. Terminal illness may extend from any of these sources and confronts us with the ultimate fallibility of our bodies. Whatever the origin, the phenomenological nature of the processes of being ill shapes the person's embodied experience.

Let us take several illustrative examples that fall within these three categories. Taking a personal experience first, an adult who contracts malaria will be completely incapacitated by fever, aches and chills until medication is administered to kill the parasite, and will experience a very slow process of recovery from extreme weakness to gradually regained strength. This may leave them with a heightened appreciation of the body in the short term if the parasite is of one of the varieties that cause acute (and dangerous) but curable symptoms and is treated early. It may also lead to the long-term reappraisal of the reliability of the body if not treated promptly and/or the variety of parasite is one that leads to chronic symptoms.

A person born with Cerebral Palsy (CP), will have restricted movement and is likely to spend a great deal of their childhood in physiotherapy and undergoing surgery, which will lead them to have a different understanding of their bodies in space, bodily movement and pain from that understood by the majority of society. Someone who acquires paraplegia in mid-life will have similar medical experiences to the person with CP but they will have forms of bodily and social *adjustment* to deal with – from identifying with the 'norm' to dealing with being perceived as disabled. Illness can be life-altering, body-altering and social capital altering.

Finally, a young person who develops metastatic melanoma (an aggressive skin cancer that spreads quickly) may, again, share some of the experiences of medical treatments (surgery, hospitalization) to the individuals with paraplegia or CP, and others specific to the condition (chemotherapy, radiotherapy). They also have the additional knowledge that total bodily failure is inevitable. Terminal illness, as Elias argues of modern medicalized societies, renders the body and the individual socially invisible, while at the same time the individual experiences heightened awareness of the body in crisis (**Death and Dying**).

Like giving birth, the experience of acute illness reminds us of the tenuousness of normality and intensifies our awareness that we are embodied beings. As a result we may take on the 'sick role' (Parsons 1937), that is submit to the medicalization of our bodies; or we may resist the medical models of illness – the person with CP may reject the notion of disability; the terminally ill person may reject treatments such as chemotherapy.

Each of these facets of illness is the focus of a great deal of sociological research, much of which involves qualitative approaches to the patient experience within the context of medical and institutional power. Narrative research amongst people undergoing medical treatment (Frank, 1995) and particularly palliative care – that might involve patients writing diaries, songs or poems (Romanoff and Thompson, 2006) – has been used to attempt to give voice to what Elias called the 'loneliness of the dying'. Phenomenological research into the effects of paraplegia and quadriplegia on experiences of embodiment has followed the mental and physical adaptive capacities of individuals in relation to their conditions (Seymour, 1998). Much social action and participant observation work has been done on the (sometimes very basic) differences in understanding of the meaning and construction of illness between patients, carers and practitioners using interviews and focus groups (for example, Oakley, cited under **Feminism**).

Illness and health are also relational categories that are often understood in binary opposition with each other. Health may denote a lack of illness but, as research in the sociology of health and illness has found, it also implies a range of other interpretations that have social implications based on bodily traits. An aspect of the rhetoric of the nineteenth century around the deserving and undeserving poor, persists in our categorization of those individuals who are chronically ill with those conditions at which public health campaigns are most frequently aimed. Those who smoke are often considered the undeserving ill even by those treating them. Take home oxygen cylinders cannot be given to people with advanced emphysema who continue to smoke due to the obvious danger of explosion, but this also carries the message that until the smoker stops he or she does not 'deserve', or that it is 'pointless' to supply, the treatment. Cardiologists regularly tell smokers assessed as requiring coronary artery bypass surgery that they will not be having surgery until they cease smoking. People who are assessed as morbidly obese are regularly told that surgery requiring general anaesthetic will be postponed until they lose weight, on the basis of the dangers posed to the patient (and the insurance risk to the hospital), but with an inevitable overtone that until weight is lost they are not deserving of what they are told is the appropriate care.

The way that health and illness are treated is also very largely dependent on the infrastructure and the general economic state of a given country: policy will therefore vary widely from nation to nation. For example, the UK, like much of Europe, has a health system that is predominantly public, for citizens and residents; the US system is predominantly private with only the most basic public cover for the poorest; and countries like Australia are somewhere in between, with a public health system that is available to all citizens and a parallel private system that those who can afford to are encouraged to utilize. Whether one accesses any or all of these systems, as noted at the start of this entry, may depend heavily on one's social status (Nazroo, 2001).

FURTHER READING

The readings here and under **Medicine and Science** should be consulted together.
For introductions to the sociology of health and illness (or the sociology of medicine as it is sometimes called) Annandale (1998), Nettleton (2006) and Nettleton and Gustaffson (2002) provide good introductory overviews. However, the reader should seek out locally specific publications for accurate discussions of issues related to the policies of individual health systems, which vary widely. For discussion of the body as the object/subject of discourses around health and illness see Lupton (1994, 1995) and Armstrong (2005). Ivan Illich (1976, 2001) remains a key thinker in the critique of the medicalization of the human body and the experience of illness, and writes in an easy-to-read manner. For some examples of the many sociological and anthropological studies of illness narratives, see Hardey (2002) and Snyder (2000) but most particularly Frank (1995) whose book is a landmark text.

REFERENCES

Annandale, E. (1998) *The Sociology of Health and Medicine.* Cambridge: Polity.
Armstrong. D. (2005) 'The rise of surveillance medicine', *Sociology of Health and Illness,* 17: 393–404.
Frank, A. (1995) *The Wounded Storyteller: Body, Illness & Ethics.* Chicago: Chicago University Press.
Hardey, M. (2002) '"The story of my illness": Personal accounts of illness on the internet', *Health,* 6(1): 31–46.
Illich, Ivan (1976) *Medical Nemesis: The Expropriation of Health.* Harmondsworth: Penguin.
Illich, Ivan (2001) *Limits to Medicine.* New York: Marion Boyars.
Lupton, D. (1994) *Medicine as Culture.* London: Sage.
Lupton, D. (1995) *The Imperative of Health: Public Health and the Regulated Body.* London: Sage.
Nettleton, S. (2006) *The Sociology of Health and Illness.* Cambridge: Polity.
Nettleton, S. and U. Gustafsson (eds) (2002) *The Sociology of Health and Illness Reader.* Oxford: Polity.
Snyder, L. (2000) *Speaking Our Minds: Personal Reflections from Individuals with Alzheimer's.* New York: W.H. Freeman and Co.

> **Definition** Identity is the sense of 'self' or personhood that is con-
> structed within a social complex. It may be perceived solely in terms of
> the individual, it may be perceived in terms of group – or other –
> relations, but it is inevitably caught up in the interplay of our own and
> others' perceptions of the self. In this, identity and the body are inextri-
> cably linked.

There are a variety of ways of understanding identity. From a psychological standpoint, identity is generally conceived as an internal intellectual process linked to stages of development and how we form
knowledge about ourselves and the world (see the discussion of Freud
under **Psychoanalysis**). This is, generally, explained in terms of our earliest interpersonal relationships (mother, father, siblings) which are said to
affect the way we construe and relate to others and society. Psychological
notions of identity are, by and large, universalizing and can imply that
certain traits are immutable. Early social theories of identity such as
Cooley's (1902) 'looking-glass self' were related to these psychological
developmental approaches as is Mead's (1934/1962) 'me' and 'I',
despite its emphasis on socialization (see also **Appearance and Beauty**).
However, psychological understandings of identity tend to be highly
individualizing and do not provide sufficient explanation of the individual's identity as a member of the group or a society, even if they have
much to say about the individual's capacity to function within a social
complex. Goffman's (1971) idea of identity as social performance or
'mask', whereby we adapt that performance for a given audience (private, public, home, work), introduced the notion that identity is not as
static as is often assumed.

Across these theories we can already see the embodied nature of
identity. Cooley and Mead's understanding of identity requires self-
awareness, a reshaping of both behaviour and appearance in response to
recognizing our own and/or others' views of our bodily cues. We
become acutely aware of our bodily presentation. Similarly, Goffman's

social masks require both the monitoring and re-presentation of ourselves through the management of embodied gestures and behaviours. The conscious (or subconscious) appropriation of a given identity may be intellectual but the social projection of that is fundamentally embodied in practice.

In broad terms, identity can be said to be the result of the material and/or intellectual connections we make with others, with whom we have something in common. One of the clearest examples of such common connection is national identity. Anderson (1991) has characterized this kind of identity as our self-selecting membership of what, in post-modern societies, is an 'imagined community'. We relate emotionally and materially to an anonymous mass of people, very few of whom we may ever meet or talk to – even though we may live next door to them – but with whom we believe we have a shared understanding of what it is to be of that nation.

Identity need not be – indeed rarely is – constituted at a single level. For example, national identity can be incredibly complex. In a multicultural society, this may involve not only identification with the geographical boundaries within which one lives but also (sometimes *rather*) identifications with one or multiple lands in which one does not and may never have resided. These kinds of diasporic connections become more complex and more common as globalization intensifies and people move more readily between nations. The mutability of national identity is a clear example of how it is no longer possible to understand identity, of any kind, as fixed. Just as affiliations to nations have become more abstract, the increasing reflexivity of everyday life in developed countries leads to the further fracturing of identity into the reflexive identities of the post-modern individuals, who take on the responsibility of self-construction as a method of (self-) control in a world in which the certainties (work, family, community) of prior social formations have fractured (Giddens, 1991).

Even within a seemingly straightforward national identity there may be multiple identities that interleave within and over that national identity: ethnic, gender, sexual, disability, religious, political ... identities may take precedence over any allegiance to country (see also **Difference**). Any of us has multiple identifications or identities at any one time, that inform and contribute to the self and these shape and are shaped by other people's perceptions of us. Identity is therefore also formed on the basis of rejection, on what we are *not*. For example, fundamentally, I am *not* male. This can be closely followed by any number of other *nots*, as well as positive assertions of what I am.

Others perceive our identity through our self-presentation, in which our bodily presentation is implicated. Bourdieu (see **Habitus**) argued that our class identity is visible in the way we hold our bodies, what we wear, our bodily actions, our choice of sport or leisure pursuits and where we live, amongst a whole complex of embodied attributes. The same may be said of identity other than class: skin-colour, gender, sexuality, ability/disability and so on. Identity may be with a nation, it may be with an ethnic group, it may be associated with a gender or a sexual preference, it may lodge in a loose grouping on the basis of bodily habits or outward markings (**Modification/Dysmorphias**), but it is hard to think of a form of identity that does not involve some embodied aspect. Even in a multicultural society national identity hinges on physical and/or geographical location (or the '*not*' of where we are located).

All manner of what might be called difference is linked to identity (**Class/Caste, Colonialism/Post-colonialism, Difference, Disability/ Ability, Race/Ethnicity**). Post-modern constructions of identity hold that none of these is fixed, therefore identity is not fixed. Identity has been assumed to be immutable in historical, positivist understandings because bodies have been assumed to be immutable in relation to all these categories. While he did tend to assume *a* body, undifferentiated on the basis of gender or age, Foucault has nevertheless shown that the dominant understanding of the body is itself a historical construction (**Medicine and Science**) that has changed over time. All the embodied aspects of identity are therefore open to adaptation, conscious presenta-tion and re-presentation (**Modification/Dysmorphias, Performativity**).

Identity is also important to the body in society on the basis of dominant dualistic understandings of the body as a lesser material adjunct to the controlling mind (**Dualism**). All the embodied aspects of identity mentioned above bring to the fore the embodied nature of identity formation. This rejects the abstract construction of identity as an intellectual phenomenon rather than a phenomenological and embodied quality. The political theorization of identity, at least since Hobbes, has been as a facet of the mind. And yet, as sociology and par-ticularly the sociology of the body has shown, much of the prejudice and oppression consequent on the ascription of non-ideal identities has been on the basis of bodily traits (**Class/Caste, Gender/Sex, Nature/ Culture**, etc.).

FURTHER READING

See also the readings for **Class/Caste, Colonialism/Post-colonialism, Difference, Gender/Sex** and **Nature/Culture**.
There are many intellectual theories of identity, which have little to say about the body or bodily effects and yet have bodily ramifications, such as Cooley (1902) and Mead (1934/1962). Some of the key theorists who do attend to the embodied nature of identity are Anderson (1991), Giddens (1991) and of course Goffman (1971). Goffman, in appealing to the physical means by which we shape our behaviour, brought the body into identity and is therefore a key further reading. Crossley (2001) takes the body *as* identity, arguing that we are our bodies. Burkitt (1999) has approached the intersection of the body and identity in modernity, arguing for identity as embodied and relational, through the interplay of body and thought. I also include here Hallam et al. (1999) because, as much of my own writing testifies (Cregan, 2007a, 2007b, 2009) I believe that *the dead are part of the community*, as we prove through our treatment of and the ceremonies we perform upon their bodies as well as our remembrance of them.

REFERENCES

Anderson, B. (1991) *Imagined Communities*. London: Verso.
Burkitt, I. (1999) *Bodies of Thought: Embodiment, Identity and Modernity*. London: Sage.
Cooley, C.H. (1902) *Human Nature and the Social Order*. New York. Charles Scribner and Sons.
Cregan, K. (2007a) 'Early modern anatomy and the Queen's body natural: The sovereign subject', *Body & Society*, 13(2): 47–66.
Cregan, K. (2007b) 'Remembering the dead', in *Globalism Institute Annual Report, 2006*. Melbourne: RMIT University.
Cregan, K. (2009) *The Theatre of the Body: Staging Life and Embodying Death in Early Modern London*. Turnhout, Belgium: Brepols.
Crossley, N. (2001) *The Social Body: Habit, Identity and Desire*. London: Sage.
Giddens, A. (1991) *Modernity and Self-Identity: Self and Society in the Late Modern Age*. Cambridge: Polity.
Goffman, E. (1971) *The Presentation of Self in Everyday Life*. Harmondsworth: Penguin.
Hallam, E., J. Hockey and G. Howarth (1999) *Beyond the Body: Death and Social Identity*. London: Routledge.
Mead, G.H. (1962) *Mind, Self and Society*. Chicago: University of Chicago Press. First published 1934.

identity

···· Media and Representation ····

> **Definition** The media is a shorthand term for the various forms of mass communication through which we gain knowledge about the world and ourselves: that is, newspapers, television, magazines, radio, film; the online forms of each of these more traditional media outlets; as well as new and emerging media such as blogs, and a range of social media and instant messaging feeds.[5] Representation is a functional aspect of the media – within any communication the message is implicitly and explicitly shaped by a variety of influences: authorial preference, editorial vision, political climate, and socio-cultural context. As Marshall McLuhan said in the 1960s, the medium is the message.

Clearly media don't just provide information in a raw form, the messages that all these media purvey are already shaped by the human beings who control and work in the media and they are products of social complexes with pre-existing ideas and agendas. So news is never just news, it is always an editorialized representation in one form or another. This may range from (but is not limited to) what the camera operator or photographer chooses to capture; the choice of angle at which a still photograph or a moving image is shot; the framing headline, title, caption or voice-over which tells us how to interpret what is presented in images and in text; the ranked placement of items within the wider context of a given media source; the kind of language and/or additional music used; and the intended and actual audiences. The work of John Berger (1972) has been crucial to opening out thinking about the meaning of representations and social, political and historical content and contexts that are embedded in them.

Because representations in the media always go further than a straightforward presentation of news, they are therefore of great interest to sociologists and has a particular place, deserved or not, in the conception of the body in society. Under **Appearance and Beauty**, and **Feminism**

---

[5]I am consciously avoiding the use of proprietary names – the main players are well known.

there is some discussion of the media as one of the most powerful ways of presenting ideals of how we 'should' be, to society at large. It presents those external opinions of worth and approval that constitute Goffman's virtual social identity, to which Cooley's 'looking glass self' or Mead's 'I' might adhere (**Identity**). The media has been criticized for peddling a plethora of messages, that we are: too fat (reality weight loss contests, fashion magazines, dieting websites); too thin (current affairs, women's magazines, public health promotions); too old (cosmetics advertising, lifestyle magazines); too young (news and current affairs); not beautiful enough (reality modelling competitions) – but suddenly beautiful after plastic surgery (reality makeover programmes) and so on. Many of these messages exhibit the force of ideas of post-modern self-realization as a socially produced and context-dependent ideal. That is, each carries in it one or more ideals of bodily perfection but those ideals vary over time and between cultures.

Social research around identity formation and body image has shown that the power of social ideals is quite real and that the promulgation of representations has effects on wider identity in terms of affecting female, and increasingly male, body image (Bordo, 1999; Millett, 1977). Representations need not refer only to ideals of perfection. In the case of representations of ageing, they can reflect other kinds of gendered social 'truths', that promote the enduring vitality of ageing men (Viagra) and the frailty (osteoporosis) or bodily failures (incontinence) of ageing women. These are not new constructions of gendered bodily qualities, representations in the media return to well-worn tropes and stereotypes. Social research has also shown that there is no straightforward cause and (negative) effect between the media message and individual actions, as might once have been claimed within the writings of some second-wave feminism (**Feminism**). Rather, there has been increasing recognition that the public at large and sub-groups within that wider society have agency and are able to critically reflect on what is presented to them. Individuals may still adhere to a given message and aspire to a given ideal, but not necessarily as passively as may once have been argued (Baehr and Gray, 1996). The media is nevertheless a powerful disseminator of body images and bodily ideals, and a vehicle for promoting what Elias would have called 'manners' or what Foucault would have called mechanisms of surveillance. In any socio-political context we will simultaneously absorb cultural mores, reproduce them, but also be selective in our adherence to them, or in some instances utterly resistant to them.

Social media and instant feeds of news (and nonsense) have a number of ramifications. They have been instrumental in a number of recent political uprisings, for example, in 2011 mobile phones were used to mobilize massed protests across Egypt, Libya and Yemen and to send graphic images of reprisals against those protests to external media outlets. These new media have the potential to excite and facilitate conscious political agitation that is expressed in more traditional ways – face-to-face battles, bloody and bloodless coups. They are also used to organize what might have been called 'happenings' in the 1960s, that is, flash-mobs which may have intentions that are political, religious, aesthetic, whimsical, or commercial. That is, new media are bringing together otherwise loosely connected or disconnected (post-modern) individuals with a single interest in common, in contradistinction to the organized socio-political movements whose aim was to reform governments that were more typical of prior social formations. Nevertheless, both are manifestations of people power and involve massed embodied actions.

FURTHER READING

One of the key texts in the semiotics of imagery and representations is John Berger's *Ways of Seeing* (1972), and it underpins many of the critiques of visual representations of the human body in the media. Baehr and Gray (1996) offer a collection of critical readings of the effects of media representations on women's self-image. The further reading under **Anorexia/Bulimia/Obesity** and **Feminism** should be consulted for writings related to the effect on women of popular images related to ideal body images. Some writings on specific effects of media and representation include Blaikie (1999) on ageing bodies, Bordo on the male body (1999) and Urla and Swedlund (2000) on the globalization of a particular iconography of an unattainable female body.

REFERENCES

Baehr, H. and A. Gray (eds) (1996) *Turning It On: A Reader in Women and Media*. London: Arnold.

Berger, J. (1972) *Ways of Seeing*. Harmondsworth: Penguin.

Blaikie, A. (1999) *Ageing and Popular Culture*. Cambridge: Cambridge University Press.

Bordo, S. (1999) *The Male Body: A New Look at Men in Public and in Private*. New York: Farrar, Straus & Giroux.

key concepts in
body and society

Millett, K. (1977) *Sexual Politics*. London: Virago.

Urla, J. and A.C. Swedlund (2000) 'The anthropometry of Barbie: Unsettling ideals of the feminine body in popular culture', in L. Schiebinger (ed.), *Feminism and the Body*. Oxford: Oxford University Press.

Medicine and Science

Definition Medicine is the field of knowledge that is applied to disease, illness and infirmity in the human body. Historically, healing has been practised by a variety of professionals in a number of systems, all of which except the increasingly dominant biomedical-scientific approach are now patronizingly relegated to the status of 'traditional'. Science, as commonly understood, is the pursuit of 'truths' through the formulation of hypotheses that are tested against the empirical observation of the natural world. Medicine is often thought of as scientific, which it was not always, and even today diagnosis and treatment can often be seen more as an 'art' than as a pure science.

It is hard to over-estimate just how much the developed world's (and increasingly the developing world's) dominant understanding of the human body is, at the core, a biomedical (that is, biological and medical) and scientific view of the body. That is not to say that other ways of understanding the body in a holistic non-medical sense do not exist – clearly they do in Traditional Chinese and Ayurvedic medicines – merely that the view of the body that has the greatest power and influence in the modern world is that formed within Western biomedical discourse. All the major concerns we have with the body in social theory come down to matters on which medical science has much to say. Gender is a social category but medicine and science, since their emergence in a modern form in the late seventeenth century, have worked hard to find material bases for gender attributes, dividing masculine and feminine domains into scientifically justifiable male and female 'facts'. Gender reassignment (which, in practice, is the attempted reassignment of the organs of *sexual* reproduction), body dysmorphia, gay genes – all are medicalized ways of attempting to explain and exert dominance over the human body, to define it in rationalistic terms.

It is, again, Foucault (see **Discourse, Power**) who has been one of the most influential writers on the social scientists who have been analysing and critiquing biomedical and scientific ideas of the body since the publication of his *The Birth of the Clinic* (1975). In this book Foucault rewrites the history of medicine, undoing the positivist narrative that has characterized ideas of medical and scientific endeavour since the eighteenth century. He deliberately turns on its head the notion that science, and medical science in particular, improves by overcoming mistakes, and that prior medical systems were based on ignorance or 'bad science'. Instead, he looks to the shifts in systems of meaning (epistemic shifts) that have culminated in modern Western medicine. In doing so he gives equal weight to each of the stages of medical knowledge, demonstrates that each had its own coherent world-view and shows how the slow and uneven movement from one system to another was related to the wider shifting social formations in which Western medicine functioned.

The effect that these epistemic shifts in medical theories had was particularly important for the understanding of the human body in society; for biomedicine (more recently known as bio-psychosocial medicine) has become the primary means of approaching and interpreting the body. The core features of the epistemic shifts that Foucault describes are the medical 'gaze' – medical perception – and the importance of the gaze for the abstraction of the body. The closer doctors came to the body in the ways in which diseases were diagnosed – from feeling the pulse to biopsy – the further away they were drawn from the embodied patient. The further the medical gaze penetrated into the body using increasingly techno-scientific means – from anatomical dissection, to the stethoscope and eventually the X-ray – the more *abstract* have its representation and its understanding become. Foucault claims that with the gradual emergence of the medical establishment many prior medical forms, including the leper house and the infirmary, were superseded as were earlier surface diagnostics.

Not only the names of diseases, not only the grouping of systems were not the same; but the fundamental perceptual codes that were applied to patients' bodies, the field of objects to which observation addressed itself, the surfaces and depths traversed by the doctor's gaze, the whole system of orientation of this gaze also varied. (Foucault, 1975: 54)

Up until the early seventeenth century, the majority of healing was performed by traditional healers, whether family members or 'cunning' people. For the desperately poor there were charitable institutions like the infirmary, where the sick were attended by clergy; and for the rich there were university educated physicians for ailments treated by medications or barber-surgeons for setting broken bones, blood-letting and anything involving cutting into the body.

Surgeons were mechanicals who applied external treatments. Physicians were scholars who diagnosed by symptoms and administered internal medications. Their practices were based in theories that expressly avoided contact with the body. Physicians ran the 'clinics' or hospitals, but, on Foucault's timeline, medical practice changed radically in the last years of the eighteenth century when Linnaean taxonomies became the dominant form of medical understanding. Medicine became observational and 'experimental' – that is empiricist, identified and classified by genus, taught theoretically instead of by an insistence on an unquestioning scholastic reverence for texts: 'Once one defined a practical experiment carried out on the patient himself, one insisted on the need to relate particular knowledge to an encyclopaedic whole' (Foucault, 1975: 71). Combined with this, medical healing (very) gradually moved out of the home and into the hospital, which had once been the site of treatment only for society's poorest and most feared.

Hospitals were increasingly funded by rich benefactors and therefore continued to be charitable institutions, as they had been under the aegis of the various religious orders that had initially set up the lazar houses and hospices in the Middle Ages. However, there was a different tenor to the arrangement once capital entered into the picture. The rich gave the funds that made the hospitals possible but the poor repaid in kind by providing the means for disease to be studied and experimentally treated in ways that ended up benefiting the rich. We can see in Foucault's example, the beginnings of the experimental scientific medicine that we live with to this day, where teaching hospitals – historically, by their nature public hospitals – are used for research and experimental procedures, which are by and large conducted on those who have least choice in life. Once a treatment is shown to have an application the people most likely to have access to it are those with the income to pay for it.

To give an example not dealt with in *Birth of the Clinic*, it is a simple fact that plastic surgery techniques (nose, jaw and cheek 'jobs') have become possible because of what has been learned from both the emergency treatments applied to burns victims, and through the reconstructive surgery on trauma victims and those with cranio-facial anomalies. What has become relatively standard orthopaedic surgery (hip and knee replacement) has learned much from battlefield surgery or the treatment of road trauma victims. Embryonic stem cell technology would not exist without IVF.

Foucault's major point is that medicine shifted away from being dependent on external signs towards looking (and listening) into the body to interpret what was clearly visible on the surface. That looking into began with anatomical dissection and the extrapolation from the evidence of the dead body to living structures and systems. This led to a process of imaginative visualization – the medical 'gaze' – long before it was possible to look directly into the living body.

The gaze led to the visualization of internal structures, symptoms and pathologies. What the sufferer felt or believed came to mean less and less: it was the physician's observations that lent coherence to disease processes. The medical gaze structured them, much as 'natural history' structured and classified the natural world (Foucault, 1975: 89). But observation alone was not sufficient, it had then to be interpreted through an authoritative language or discourse.

> In this regular alternation of speech and gaze, the disease gradually declares its truth, a truth that it offers to the eye and ear, whose theme, although possessing only one *sense*, can be restored, in its indubitable totality, only by two *senses*: that which sees and that which listens. (Foucault, 1975: 112)

Thus, the body came into a new kind of existence through the abstracted visualization and auralization of its symptoms, its boundaries, its depths and cavities. What we would now call a 'clinical history' as a means of diagnosis is an outcome of this process. In the general sense of the word, that visual cognition and its consequent discourse abstract embodied disease experiences into the hands, eyes, ears and mouth of the physician (Foucault, 1975: 119). And in the analytical sense, the symptoms and the experience of disease are abstracted away from the body in which it is housed. It becomes an entity in itself under the gaze of the physician, over which he has the power of bringing into being. But, most importantly from Foucault's point of view, this led to an epistemic shift: medical discourse and medical knowledge moved into a new phase.

Paradoxically, the whole notion of the ailing body shifted from diagnosing from symptoms or external evidence and verbal inquiry – whereby, the patient had the power over what ailed him or her – to a surrendering of that power to a doctor. And it was the doctor who at once projected beyond the surfaces of the body, laying on hands and ears, intruding with a penetrating gaze, while at the same time rendering the body more abstract and more distanced both from the patient, and from himself.

Though these are not Foucault's terms – nor particularly in sympathy with them – it also identifies a moment in the intensification of the abstraction of the human body that is at the heart of the medical way of understanding being that is dominant in the contemporary world: techno-scientific medicine. Foucault identifies the instrumental means of representing bodily processes that were the first step in the on-going process of the analytical abstraction of embodiment: the body as read and interpreted by ultrasound, X-ray, heart monitoring, brain wave monitoring, and by ultrasonic or magnetic resonance brain and full body scans.

Foucault rightly notes that something as simple as the 'stethoscope, solidified distance, transmits profound and invisible events along a semi-tactile, semi-auditory axis' (1975: 164). It sets up a physical and moral distance between the doctor and the patient. The result is the physician's ability to 'see' into the body is based on knowledge extrapolated from firsthand experience of dissecting (dead) bodies. The bodies of the dead are maps to the illnesses of the living. 'It is when death became the concrete a priori of medical experience that death could detach itself from counter-nature and become *embodied* in the *living bodies* of individuals' (Foucault, 1975: 196). So, in essence, the 'modern' body is patterned on, modelled on, interpreted through, the corpse. Ironically, this eventuates in a medical science that is determinedly at war with death (see Ariès, 1981; Elias, 1985).

FURTHER READING

Foucault and Illich (see **Health and Illness**) were key to starting the debates around the power and orthodoxies of medicine, they are clearly written and are good places to start reading further into the body in medicine. Turner and Samson (1995) picked up where Foucault left off, looking at the social construction of medical knowledge in late twentieth century society. Williams (2003) is an excellent overview and introduction to medical sociology. Harding (1986) was one of the first to bring feminist questions to the construction of scientific discourses, including medicine. Those who have followed on in exploring the social construction of medical knowledge systems include Cartwright (1995) and Birke (1999) who take feminist cultural studies approaches to the topic. Sawday's (1995) book is a widely cited, historically situated cultural/literary studies reading of anatomical illustrations and poetic imagery that follows the shift in medical understanding that came with the rise of dualism. My own (2009) book on drama, anatomical dissection and the law is similarly a cultural history of medical power that also offers insight into some of the people who were subjects of one particular anatomy theatre.

REFERENCES

Birke, L. (1999) *Feminism and the Biological Body*. Edinburgh: Edinburgh University Press.

Cartright, L. (1995) *Screening the Body: Tracing Medicine's Visual Culture*. Minneapolis: University of Minnesota Press.

Cregan, K. (2009) *The Theatre of the Body: Staging Life and Embodying Death in Early Modern London*. Turnhout, Belgium: Brepols.

Foucault, Michel (1975) *The Birth of the Clinic: An Archaeology of Medical Perception*, trans. A.M. Sheridan Smith. New York: Random House.

Harding, Sandra (1986) *The Science Question in Feminism*. Ithaca, NY: Cornell University Press.

Sawday, J. (1995) *The Body Emblazoned: Dissection and the Human Body in Renaissance Culture*. London: Routledge.

Turner, B. with Colin Samson (1995) *Medical Power and Social Knowledge*, 2nd edn. London: Sage Publications. First published 1987.

Williams, S. (2003). *Medicine and the Body*. London: Sage.

···· Modification/Dysmorphias ····

Definition Body modification can have a number of meanings, which will be grouped here into three generalizing categories. The first is bodily marking. This may be the result of traditional or tribal practices – such as scarification, piercing or tattooing – or the use of those practices by non-traditional and non-tribal people. The second is bodily enhancement.

This refers to the conscious reshaping of the body either through diet and exercise or through elective cosmetic/aesthetic surgery. The third is body modification. This can sometimes be used to refer to cosmetic surgeries but here it is being used specifically to refer to the surgical treatment of body dysmorphia and to gender reassignment.

Traditional or tribal bodily marking – such as scarification, piercing or tattoos – mark the entry of a member of social group into a particular stage of life and/or social belonging within that group (Brain, 1979). These marking practices generally embody the taking on of a new level of responsibility within and towards the group and often signify a movement into adulthood. They signify a direct connection to others. Each of these kinds of bodily marking has also been appropriated from traditional or tribal contexts by people from post-colonial, post-modern societies. Various forms of piercing to display jewellery have come and gone in Western societies through traditional and modern social formations but tattooing had not survived beyond pre-traditional social formations. The modern European adoption of tattoos is said to have been brought back by seamen who took part in explorations between the fifteenth and nineteenth centuries and encountered cultures who practised tattooing, although there is evidence that it was a practice known in tribal Europe that had fallen into disuse until re-encountered (Caplan, 2000). They were famously adopted by members of European Royal families in the late-nineteenth century, both male and female, but until the late twentieth century they were largely associated with out-groups (rebels). Since the 1980s they have become increasingly common as personal statements of identity, or decoration (Sanders and Vail, 2008), where the original meaning is emptied out and a new meaning of post-modern dissociated belonging is applied. The desire to tattoo or modify can be seen as an expression of autonomy but it has also drawn a lot of attention from psychologists in relation to self-harm (Rothman and Rothman, 2003), and from psychoanalytic theorists in its potential for remaking the self (Lemma, 2010). Hence, the same tattoo may still mark entry into a tribal clan or it may be the result of a post-modern aesthetic decision.

Bodily enhancement might be done through diet and exercise (Bordo, 1993) involving a conscious reshaping of the body to fit an ideal the individual wants to realize. The enhancement of the body through diet and/or exercise involves self-regulation to a high degree, and may be a conscious response to social models of desirability (**Appearance and Beauty**); in response to public education campaigns (**Health and Illness**), or at the behest of a medical practitioner (**Medicine and Science**). Those social models of desirability may cross cultures and involve the reshaping of the body to meet a dominant Western model of beauty that culminates in the erasure not only of the beauty standards of another culture, but also the visible signs of cultural specificity in the individual (Miller, 2006). There are ambiguities and contradictions in this aspect of enhancement, whereby the same practices may be understood in divergent ways, as healthy and unhealthy: the obsessive exercise component of bulimia and the moral panic over obesity are examples that come to mind (see also **Anorexia/Bulimia/Obesity**).

The body may also be consciously reshaped and refined in aspects that are not amenable to change via diet and exercise. This may include the use of implants or the removal of what is deemed to be excess (Davis, 1995). Breast augmentation (implants) and rhinoplasty (nose-jobs) have been available since the 1960s and have gradually moved through the social scale, along with other aesthetic procedures. Thanks to surgical 'holidays' to South East Asia for cosmetic procedures, that cost little more than a holiday in Bali, what was once the self-indulgence of the rich has become an aspirational consumption for the many. Cheek, chin, breast, penile and buttock implants, rib removal, nose re-modelling, jawline shaving, brow lifts – all mould the structure of the body to order. This may also be in combination with less invasive techniques such as Botox injections and liposuction. These procedures have been the subject of extensive social research and also activism (Elliott, 2008). Women have been the main consumers of these procedures but men are increasingly taking part and there are many questions to be asked around identity formation and consumption in this regard. There are a number of artists who have undergone repeated surgical enhancements as theatrical/identity performances. These performances are intended to question the understanding of the human body as 'stable' and a 'given' (**Performativity**).

Bodily modification, as defined here, is undergone surgically like these latter forms of enhancement. They are invasive procedures that involve substantial bodily rearrangement that is inextricable from identity formation (Featherstone, 2000). Included in this definition there are procedures such as gender reassignment or the surgical treatment of body dysmorphia. Gender reassignment (see also **Gender/Sex**) is a bodily modification that is effected both bio-chemically and surgically. It may be done in infancy to reassign incompletely formed male genitals (Parens, 2006) or it may be done electively in adulthood. In adult reassignments, hormones are used to rebalance to the appropriate levels for a male or female appearance: more or less hair, coarser or finer skin, more or less body fat, the promotion or depletion of mammary tissue (Oudshoorn, 1994). Once a biochemical and psychological regimen has been undergone, generally over a minimum period of two years, surgical reassignment may (or in some instances may not) take place. Excess breast tissue is removed or implants introduced, and the external genitalia remodelled to approximate the appearance of male (penile implants) or female (penile inversion to form a vagina) genitals.

Children are not accorded these niceties, the decision and/or recommendation to reassign sex being in medical hands, with parental decision-making and consent required. As we saw under both **Genetics** and **Gender/Sex**, intersex reassignment of outward appearance of sex is generally done to remove an incompletely formed penis so the child can be raised as a girl. I discuss elsewhere the ongoing physical treatment required to maintain that narrative, but there is increasing disquiet in some circles around such decisions being made so early in life and without any reference to the embodied individual who will live with the consequences (Parens, 2006). It is not only in gender reassignment that this is an issue. Surgery and other medical treatments to 'normalize' children occur for numerous reasons, some of them involving illness and others purely cosmetic. This raises ethical issues over who has the right to make such fundamental bodily decisions for those who are not considered able to make legal decisions for themselves (see also **Ageing and Childhood** and **Youth and Children**).

FURTHER READING

See also the readings under **Gender/Sex**, **Identity**, **Queer** and **Sexuality**. Featherstone's (2000) collection is an early and interesting selection of essays that theorize the meaning of body modification as a social artefact. Brain (1979) takes a 'collector's' approach to identifying forms of bodily decoration, some of which are also modifications, from around the globe with some anthropological discussion. As noted under **Appearance and Beauty**, Gilman (1999) is notable for his work on the history and socio-cultural politics of aesthetic surgery. Davis (1995) and Elliott (2008) contribute to the debates around the wider effects of fashions in cosmetic surgery, on women and post-modern society, respectively. Parens (2006) is concerned with the ethics of surgical modification on children and Rothman and Rothman (2003) are concerned about any kind of medical modification of the body. On tattooing, see Caplan (2000) for the history, Lemma (2010) for a psychoanalytic approach, and Sanders and Vail (2008) for a cultural studies critique.

REFERENCES

Brain, V. (1979) *The Decorated Body*. London: Harper & Row.

Caplan, J. (ed.) (2000) *Written on the Body: The Tattoo in European and American History*. London: Reaktion Books.

Davis, K. (1995) *Reshaping the Female Body: The Dilemma of Cosmetic Surgery*. New York: Routledge.

Elliott, A. (2008) *Making the Cut: How Cosmetic Surgery is Transforming our Lives*. London: Reaktion Books.

Featherstone, M. (ed.) (2000) *Body Modification*. London: Sage.

Gilman, S. (1999) *Making the Body Beautiful: A Cultural History of Aesthetic Surgery*. Princeton: Princeton University Press.

Lemma, A. (2010) *Under the Skin: A Psychoanalytic Study of Body Modification*. New York: Routledge.

Miller, L. (2006) *Beauty Up: Exploring Contemporary Japanese Body Aesthetics*. Berkeley: University of California Press.

Parens, E. (ed.) (2006) *Surgically Shaping Children: Technology, Ethics and the Pursuit of Normality*. Baltimore: Johns Hopkins University Press.

Rothman, S and D. Rothman (2003) *The Pursuit of Perfection: The Promise and Perils of Medical Enhancement*. New York: Vintage.

Sanders, C. and D. Vail. (2008) *Customizing the Body: The Art and Culture of Tattooing*. Philadelphia: Temple University Press.

key concepts in
body and society

Nature/Culture

128

Definition Nature and culture are two interconnected ways of understanding and describing the world that are as old as the stories human beings tell about themselves. They form a pair of binary opposites, that is, opposite terms that cannot be dissociated conceptually because the definition of each depends on the existence of the other. Nature refers to what has yet to be cultivated or civilized and culture is the means of taming or bringing nature under control (see also **Civilizing Processes**). Nature is associated with the natural (non-human/yet-to-be-human) world and culture with human traits, activities and knowledges.

Over the past 30 years or so, culture has increasingly come to define the different social structures and networks that characterize given groups of people or by which identity is conveyed or actively formed. This might be on the basis of nationality (French culture), diaspora (multiculturalism), group identity (tattoo culture, deaf culture) and artistic endeavour (high culture, popular culture) to name just a few. The word is used so broadly and so frequently that it risks becoming a term with little content, much like the word 'community'. Nevertheless, when the term is used in these ways it often relates to a group identity (whether internally or externally constituted) that is at least partly linked to bodily traits or experience. The roots of the bodily associations allied to nature and culture are, as noted in the definition, as old as the cosmological stories human beings tell about themselves. Nature and culture are in the Garden of Eden, they are in the Dreamtime and they are in the Lele cult of the pangolin.

Before science became the dominant way of describing the world in early modern Europe (see **Discourse**), nature and culture were perceived as complementary, although unequal, opposites. Each had respective stereotypical qualities or associations: nature was wild, chaotic and unbounded; culture was civilized, orderly and contained. Nature was also allied with femininity and culture with masculinity. In all these pairings culture was superior to nature. 'Nature' was often personified as a naked woman in the Renaissance and was seen as a force to be cultivated (made cultured) and controlled, according to divine right, by Man. Culture, when applied to nature, was believed to 'civilize' behaviours and peoples. With the rise in the dominance of science, these kinds of associations made with and between nature and culture became quietly absorbed into the knowledge systems of the natural sciences, with the effect that qualities such as gender became absorbed into the body and thereby welded to sex categories (Cregan, 2009; Sawday 1995; Schiebinger, 1993). Not until the late twentieth century was this challenged by sociologists and feminists (Oakley, 1972; Sydie, 1987) (see also **Gender/Sex**).

The rationalist philosophers of the seventeenth and eighteenth centuries applied scientific approaches to nature with similar consequences (Lloyd, 1993). Rational (European) human beings felt obliged to bring their culture to the 'savage' worlds they explored and conquered. Settler societies imposed the values of culture onto the social structures they perceived as less cultivated, thereby bringing all those nature/culture binary associations to their understanding of the peoples they colonized (**Colonialism/ Post-colonialism**). There were less derogatory associations – eighteenth-century French educationalist philosopher Jean-Jacques

Rousseau's idea of the noble savage being one. This is a romanticized idea of children – and by extension tribal peoples who are child-like – existing pure and untouched in a state of nature, who nevertheless require guidance in progressing to adulthood. Rousseau held nature up as being preferable to certain forms of culture but at the same time his construction of nature is patronizing and infantilizing, particularly when applied to peoples overrun by colonists. This can be paired with less flattering constructions of natives and savages by explorers and settlers, which frequently focused on bodily traits. The 'Hottentot Venus' is a case in point, an African woman who in her own culture was a beauty. Images of her naked form, grossly over-exaggerating her exposed genitals and her general bodily proportions, were held up for ridicule and the titillation of European sensibilities (Hobson, 2005). She stood in stark contrast to contemporary female nudes depicting Nature as a European ideal through the body of white women whose genitals are either hidden by wisps of fabric or, when visible, are as anatomically accurate as that of a Barbie Doll.

Culture in relation to the body in society involves all of these aspects and more. We cultivate (enculture) our bodies in our everyday grooming practices. Elias' theory of manners (**Civilizing Processes**) is a narration of the effects of culture on nature, that is, the rules that Erasmus recommended for the civilization of boys were directly linked to notions of bodily regulation through (masculine) cultured pursuits as the fit form of training for manhood. Although manners have changed, the idea that there are forms of behaviour that are appropriate in particular situations and that knowledge of these is linked to greater sociability success persists.

In Bourdieu's theories one of the key factors in the fields of play of a given habitus are the cultural pursuits with which the individual identifies (**Habitus**). The cultural pursuits one favours directs where one's body circulates in public spaces. For example, a person whose taste includes collecting contemporary art will be likely to attend individual galleries where new art work may be bought. Another person whose cultural sphere valorizes football may attend matches in massive stadiums and/or take to a local playing field on a weekend. Bourdieu, along with Elias, recognizes that social success is dependent on taming bodily 'nature'.

FURTHER READING

See also the readings under **Gender/Sex** and **Medicine and Science**. Schiebinger (1993) argues that the scientific approach to studying the natural world was a highly gendered project that sexualized and feminized as it 'discovered' new worlds (see also **Colonialism/Post-colonialism**).

Jordanova (1989) similarly critiques the sexualization inherent in the scientific gaze in historical context, specifically in relation to anatomical dissection. Macnaughton and Urry (2001) by contrast take a sociological approach to the construction of nature and culture in more recent discourses on land, multiple notions of nature and social practices that are not related directly to the body in society but which nevertheless inform debate around embodiment. As can be seen under **Gender/Sex**, Oakley (1972) contributed to the demystification of the gender/sex distinction in which nature/culture associations were key, an agenda explicitly approached by Sydie (1987).

REFERENCES

Jordanova, Ludmilla (1989) *Sexual Visions: Images of Gender in Science.* Madison: University of Wisconsin Press.
Macnaughton, P. and J. Urry (2001) *Contested Natures.* London: Sage.
Oakley, Ann (1972) *Sex, Gender and Society.* London: Temple Smith.
Schiebinger, Londa (1993) *Nature's Body: Gender in the Making of Modern Science* Boston: Beacon Press.
Sydie, R.A. (1987) *Natural Women/Cultured Men: A Feminist Perspective on Sociological Theory.* Milton Keynes: Open University Press.

Pain

pain

Definition Pain is a bodily sensation that, except in very specific and rare neurological conditions, we have all experienced at some time in life. It is the result of the excitation of nerve endings within the affected part of the body, which sends messages to the brain which are interpreted as painful. As a neurological signal in a mechanistic body (**Dualism**), it is a warning mechanism that can denote illness within the body and that will prompt withdrawal from an external stimulus that is damaging to the body (for example, excess heat or sharp objects). Pain can also be felt as an emotion, as a combination of mental and physical anguish. When pain is persistent it can affect both our identity and our phenomenological experience of the world.

At the beginning of *Discipline and Punish*, Foucault details the fate of an attempted regicide in early modern France, describing the lengthy retribution as inscribing pain into the body with each act of torture and mutilation. Sovereign law is written into the criminal's body as a visible expression of state power. Taking contemporary torture as a large part of her case, Elaine Scarry (1985) makes a similar point about the uses of pain as a means of both undoing the victims' identity (or world) and of remaking it in a wider complex of political acts. Mounting a provocative argument around pain, Scarry argues that in acts of torture, pain can be a means of bringing us into being, giving the sufferer an identity in the moment of torture that defines them not only in the moment but also into their futures. When torture ceases and the tortured person returns to some level of normality the act of torture continues to affect their identity. The physical act leaves psychological scars that continue to affect the body for years afterwards.

Modern (or post-modern) torture is less a visible expression of Foucault's sovereign revenge on a revolutionary subject; it is much more a secretive, private expression of the modern nation-state. However, in each instance what is at stake and being expressed is political power wielded on the body of the individual. Foucault's victim does not survive to remake his world, but in those instances where torture is survived, Scarry argues that they come to remake themselves through the experience and reorganization of that pain into projected objects of re-creation, such as narratives. Scarry's approach draws heavily on psychological and psychoanalytic frameworks, whereas the social constructionist approach of Foucault does not, but they come to a similar point. The embodied experience of pain can be a creative, re-constituting experience. This understanding of re-constitution of identity permeates many areas of debate around the meaning of pain for the body in society and the sociology of the body.

From a dualistic perspective (**Dualism**) pain is understood as a physical symptom or reaction. According to Leder (1990), in everyday experience our bodies *dys*-appear such that we go about concentrating on the mental perception of the world rather than being mindful of our bodily experiences in the moment. This falls apart in the experience of pain. We are made acutely conscious of the bodily experience of discomfort and, as common idiom has it, we may feel our bodies have let us down.

One of the main areas where this has found expression in both theory and in research practice is in the sociology of health and illness (**Health** and **Illness**). For those living with chronic illness, pain can become a central part of their existence which both they and those who see them suffering can take as defining their identity, reversing the dualistic relationship and putting the body in a place of influence in relation to the mind (Jackson in Csordas, 1994). This is especially evident in the perception of people suffering from mental pain, such as chronic depression. The person who experiences the feelings of profound unhappiness is named within a diagnostic system. While mental health professionals may endeavour to use phrases like 'suffering from depression', more commonly this easily becomes hardened into 's/he *is* a depressive'. The effects of mental pain and suffering (Wilkinson, 2005) are evident at the individual and the social level. The concrete effects of mental pain can be enormously socially disabling, as is recognized in burgeoning public mental health campaigns.

As we saw under **Death and Dying**, living with chronic pain associated with a terminal illness can become the major focus of one's medical treatment and therefore of one's life. Living with chronic pain unrelated to a terminal condition, as Seymour (1998) showed in her study of wheelchair users, can mean a complete mental and physical readjustment in the phenomenological understanding of the body. Pain in these circumstances can lead to the reshaping of the body and therefore affect our social presentation. In the lived experience of chronic pain we can come to hold ourselves to lessen the discomfort and this kind of continual rearranging of our posture can have long-term effects, curving spines, pinching brows, deepening furrows in brows. It can permanently change our way of moving. We can immediately see how this might affect our social relations and our identity. Conversely, the relief of pain can relatively quickly relax out those tensions. We can see this most starkly in the complete relaxing out of facial lines in a comatose patient or the shift in facial expression on an injured person when administered opiates.

What sociological and anthropological research has also shown us is that there are aspects of Scarry's and Foucault's observations that can be used to affect the lives of people in pain, whether it is psychological or physical. Perhaps because it takes the sufferer's attention away from the presence of the feeling, creative outlets such as narratives, poetry, songwriting and diaries conducted in research both in psychiatric and palliative care wards have been shown to improve the sufferer's sense of self and their experience of the pain (Baikie and Wilhelm, 2005). Pain has also come to have an impact from the researcher perspective as well.

pain

Ellingson (2006), as a cancer survivor, has written extensively of her own experience of pain as she conducted research in hospital wards. It changed her research practice, made her more acutely conscious of her effect on the collection and interpretation of qualitative data, and ultimately led to a revision in her research practice. So, in her case at least, pain has influenced the course of phenomenological research into pain and brought the body to the fore of her social research.

Pain also operates within a complex of cultural and religious contexts, with varying responses or judgements in relation to the experience of pain. In traditional Christianities, suffering can be understood almost as an obligation. This is based on Christ's example of enduring pain and dying on the cross; it is handed down through the example of saints who undertook acts of physical mortification, and relatedly it is connected to ecstatic experiences – so, extreme pleasure as a result of pain. Pain then shows holiness and religious observance. There are many other cosmologies that similarly value a capacity to endure physical and mental torment.

Culturally, pain can have different meanings and expressions. For example, responses to pain can be gendered with masculinity, implying men have a greater capacity to bear pain and women a lesser. Different cultures value the ability to endure ritual pain – in bodily ceremonies that exact flesh and blood (fire walking, scarification, ritual circumcision). In modern cultures, the expression of pain may be culturally inflected with religious values even when a society is highly secularized, with the open expression of pain acceptable or expected in some cultures and discouraged where more dour (Calvinistic) principles of stoic endurance are perpetuated, even if the religious observances are not (Lingis, 1994).

FURTHER READING

See also the readings for **Discourse** and **Health and Illness**.
Scarry (1985) is a key further reading in this area, and deals with the meaning of pain in the construction of identity – through acts such as torture. So too is Leder (1990), whose study of the *dys*-appearance of the body and its reappearance in pain is a landmark text. Similarly, a quarter of Csordas's highly cited collection (1994) is devoted to the effects of pain on bodily phenomenology, in illness, violent crime and torture. Seymour (1998), as noted also in several other sections, follows the adjustments and readjustments in daily life of adults living in wheelchairs. Baikie and Wilhelm are psychologists (2005) who have used and shown the efficacy of narrative

therapy in clinical settings. Wilkinson's (2005) book looks at pain from the perspective of the social meaning of suffering, a term which covers both mental and physical experiences of pain. Lingis (1994) offers a philosophical meditation on Eurocentric notions of pain and the difference in both the acceptance and expression of pain across cultures.

REFERENCES

Baikie, K.A. and K. Wilhelm (2005) 'Emotional and physical health benefits of expressive writing', *Advances in Psychiatric Treatment*, 11: 338–46.

Csordas, T. (ed.) (1994) *Embodiment and Experience: The Existential Ground of Culture Itself.* Cambridge: Cambridge University Press.

Ellingson, L. (2006) 'Embodied knowledge', *Qualitative Health Research*, 16(2): 298–310.

Leder, D. (1990) *The Absent Body.* Chicago: University of Chicago Press.

Lingis, A. (1994) *Foreign Bodies.* New York: Routledge.

Scarry, Elaine (1985) *The Body in Pain: The Making and Unmaking of the World.* Oxford: Oxford University Press.

Seymour, Wendy (1998) *Remaking the Body: Rehabilitation and Change.* Sydney: Allen & Unwin.

Wilkinson, J. (2005) *Suffering: A Sociological Introduction.* Cambridge: Polity.

Performativity

Definition Performativity is a theoretical concept that describes how we present ourselves to the world. It is closely associated with arguments around the meaning and expression of gender (see **Gender/Sex**). Males may be masculine and females may be feminine, but males may also be feminine and females masculine, within a continuum of degrees of expression. That is, gender is something that can be played with and acted out or performed. On this account, normative heterosexuality is as much a performance as any expression of sexuality and gender is mobile, unfixed and unstable.

Judith Butler, a North American cultural theorist and philosopher, came up with this theorization in *Gender Trouble* (1990) to disrupt boundaries and to explain how gender is not welded to biological sex. Using drag queens (gay men dressing as women in performance), transvestites (people dressing and living as an alternate gender) and transsexuals (people who have had their bodies hormonally and surgically altered) to illustrate her case, Butler argues that gender is always performed. When we express our identity through our bodies we can be said to be 'performing' ourselves.

Butler was reacting not only to patriarchal assumptions about sex and gender but also to earlier influential feminisms, such as De Beauvoir's, that were based in heterosexual women's experiences of oppression and their critiques of gender and gender attributes (**Gender/Sex**). Butler is right that early feminisms had a tendency to be universalizing about the category of 'women', thereby suppressing differences between women such as race, class and sexual orientation. Gender is not dependent or necessarily linked to bodies and, she asserts '*man* and *masculine* might just as easily signify a female body as a male one, and *woman* and *feminine* a male body as easily as a female one' (1990: 10). This is a postmodern move, deconstructing the binary oppositions of male/female, masculine/feminine and finding the continual uncertainty of meaning such as those Derrida identified in specific linguistic terms (for example, the Greek root of the word drug (*pharmakon*), which can equally be a helpful medicine or a harmful poison).

Butler's stance is political. As an activist lesbian philosopher she wants to overcome the oppressive tendencies of hetero-normativity. Just as patriarchy is oppressive of women in general, homogenizing feminisms that don't pay sufficient attention to the many differences between women become part of the problem by giving legitimacy to patriarchal categories. She also wants to use the work of Foucault, who relies on ideas of social construction, and combine it with re-readings of psychoanalytic theory by feminists such as Kristeva, Irigaray and Wittig (see **Psychoanalysis**). In this she sets herself a hard task, for the former insists on the importance of social and historical context while the latter are by their nature universalizing and indeed she does not find Kristeva's theories uniformly helpful.

Nevertheless, she takes Foucault's notion of the repressive hypothesis and applies it to the Freudian notion of the incest taboo, a key moment in psychoanalytic theory that marks early repression of sexual desires. The 'repressive hypothesis' is a broad claim that the more sex became a subject to be repressed from public discourse, the more it became the subject of endless chattering in the confessional before religious authority and in medical diagnoses in the doctor's office (see **Discourse**). The incest 'law' is what is at stake in the Oedipal moment, that is, the moment when a child rejects the early maternal sphere and moves into the paternal order. This is intimately linked to shifts in language acquisition. She argues that the historical moment of Freud theorizing about incest taboos is within Foucault's period of endless chatter in the doctor's clinic and that in that chatter the taboo *creates* heterosexuality and homosexuality in precisely the same moment. So Butler's point is that Freud's theory of the incest taboo, which is supposed to mark the moment of sex/gender differentiation, is already informed by the sex/gender distinction.

The explanation given here is extremely condensed. Butler spends two-thirds of *Gender Trouble* leading the reader through a long re-reading of heterosexist hegemony because she wants to find a way of expressing embodiment that can account for what has become known as the queer body (see **Queer**): an account of embodiment that is neither homo- nor hetero-sexual. She does so by appealing to linguistics and 'language games', specifically 'performative utterances'. 'Performatives' in language games bring meaning into being. If language is 'written' on or can be read via the social body – which various body theorists claim is the case, including Foucault, Bourdieu and Douglas – Butler claims that one can bring one's own body into being through language. Thus we arrive at the notion of bodily performativity, the re-inscription of the body to match the individual's conception of gender and/or sex. Butler argues that bodily signification, or signification through or on the body, brings coherence to being.

> Such acts, gesture, enactments [as are produced on the surface of the body to signify internalized identity] generally construed, are *performative* in the sense that the essence or identity that they otherwise purport to express are *fabrications* manufactured and sustained through corporeal signs and other discursive means. (1990: 173)

So, embodiment is, then, open to reconstruction. And in the terms of the 'language games', the appropriate type of utterance to make a successful move in the game is the 'performative'.

While there are problems in the way Butler goes about constructing this idea on the basis of three quite distinct notions of language, one can see how this theorization of the impermanence and fluidity of the sex/gender distinction would be extremely useful in legitimating difference.

performativity

It is undeniable that hetero-normativity can and has been used to oppress people who don't fit into its categories when they are expressed in hard-edged forms. Performativity then should be read in conjunction with the areas in which it has had the greatest influence in writings on the body in society. It is at base a feminist critique of gender and therefore has immediate relevance for feminism and being based around unsettling notions of gender and sex is an extension of that category. Performativity has also been used extensively in arguments around the body in relation to sexuality, identity and queer theory.

FURTHER READING

The central texts for further reading related to performativity remain Butler's (1990, 1993), as the theorist with whom the concept originated. Examples of the application of notions of performativity can be found in the readings under **Feminism, Gender/Sex, Queer** and **Sexuality**.

REFERENCES

Butler, Judith (1990) *Gender Trouble: Feminism and the Subversion of Identity*. New York: Routledge.
Butler, Judith (1993) *Bodies that Matter: On the Discursive Limits of 'Sex'*. New York: Routledge.

Phenomenology

Definition Phenomenology is a branch of philosophy, originating with Husserl and expanded by Heidegger, that explains knowledge about the world as based in lived experience, that is, in terms of sensory perception in the moment. In phenomenology, the mind is not privileged over the body as in dualism. Rather, the fact of the body in the world is a prerequisite for any perception and the world is understood to be always

> simultaneously perceived through the bodily senses and the mind. It is, therefore, an embodied philosophy and has direct applications for the interpretation of the body in society.

Phenomenology in philosophy raises questions about identity (self/subject and the world/object) at the same time as it explains how knowledge is formed about the world (ontology). It puts the power of knowledge creation into the senses of the perceiver: the world *is* what we perceive. This is a clear rejection of positivist notions that the world and facts about it are 'out there'. So, it is an embodied philosophy that is in sympathy with sociological attempts to explain how people understand and create their (social) worlds. It has been particularly important in qualitative social research methodologies, where in 'order to grasp the meanings of a person's behaviour, *the phenomenologist attempts to see things from that person's point of view*' (Bogdan and Taylor, 1975: 14, emphasis in the original).

Phenomenological thought was brought into sociology by Alfred Schutz. However, it is the work of French philosopher, Maurice Merleau-Ponty, as applied in sociology, that is perhaps best known in the study of the body in society. Husserl, the progenitor of phenomenology, posited that the world is created by people as they perceive it. Merleau-Ponty was interested in how those creations 'arise' through our physical being-in-the-world: 'Our body is both an object among objects and that which sees and touches them' (*Sense and Non-Sense*; 1961/1984: xii). This was not intended as a simple reversal of dualism. Rather, Merleau-Ponty was interested in the primacy of the body as the sensing object and the simultaneity of, and the negotiation between, the mind and the body in perception of the world. In this, embodied actions and interactions (intercorporeality) are central to our building up of our knowledge of the world. So, the body is social (in the world, creating the world) and relates to other bodies that are in the world, creating the world.

Merleau-Ponty's concept of phenomenology is, then, directly applicable to the study of the body in society. A range of sociologists have used his ideas in looking for a way to talk about embodiment and social processes. The attraction of phenomenology, in this sense, is that unlike discussions that concentrate on theorizing and explaining the body as an object in society and how it is written on or into meaning, phenomenology attempts to explain the body in movement and action in creating our social world. Phenomenological approaches to the body attempt to bring the mind and body back together in approaching embodied experience.

These notions have been used in a wide range of studies based on bodily experience and knowledge production, ranging from community engagement projects on the experience of participating in local arts festivals to studies of illness and adapting to acquired disability. Indeed, illness or disability, as Leder (1990) has noted, constitute disruptive moments that make us aware of the body as an object and interrupt the phenomenological flow of perception.

As noted above, phenomenological approaches have been extremely important to qualitative research that seeks to take into account multiple points of view, to build up a broader picture of social phenomena. However, phenomenology as a means to explaining the body in society is not without its critics. It can be seen as being overly concerned with the perceptions or point of view of the individual. The body and mind are framed holistically but the inter-corporeality of multiple points of view is not necessarily sturdy enough to account for group action or group agency. There is little in phenomenology to account for the effects of power in, on and/or between bodies (**Power**). That is, it explains actions in the world (of individuals) but cannot account for social agency or social structure. Indeed, one of the more potent criticisms is that it is essentially an explanatory frame, a heuristic device, with no capacity for social change. In common with more psychologically oriented concepts around body and society, it also has a tendency to be universalizing in its terms and in understanding how bodies and minds interact. Neither the mind nor the perceptual body are nuanced, Merleau-Ponty's phenomenological body is 'the body', which flattens out difference on a range of bases: including, but not limited to, gender, race/ethnicity and ability (see **Disability/Ability**, **Difference**, **Gender/Sex, Race/Ethnicity**). Nevertheless, this does not mean that it is not possible to make attempts to introduce greater nuance to 'the body' of phenomenology, and it remains an important concept in the body in society.

As Shilling (1993) and Turner (1996) have argued, there is a place for bringing approaches to lived experience into concordance with pragmatic attempts at social change. Phenomenology certainly provides a basis for interrogating how individual embodied perception of the world *varies* when there is either a physical or psychological dissonance between the mind and the body. One excellent example of a phenomenological study of the variability of embodiment is Wendy Seymour's study of people living with acquired physical disabilities, specifically para- and quadriplegia, where their perceptions of their bodies and their ability to adapt in a situation of dissonance is inspirational to say the least. Illness and disability have been mentioned as phenomenologically 'different' ways of experiencing the body and to this can be added a number of conditions that contest common assumptions about perception. As Shilling has noted (2008) transgender identity is characterized by a phenomenological dissonance between the individual's body as lived and the mind's belief about gender identity, and other forms of body dysmorphia provide similar evidence of phenomenological variability.

FURTHER READING

See also **Death and Dying**, **Health and Illness** and **Pain**.
As noted above, Schutz (1932/1967) can be credited with introducing phenomenological approaches to studies of the social world. However, it is Merleau-Ponty (1984, 2001) whose writing on phenomenology and bodily sensations has become more frequently appealed to in the study of the body in society. The collection compiled by Csordas (1994) provides a selection of essays giving practical examples of how phenomenological studies apply to the construction of culture and self through the body. As mentioned under several categories, Seymour's (1998) book-length study of the experiences of people with acquired disabilities gives an extended example of phenomenological practice.

REFERENCES

Csordas, T. (ed.) (1994) *Embodiment and Experience: The Existential Ground of Culture Itself*. Cambridge: Cambridge University Press.
Merleau-Ponty, Maurice (1984) *Sense and Non-Sense*, trans. H.L. Dreyfus and P.A. Dreyfus. Evanston, IL: Northwestern University Press. First published 1961.
Merleau-Ponty, Maurice (2001) *Phenomenology of Perception*, trans. C. Smith. London: Routledge. First published 1962.
Schutz, A. (1967) *The Phenomenology of the Social World*. Evanston, IL: Northwestern University Press. First published 1932.
Seymour, Wendy (1998) *Remaking the Body: Rehabilitation and Change*. Sydney: Allen & Unwin.

Power

Definition Everyone knows what power is in the general sense – the possession or exertion of an ability to direct or control, whether the object of that control is an individual, political regimes, social systems, or abstract concepts. In terms of the human body in society, power can be exerted upon the bodies of individuals for any of these reasons (and more) and it can also be exerted through knowledge systems (**Discourse**) to frame, define, manoeuvre and control the body as a material entity and to shape the way we understand embodiment as an abstract concept.

There are many ways of speaking about power in sociology. However, in relation to the human body in society it is, again, Foucault who has been one of the most influential thinkers on the analyses and conceptualizations of the body as an object caught in structures of power. He described a number of strategies by which power may be exerted, generally through the formation of specialized languages based around an area of knowledge – what he termed a 'field of delimitation' or 'episteme' (see **Discourse, Medicine and Science**). To be able to exercise power in that field one needs to be an expert (an authority of delimitation) through the access to the language or discourse that comes with that expertise. Foucault described the power of medical knowledge to re-invent the human body as the subject of the medical 'gaze'.

For Foucault, power is diffuse. No individual is capable of controlling it, and we are all subject to and curtailed by various systems of power. This diffuse power lies in systems of knowledge and the structures that uphold those systems. The individuals or groups who have access to and authority over a given system are thereby empowered but they are still contained within those system(s). They are as subject to the effects of that power as anyone else. Bourdieu's notion of habitus and fields of play make a similar point about the ability of definition to lie within a (for him class) group, with similarly disempowering consequences as far as moving beyond the group into which one is born. However, Bourdieu also understood that individuals could consciously manipulate power when they were experts in their field of play and that their social/group success depended on their capacities to '*play the game*'. In the case of both these thinkers, the power they wrote of had a concrete effect on the body.

If we look at Foucault's study of judicial authority in *Discipline and Punish* (1991) we see another diffuse system of power that has contributed a key concept to sociological analysis. In approaching bodily control and power in relation to the criminal, Foucault re-introduces us to a penal structure that was never fully implemented in its original design, but the intent of which can be found on the street corners of most modern cities: the Panopticon.

Foucault traces a genealogy of criminality and judicial authority along the same time span as he applied in relation to medicine, following the epistemic shifts that led from traditional to modern understandings of crime and punishment. We do not need to follow this whole trajectory to understand the purpose of the Panopticon but it is worth noting that in the late eighteenth and into the nineteenth century there was an upsurge in reformatory theories of law and punishment. Up to this time prison was a place where the offender lived, in squalid conditions, awaiting punishment. Physical punishment directly applied to the body of the criminal, often visceral and bloody, was the standard but the law and prison reform movements which emerged in the late eighteenth and early nineteenth centuries were more concerned with affecting and retraining the mind of the criminal. 'Treatment' and rehabilitation, which became fashionable in the nineteenth century, only makes sense in a world in which the mind is separable from the actions of the body, that is once the idea of Cartesian dualism has taken hold (see **Dualism**). Yet, as Foucault describes it, the body is still central in the 'new tactics of power' (1991: 23–5).

The push towards a medicalization of aberrance and the medical 'gaze' meet in the power structures of the Panopticon. Literally, the panopticon is a building, or rather exists in a structural plan for a prison devised by a nineteenth-century Englishman, liberal philosopher and social reformer, Jeremy Bentham. The design consists of separate cells for each criminal – in which they are constantly visible through a grilled front. The cells are arranged in a circular array facing towards a central tower. Prison guards, who are not visible, watch the prisoners from this tower. The power of the panopticon lies in self-regulation.

The supposedly 'penitent' prisoner cannot see the warders – never knows for certain if the warder is actually watching or even in the tower – but under the unseen but all-seeing eye is prompted to regulate his or

power

her behaviour *as if* s/he is under observation. The theoretical approach behind it is clearly recognisable in contemporary prison design and management, and indeed in all contemporary social surveillance techniques such as CCTV cameras in public spaces. What in comparison to flaying and torture at first appears to be a 'lenient' and 'redemptive' system of rehabilitation actually relies on absolute authority. Foucault uses the term 'panopticon', like 'the gaze', to describe the full political outcome of the absorption into oneself of self-regulatory behaviour that stems from the belief that one is always being watched.

The impetus behind the panopticon is not merely diagnoses or treatment: it incorporates a mentality of training that goes beyond prosecution and incarceration. This manifestation of power extends to a range of arenas in which docile bodies are trained into submission: for example, in military service, and in educational models. 'A glance at the new art of punishing clearly reveals the supersession of the punitive semio-technique by a new politics of the body' (Foucault, 1991: 103).

The effect of the prison on criminal bodies is extended to the effect of power on and through the body in society. The carceral becomes a part of society in general, based in a new system of law, and a new system of general self- and other-control. For Foucault, the deeper lesson to be learned is that the prison is not the only imprisoning object in society, it is 'linked to a whole series of "carceral" mechanisms which seem distinct enough – since they are intended to alleviate pain, to cure, to comfort – but which all tend, like the prison, to exercise a power of normalization' (Foucault, 1991: 308). Those carceral mechanisms include medicine, education and religion.

These notions of diffuse power exerted through the panoptic gaze, surveillance and self-regulation have formed a cornerstone of research into contemporary law, policing, criminality and social control, whether in following the method or in critical response. Habermas, amongst others, is critical of the lack of space left in Foucault's description of power for agency or action on the part of those subjected to this power. If we are all caught in the web of power how are we ever to affect social change? Nevertheless it is Foucault's discursive construction of power that has dominated discussion of power in relation to the body in society, whether followed or critiqued.

FURTHER READING

One of the greater exponents of Foucault's method in the sociology of the body is of course Bryan Turner, whose *Medical Power and Social Knowledge* (1995) is a key text in the field. The dynamics of power is the focus of much of Foucault's writings but the clearest expressions of it can be found in his meditations on panopticism (1991), discourse and knowledge production (1994), and governmentality (1980).

REFERENCES

Foucault, M. (1980) 'Governmentality', in *Power/Knowledge: Selected Interviews and Other Writings 1972–1977* New York: Vintage.

Foucault, M. (1991) *Discipline and Punish: The Birth of the Prison*, trans. A. Sheridan. London: Penguin.

Foucault, M. (1994) *The Archaeology of Knowledge*, trans. A.M. Sheridan Smith. London: Routledge.

Turner, B.S. with C Samson. (1995) *Medical Power and Social Knowledge*. London: Sage. First published 1987.

Private and Public

Definition Private and public are relative terms. At different times in history and in different cultural contexts there may be little in one's life that could be considered private, in the sense of being unavailable to, inaccessible by or hidden from others. In Western societies, privacy has come to be associated with domesticity, interiority and modernity. Public is likewise a historically and socio-culturally dependent term, which implies everything that is not private. It also carries connotations of political activity – of public life, public commentary – and what is available, accessible and open to the scrutiny of others. In relation to the body in society, private and public spheres are contexts in which embodiment takes on specific meaning and is the basis on which embodied acts are considered appropriate (or not).

In modern and post-modern social formations, when we refer to the private world we generally mean the domestic or private spaces, and/or the internal life of the individual – something that is closed off or restricted from general view. When we speak of the public realm, we are generally referring to the political/social sphere, freely accessible spaces, the outward life of the individual in a social context – something that is open and largely unrestricted from the general view and in which large sections of a population may take part. The same is not the case for prior social formations, whether in examples taken from the history of developed countries or in the cultural contexts of contemporary developing countries.

Elias has argued that in terms of the human body where we are, in public or in private, affects the disposition and the socio-culturally acceptable functioning of bodies. Added to this, acceptability can be judged on the basis of our status as individuals or in relation to our membership of a particular social grouping. With variations across cultures and societies, what is considered appropriate bodily behaviour in the private realm may not be acceptable in the public realm, and vice versa, particularly in relation to basic bodily functions. Success or failure to abide by a given cultures' understanding of what is appropriate to each sphere can determine an individual's acceptance within that culture. Elias traced the changing modes of social acceptability (manners) in Western European culture from medieval times to the early twentieth century (**Civilizing Processes**). Many of those rules were about guiding behaviour in public, for example the rules on eating, but there are a number that Elias describes as moving from the public into the private realm. Elias' general thesis is that such rules begin with the upper classes but gradually move through the social ranks to become common social expectations. The two most obvious examples of such acts of 'closeting' were the shifts in toileting and in sleeping behaviours.

In a medieval feudal court, urination and defecation were not private acts (Elias, 2000: 109–21). Urination was performed wherever it was convenient and urine was collected as an important product (uric acid) used in dying cloth and thread, particularly wool. Indeed, in the sixteenth century it was considered dangerous to hold in urine. One can still see in many castles open chutes, that extend down external walls, that were used for defecation (and the disposal of rubbish) by those who lived in the upper reaches of the castles: that is, the upper classes. Those who lived and worked on the lower levels, or on the fringes, must have done much as cultures with minimal sanitation do today, relieved themselves where it was convenient. It would be easy to assume that this meant life was extremely smelly and dirty, but having witnessed their voraciousness in rural villages and the disappearance of any and all detritus into their gullets, where pigs were kept this was not necessarily the case.

Filth and odours came with greater density of housing. With shifts in social formations and consequent alterations in manners and forms of housing, bodily evacuation became more regulated and, gradually, more private. Cabinets with drawers holding a china dish, ceramic jugs for pissing in while travelling in coaches and chamber pots under the bed all brought toileting processes in from the possibility of public view. In the first instance, this was to private rooms such as a bedroom, where one might be assisted by a servant (a titled position in a royal household). Eventually a separate room, often separated from the house, was deemed necessary. Conversely, the disposal of waste matter became more public, flowing into public gutters and eventually into public-health mandated drains and sewers from the mid-nineteenth century onwards.

Sleeping arrangements underwent a similar transition, from a shared, often communal experience to a highly segregated and individualized one (Elias, 2000: 136–42). The congregating of bodies in sleeping arrangements to share warmth is extremely logical. Shared sleeping arrangements were common when the bedding might consist of straw and for the majority of people there was no differentiation between day-clothes and bed-clothes. Even when beds became more common throughout the classes, bed-clothes (sheets and blankets) remained costly items well into the nineteenth century and the warmth of another human body was a sensible guard against the elements. However, it also brought with it a new set of manners. By the sixteenth century undressing was likely to be involved in sharing a bed, in the upper classes at least, and how one behaved in the presence of another undressed person became important. This was all the more important as one might find oneself sleeping with a stranger if travelling and stopping at inns. Sleeping arrangements, while no doubt always open to moments of sexual exploration also became an object of greater concern in terms of warning against the temptations of the flesh. Alan Bray (1982) has examples from early modern English legal cases of (male) apprentices sharing beds with other servants or their masters, who became sexually involved, both con-sensually and against their will. By the nineteenth century, sharing a bed was a practice largely confined to family members (unless one was a servant or impoverished) and the notion of a bed as a private realm moved throughout the social ranks. Sharing a bed became a sign of poverty.

These are good examples of the shifting nature of private and public bodies. There are connections in the first example of other ways in which bodies may be considered public, that is, in terms of public health. The rise of public health in the wake of epidemics of diseases that thrived in conditions of overcrowded habitation and poor sanitation – such as cholera and typhus – propelled sanitation reform movements in the nineteenth century that oversaw the rebuilding of whole sections of cities to remove tenements and introduce public drains for the removal of waste matter. Private bodily functions became public and political matters and, in turn, bodies were regulated within the private realm by the location of plumbing and sanitation within homes (Sennett, 1994). Sennett (1974) has also convincingly traced the movement of general social interaction from being more based in an idea of the 'public man' to the more private and less interconnected social lives we are familiar with today. Death in developed countries has similarly moved from being more public into the private and professionalized realms (**Death and Dying**). These are the antecedents to the public and private bodily realms of contemporary societies in developed countries. Public and private bodies continue to have different meanings in other societies and cultures (Strathern, 1996).

FURTHER READING

For further reading on the progression from the public to the private realms of sleeping arrangements and toileting practices, Elias is a good place to start. With respect to a wider range of examples of shifts in understandings of the private and public domains, particularly in relation to architecture, Sennett's *Flesh and Stone* (1994) is an excellent collection. Sennett's writing on *The Fall of Public Man* (1974) should also be consulted as a key text in the area. For a comparative study of the meaning of tribal and Eurocentric embodiment, see Strathern (1996).

REFERENCES

Elias, N. (2000) *The Civilizing Process: Sociogenetic and Psychogenetic Investigations.* Oxford: Basil Blackwell.

Sennett, R. (1974) *The Fall of Public Man*. Cambridge: Cambridge University Press.
Sennett, R. (1994) *Flesh and Stone*. New York: W.W. Norton.
Strathern, A.J. (1996) *Body Thoughts*. Ann Arbor: University of Michigan Press.

Psychoanalysis

Definition Psychoanalysis is a theoretical approach to the workings of the human mind, first formulated by Sigmund Freud, which posits various universalizing propositions around the formation, development and expression of the human psyche. Those universalizing propositions are both normative (related to 'normal' developmental phases, e.g. the Oedipal stage) and of pathological importance (related to imperfect development, e.g. the Oedipal complex). While in many ways diametrically opposed to social inquiry in its emphasis on the psyche of the individual – as distinct from locating inquiry in the individual in social relations – psychoanalysis is nevertheless important to the body in society, as it has been adapted by later theorists of the body whose work is influential within sociology (see especially **Cyborgs, Feminism, Performativity**).

Psychology is the study of human behaviour that is inextricably linked with the mind/body division (see **Dualism**), whereby the mind or the brain is seen as controlling and determining the actions of a materialistic body. Psychoanalysis is the brainchild of Freud (Gay, 1995), and is closely allied with psychology and psychiatry, and is an approach to understanding human actions and behaviour as products of the mental attitudes of the individual. In proposing universal categories – across time, space and culture – it is easy to see a basic tension between psychoanalysis and the located, contextual nature of sociological approaches.

To express his universalizing categories, Freud used tropes from ancient mythology to describe and define what he believed to be the fundamental ways in which all humans think (and interact). For example, his Oedipus complex is named after the story in which Oedipus, separated from his parents at birth, meets them as an adult when he kills his biological father, Laius, and marries his biological mother, Iocaste. When their biological connection is revealed, Iocaste kills herself and Oedipus blinds himself. Freud takes the incestuous marriage narrative and relates it to early childhood developmental stages as being based on primal sexual drives. The Oedipal 'crisis' is concentrated on the moment of a shift, from the (male) infant's close identification with the mother to a rejection of her. In the course of 'normal' development boys are said to reject the maternal sphere and re-identify with the paternal at the moment of the Oedipal crisis. Freud took the existence of these stories in ancient Greek culture as evidence of the universality of their themes and from there assimilated them into a wider theorization of the developmental stages of all humans. What this obliterates, of course, is the (patriarchal) social context of the original myths and the veneration and promulgation of Athenian values in eighteenth and nineteenth century European culture, of which Freud was a product. In other words, it is blind to the very real political effects of historical and social contexts.

Roughly contemporaneous with Freud's early work was the development of the Grand Theories of sociology. As Shilling notes, Grand Theory's concentration on social complexes, rather than individualities, had the ironic effect that in the same move that individualizing psychology was relegated by those thinkers to the (unimportant) pre-social world, so too was the body as a natural given (Shilling, 1993: 24–5). So, early sociological thinking did not pay overt attention to bodily matters, while psychoanalysis did.

Psychoanalysis has mutated a great deal since Freud's time, as have social and psychoanalytic theories. It has become important and influential far beyond the sphere of defining mental development or applying 'talking cures' to pathologies. As Foucault observed, psychoanalysis was a part of the medico-legal complex that simultaneously disapproved of the public discussion of sexual matters but was tireless in discussing it in the privacy of the clinic, or the confessional (Foucault, 1990). Many second-wave feminists (**Feminism**) rejected Freud's psychoanalytic theories on the justifiable grounds that they were inherently sexist. Others, such as Juliet Mitchell in *Psychoanalysis and Feminism* (1974), attempted to give their own reinterpretations of those theories in ways that could be accommodated into left feminist politics by positing a psychology of femininity.

In contemporary theory, French psychoanalyst Jacques Lacan has probably been the most influential writer on those psychoanalytic theorists whose work is in turn used within sociology, and consequently on the interpretation of the body in society. Lacan was interested in the connection between the acquisition of language and the various stages of psychological development, in particular in how (and whether) meaning is formed before an infant has acquired language. Lacan's linguistic re-interpretation of Freud has in turn been appropriated and reformulated, initially by French feminists such as Julia Kristeva, Hélène Cixous, Monique Wittig and Luce Irigaray (**Feminism**). These feminists, in turn, have influenced the writing of Anglo-American feminists such as Judith Butler (**Performativity**), Donna Haraway (**Cyborgs**) and Liz Grosz (**Feminism**), whose own work has gone on to influence many others who are directly involved in social research. For example, Butler's theories on performativity are deeply indebted to psychoanalytic theoretical concepts as appropriated to feminism by Kristeva, Cixous and Wittig, in combination with aspects of Foucault's notion of power/knowledge (**Power**). Haraway was originally avowedly Marxist-feminist, but in her cyborg theories she shows her indebtedness to psychoanalytic theory, particularly as used by Butler. These feminists, who have been so influential on understandings of the body in society, take from psychoanalysis notions of identity and self as acts of potentially conscious self-creation.

These theories inform both the analysis of and the approach to acquiring knowledge about the body in society, not least through the revision of qualitative research methodologies and methods. The body in society is, for some, an individualized project. For example, there are some feminist social research methods that rely heavily on personalized narratives that take a psychoanalytic approach. This comes out of a stream of thinking that is concerned to find voices for women's experiences that have been suppressed or ignored in many other studies, both historically and in the present. Other groups who have similarly been excluded from mainstream research (**Gender/Sex, Queer**) are also committed to putting their narratives and experiences on the public record. These are important political moves to broaden our understanding of the human condition which, historically, has often been very narrowly conceived. However, taking such an individualized approach can, sometimes, be at the cost of examining the social. Tensions therefore remain in using such individualizing approaches to social questions.

Freud, frequently called the 'father' of psychoanalysis, was a prolific writer and there are numerous of his own works readily available in translation, as well as general introductions to his work, such as Gay's (1995), that the reader may find useful. Mitchell's (1974) attempt to revivify psychoanalysis for feminism is another early key text. Several key reinterpretations of Freud's work by feminists that are invoked in the study of the body in society include Liz Grosz's philosophical work on material bodies (1994, 1995); Kristeva's theorizations around the rejection of bodily matter as 'abject' or polluting (1980); and Butler's writings around gender mobility (see readings under **Performativity**). See Howson (2005) for a sociologist writing on the intersection of feminism, body studies and psychoanalysis.

REFERENCES

Gay, P. (1995) *The Freud Reader*. London: Vintage.

Grosz, Liz (1994) *Volatile Bodies: Toward a Corporeal Feminism*. Bloomington: Indiana University Press.

Grosz, Liz (1995) *Time, Space and Perversion: The Politics of Bodies*. New York: Routledge.

Howson, A. (2005) *Embodying Gender*. London: Sage.

Kristeva, Julia (1980) *Powers of Horror: An Essay on Abjection*, trans L. Roudiez. New York: Columbia University Press.

Mitchell, J. (1974) *Psychoanalysis and Feminism*. London: Allen Lane.

Queer

Definition Queer's original meaning is 'odd' or 'irregular' but it became an insulting term for gay men, in English, around the 1920s. The political revivification of the word queer reclaims a term of vilification, in the way many marginalized or oppressed peoples have turned insults into empowering weapons of identity-formation. In doing so, queer has come to mean more than 'gay man'. As an identity, at its widest, it includes all sexualities

> that are not hetero-normative. As a political practice, queering is an act of re-reading and disrupting narratives of heterogeneous hetero-normativity. As a theory and an academic practice, its agenda is to show that queerness is and always has been present across time, space and cultures.

Queer and queering are political terms that have provided a means of legitimizing the embodied realities of people who do not identify as hetero-normative. At the same time, queer is a somewhat contentious term because it tends to give the impression that gay, lesbian, transgender, bisexual, asexual … issues are homogeneous. Logically, this is no more the case than that a catchall understanding of human rights represents equally and accurately the concerns of all human beings. The plethora of UN commissions and conventions related to specific groups' concerns (women, children, the elderly, indigenous people, refugees, etc.) are testament to the diversity involved in that sphere. So, in parallel, the matters of importance to gay men are not necessarily the same as those of lesbians, any more than either (or both) are the same as those of transgender or asexual people, and nor are the matters of importance to one group of gay men (a cycling club) necessarily the same as another (a rally car club). At its most radical, queer is a statement of identity that rejects any fixed gender categories (**Gender/Sex**) or stable notions of attraction (**Sexuality**). Queer is a political claim to on-going self-invention and embodied performance (**Performativity**).

Queer Theory is a general term for the academic analytical movement, that arose in the late 1980s and early 1990s, which seeks to destabilize hetero-normative assumptions at all levels of social and political life. It does so by continually questioning, through academic inquiry, the ways in which non-hetero-normative people, and their concerns, are suppressed and oppressed. Queer Theory is particularly strong in textual studies (literature, media, film, cultural studies, history) but it is also actively applied in the social sciences. Before the term Queer Theory was coined, and before Gay Liberation emerged as a political movement in the US, in the early 1960s Laud Humphreys undertook in the course of his doctoral thesis a sociological study of heterosexual-identifying men's homoerotic encounters in public toilets, published as *The Tearoom Trade* (1975). Those encounters were both with other heterosexual-identifying men and with homosexual-identifying men. In his study, Humphreys gave a detailed account of the non-normative sexual activities of men that flourished in the urban parks of middle-America, and of the suppression of

Queer

their conflicted identity in their marital lives. The study became a landmark in sociological studies – of what was at the time called 'deviance' – that has given legitimacy to the closeted and oppressed lives of gay men both then and since. Laud Humphreys was not a Queer Theorist, but his work was a milestone in documenting suppressed Queer lived experiences.

Queer Theory, like **Feminism** and **Colonialism/Post-colonialism**, is an umbrella term for a range of critical analyses. It is a part of a wider complex of the questioning of long-held norms, sexual and otherwise, that started to gain momentum in the 1960s. In many developed countries, Gay Liberation and militant Lesbian Feminism gained prominence as forms of political activism in the late 1960s and into the 1970s, as part of a wider flourishing of social movements. As an analytical movement in the 1980s, it was at least partly based on the work of a number of key thinkers involved in post-structuralism and post-modern analysis (**Gender/Sex, Power**). The genesis of Queer Theory has direct links with areas of radical feminism, but it is also clearly indebted to the work of the French post-structuralist Michel Foucault. The first volume of *The History of Sexuality* was published in English in the late 1970s, followed by a further two posthumously published volumes, and it became an immediately influential text in critical theory, history and the social sciences. Foucault's writing is behind the intellectual work of Haraway (**Cyborgs**) and Butler (**Performativity**) along with many other theorists of the body, but this work from the latter part of his life is directly concerned with uncovering the social construction of sexualities, in the plural.

Part of the Queer Theory agenda is historical, that is, putting on the record the reality of queer lives throughout history. It does so in narratives which go beyond characterizations of sexual deviance or polite retellings of prominent moments in a quaint past. For example, in the nineteenth and into the late twentieth centuries the teaching of the Ancient Greek philosophical texts of Plato, some of which include open references to male–male love and physical attraction, defused these homo-erotics by explaining them away either as not 'really' (homo)sexual or as a cultural aberrance, as one tutor explained it to me in my own university education. Not all bodies have been equal in history: gay, lesbian, transgender and asexual experience have often been relegated to the status of titillating pathologies (Ellis, 1936; Krafft-Ebing, 1886/1965). So, one of the main streams of Queer Theory has been the unpacking of suppressed queer histories, bringing out of the archive what had been politely (and not so politely) glossed over in prior histories (Bray, 1982; Norton, 1992).

Similarly, Queer Theory has been particularly strong in literary studies. Forgotten, sidelined and forbidden narratives that survived in manuscript form or in restricted sections of libraries are one focus of such research. Other studies have focused on drawing out coded references in more public texts which a more innocent readership may not have recognized as sexually transgressive. And even where there is no overt theme of sexual or gender difference it is nevertheless possible to give a queer reading of the silences and absences in many texts. Queer biographies of the private lives of well-known authors have also been a part of that project.

Queer Theory is, logically, strongly related to sexualities in these examples from history, literary studies and sociology. But more recently it has also been concerned to claim a place for more than discrete sexualities, turning rather to notions of queerness as formulated in Butler's ideas of gender (and sexual) performativity (see **Performativity**).

FURTHER READING

There is a wide range of possible readings that give examples of queer histories. Bray was one of the first to attempt a history of homosexuality in early modern England (Bray, 1982) and Rictor Norton's (1992) history of the gay clubs in Restoration London is a fascinating retelling of the political impetus behind the stamping out of what was in the process of becoming a sexual (rather than a deviant political) crime: that is, sodomy. Epstein and Straub (1991) provide a collection of queer histories that cover a range of temporal and geographically situated examples. Jeffrey Weeks (1985) is one of the foremost queer theorists within cultural and literary studies. Seidman's (1996) reader is a broad introduction to the ways in which queer theory is being applied in a sociological framework to queer lived experiences. Stryker and Whittle (2006) provide an excellent collection of readings on transgender studies and both the history and the present political and social struggles of transgender individuals. Krafft-Ebing (1886/1965) and Havelock Ellis (1936) were two of the most influential clinicians in the pathologization of non-hetero-normative sexualities. See also the readings for **Sexuality**.

queer

REFERENCES

Bray, Alan (1982) *Homosexuality in Renaissance England*. London: Gay Men's Press.
Ellis, H. (1936) *Studies in the Psychology of Sex, Vol 2: Sexual Inversion*. New York: Random House.
Epstein, J. and K. Straub (eds) (1991) *BodyGuards*. New York: Routledge.
Humphreys, L. (1975) *Tearoom Trade: A Study of Homosexual Encounters in Public Places*. Chicago: Aldine Publishing Company. First published 1970.

Krafft-Ebing, R. von (1965) *Psychopathia Sexualis*. New York: G.P. Putnam's & Sons. First published 1886.

Norton, Rictor (1992) *Mother Clap's Molly House: The Gay Subculture in England 1700–1830*. London: Gay Men's Press.

Seidman, S. (ed.) (1996) *Queer Theory/Sociology*. Oxford: Blackwell.

Stryker, S. and S. Whittle (eds) (2006) *The Transgender Studies Reader*. London: Routledge.

Weeks, J. (1985) *Sexuality and its Discontents: Meanings, Myths and Modern Sexualities*. London: Routledge.

Race/Ethnicity

Definition Race is a discredited term that, historically, has been used to define peoples as 'other' from those doing the defining, on the basis of bodily appearance (skin colour, bone structure) and supposedly common, often pejorative traits (**Colonialism/Post-colonialism**). Race as a biological category does not exist. However, racism or the persistence of prejudices and discrimination based on the fallacy of race is very real. Ethnicity or ethnic grouping is a concept that refers to the identity of a population on the basis of a shared language, culture and cosmology and spatial location. In contemporary use, it generally refers to a group identity that is not reflected in national boundaries and often implies a tribal or traditional (pre-modern) social formation. Hence, we hear of ethnic-Hmong living in Vietnam and Cambodia, ethnic-Kurds living in a number of states of the former USSR, and ethnic-Suni Muslims living in Iraq.

We can see from the definition given above that each term is intimately related to **Identity** and this section is usefully read in conjunction with the entries on **Class/Caste** and **Colonialism/Post-colonialism**. Race is a category of identity conferred by those with dominance and power, on a people or peoples who are subordinate to that power. As is seen under **Sport** and **Sexuality**, it has been used to oppress and marginalize peoples on the basis of visible (seeming) differences. Ethnicity is a group (self) identity. It has been a basis for claiming national rights against imperial domination, particularly in nineteenth-century Europe, and as a theoretical concept became absorbed into anthropological theory. The notion of ethnicity can still be related to an allegiance to an identity linked to a nation-state, for people no longer living in that state: that is, to define diasporic communities of peoples in large multicultural nation-states (for example, Italian-American, Sudanese-Australian). Ethnicity also commonly refers to a group identity formed around the kinds of commonalities mentioned in the definition, which have never had a nation-state. Romany, Bedouin and Bushmen have strong group identities but no national borders. In all of the examples of ethnic groups mentioned in the definition above, those peoples may have always been inhabitants of these particular places but they have either not been granted citizenship within the state that has grown up around them – and often separated them where populations straddle multiple nation-states – and/or they are politically oppressed within those states. So, ethnicity and race are historically, socially, politically and contextually dependent terms that have had, and continue to have, significant effects on the body in society.

The early scientific justifications for theories of race came out of early modern theories of external diagnosis of character, that were based on evidence such as wrinkles (metoposcopy) and facial appearance (physiognomy). These were later absorbed into adaptations of Darwin's explanations of the differentiation and evolution of (other) animal species (Schiebinger, 1993). The patterning and differentiation of peoples also extend further back into ancient descriptions of the four embodied 'humours' of Galenic medicine, that were linked to highly gendered character 'types' (stereotypes). This categorization of peoples on the basis of embodied traits, which by definition cannot be avoided or exceeded, fosters intransigent prejudice and oppression. We can also see that it follows the same patterns of the normalization or absorption of constructed traits into embodied 'others' (**Colonialism/Post-colonialism, Difference, Gender/Sex**).

There are many aspects of ethnicity and race that cannot be separated from notions of modernity, and the rise of nations and nationalism (Anderson, 1991). Indeed, the second half of Elias' treatise on embodied manners (**Civilizing Processes**) is devoted to the foundation of modern nation-states. Ethnicity is the basis on which modern Europe came into being as a collection of geographically bounded nation-states, fought for on the basis of commonality rooted in a dominant language, culture and cosmology. This came at the cost of those ethnic groups that did not achieve dominance. The long-term consequences of that ethnic hatred – which is closely allied to racism – were at the heart of the atrocities committed after the dissolution of Yugoslavia. What we are concerned with here is how these concepts affect the body in society. Those hatreds were expressed through the committing of physical violence upon the bodies of people on the basis of ethnic identity.

Ethnicity is strongly related to identity and to many of the issues under **Colonialism/Post-colonialism**. Ethnicity, generally, does not refer to a dominant population within national boundaries and is not linked to power within a state. In more popular and positive (if at times patronizing) discourses around multiculturalism it is linked to diversity and inclusiveness. Such associations can be confined to notions of exoticism in dress and cuisines but where group identity is maintained by the groups concerned it can be productive. Where it carries forward ethnic tensions, it can also be unproductive.

Race is a socially produced category not a natural fact. The more science contributes to dominant understandings of genetic heritage the clearer that fact becomes. Unfortunately, racism is all too real and arose out of cultural beliefs and social concerns which were given credibility by prior scientific theories, bolstered by Darwinism, and inextricable from those social concerns and world views. Socially con-structed beliefs in hierarchies of abilities and worth, based on herit-age, skin colour, socio-economic status, etc. (see **Class/Caste, Difference**) go back as far and as wide as our knowledge of human society extends. Since the rise in dominance of Western science, from the late seventeenth century onwards, at the same time that European conquest and colonialism was experiencing a parallel rise in domi-nance around the globe, ingrained beliefs about distant and different peoples were given credibility. Credible sciences of the time – such as physiognomy and later phrenology – determined that people of particular countries had specific, natural/racial characteristics which ranged from physical features to cognitive capacities and sexual appe-tites (Schiebinger, 1993).

At base, for all the outward talk of the rational light of science and empirical observation, these categorizations were based as much on pre-existing world views as was the construction of gender. Scientists found what they expected to find and what they found under the categories they created around race was that people of particular (darker) skin shades were less intelligent, more sexually rapacious and greatly inclined to all that might be considered low or bad (**Violence**). Those peoples whose skin colour was closer to that of those conduct-ing the investigations (Western Europeans) were found to be more likely to have more positive attributes. The definition of peoples by race, in the late eighteenth and throughout the nineteenth century, led to oppression and subjugation on the basis of the interpretation of embodiment.

FURTHER READING

See also the readings for **Class/Caste** and **Colonialism/Post-colonialism**. For politically oriented discussions of ethnicity and race, particularly with reference to nation-states, nation building and nationalism, see Anderson (1991), Nairn (1977) and Kymlicka (2001). As noted under **Class/Caste**, Gans (2005) problematizes the construction of race as class in contemporary US society.

REFERENCES

Anderson, B. (1991) *Imagined Communities: Reflections on the Origin and Spread of Nationalism.* London: Verso.
Gans, H.J. (2005) 'Race as class', *Contexts*, 4(4): 17–21.
Kymlicka, W. (2001) *Politics in the Vernacular: Nationalism, Multiculturalism, Citizenship.* Oxford: Oxford University Press.
Nairn, T. (1977) *The Break-Up of Britain: Crisis and Neonationalism.* London: New Left Books.

Religion

Definition Religion, here, refers to a system of meaning that explains the world in terms of a divine or sacred cosmology. Religions may have one god (monotheism) or many (polytheism, animism). In relation to the body in society, across cultures, religions or sacred systems all have bodily aspects in their symbolic rites and rituals. For example, the wetting of a baby's head in a Baptism or Christening (in Christianity) is a bodily act that symbolically welcomes the infant into that community. Circumcision and/or scarification of boys as they reach puberty in tribal cultures confirms them as full members of their clan and begins the process of passing on sacred knowledge to them.

The person perhaps best known across disciplinary divides for theorizing around religious, or spiritual, views of the body is anthropologist Mary Douglas. Douglas wrote two books, *Purity and Danger* (1966/2000) and *Natural Symbols* (1970/1996) that are amongst the foundational texts of studies in body and society. Douglas took a broad-ranging approach to the importance of the body, of bodily rituals and of bodily substances to social constructions of the body across a range of developed and developing societies. Douglas shows how varied the perception of the body and bodily substances are across societies and at the same time how important the body remains to social understanding. At the same time she also shows that there are unexpected similarities in the social significance of the body between tribal and modern social formations, based on their interpretation as sacred or profane.

Douglas' key observations on the body are that it is a natural symbol of political power and that it is the focus of concerns about purity/sanctity, pollution/taboo and social danger. Perhaps the most interesting notion to come out of her work is that of boundary-crossing, that there are particular substances or bodily acts that can be understood as *both* pure and dangerous, that defy simple categorization.

Douglas was fascinated by the messiness of bodies and the importance of that messiness in rites and rituals. Bakhtin (1984) was similarly fascinated at the differences between the closed, 'classical' male body and the grotesquely open, 'carnivalesque' female body in early modern French literature. Douglas was heavily influenced by Durkheim and Marcel Mauss (the theorist of 'the gift'), however, she took an entirely original turn. In *Purity and Danger* (1966/2000) Douglas studied the socio-political responses to bodily parts and excretions across a number of tribal cultures, and compared those cultures' 'cosmological' (ritualistic or religious) responses to such matter with that of the cultures and institutions of industrialized societies. Her approach is based specifically on the study of sacral bodies and the importance and power of cosmologies on our understanding of the body and bodily products as well as their symbolic meaning and power. In this study of the function of pollution and taboos related to the body, Douglas contrasts dirt and impurity. Douglas argues that across time, space and societies what constitutes dirtiness or defilement may differ but *how* they are defined is common.

Douglas uses the place of the body in religion to explore comparative religions and to explore how cosmologies are similar and different across cultures. Where she was quite radical, in one sense, was in turning her study towards Judeo-Christian traditions of pollution and taboo: 'we shall not expect to understand other people's ideas of contagion, sacred or secular, until we have confronted our own' (Douglas, 2000: 29). Clearly and openly embedded in her own Catholicism, the aim of her method is to try to unpack the cultural relativism behind 'symbolic rites' and 'hygiene'.

Dirt is an objective or 'real' fact, but the reactions of an individual or a culture to it are relative. This is a highly persuasive observation – we have all come across instances where one person's idea of dirt is not the same as someone else's. At least half the arguments between teenagers and parents start with 'please clean your room' and anyone who has lived in shared student accommodation will have experienced different levels of tolerance towards what is objectively dirty. Further, dirt is not necessarily 'impure' and what is considered impure is not necessarily objectively dirty. As Douglas argues in this early work, defilement or pollution is subjective, particular to a person or a culture, and is absolute. Something is either a source of pollution or defiled, or it is not. Douglas gives numerous examples of bodily products being considered impure. For example, there is nothing intrinsically 'dirty' about urine as it is expelled from the body. Nappies (or diapers) are wet and changed, small children 'caught short' may have to urinate publicly but neither are regarded as polluting as such. Urinating in a toilet is a private function but it is not a matter of disgust until a 'dribbler' or 'hoverer' leaves a drip (or a mist) on the seat, while public urination by drunken revellers is generally regarded with disgust, and an act for which an offender may be prosecuted. Urine is perceived as polluting, depending on where and how it is expelled. This is the crux of the argument in *Purity and Danger*: that problems of pollution and taboos appear when you cross boundaries, and in particular, bodily boundaries. That is to say, by their very nature, events that cross boundaries are sources of pollution and taboo. Holiness is constituted in wholeness, in events and artefacts that do not cross boundaries, which are inseparable from the 'unity, integrity, perfection of the individual and of the kind' (Douglas, 2000: 55). The bodily matter most likely to be identified as symbolically powerful (polluting and impure or purifying and sacred) is that which crosses bodily boundaries, depending on where it issues from and whether it is contained or free-flowing.

The mistake is to treat bodily margins in isolation from all other margins. There is no reason to assume any primacy for the individual's attitude to his own bodily and emotional experience, any more than for his cultural and social experience. This is the clue which explains the unevenness with which different aspects of the body are treated in the rituals of the world. (Douglas, 2000: 122)

Some years later, after critical feedback, Douglas modified her views on the absolutism of the negativity of boundary crossing. Most importantly, while maintaining the position that boundary-crossing was central to the identification of pollution and taboo, she moved away from the position that the sacred was only identified with wholeness and impermeability. She states this most clearly in *Implicit Meanings: Essays in Anthropology* (1975) in admitting her inability to account for the reverence for the (boundary-crossing) pangolin by the Lele, which contrasts so strongly with the Biblical abomination of the pig (about which she wrote in *Purity and Danger*).

> Foul monster or good saviour, the judgment has little to do with the physical attributes of the being in question and much to do with the prevailing social pattern of rules and meanings which creates anomaly … Such a response to a mixed category is essentially a gut reaction. (Douglas, 1975: 285)

Boundary-crossing becomes a sign of liminality, and the liminal has the potential to confer either sacredness or defilement, purity or danger.

It is the symbolic systems as they relate to social forms, far more than the specific content of a taboo, with which Douglas is concerned. She wants to clarify the ways in which patterns of inclusion and exclusion are formed. While throughout her work, religions or cosmologies are the means through which this patterning is identified, she does not believe that sacred systems are intrinsic to the definition of pollution. Douglas sees in the human body, and the symbolism attached to it in various cultures, a reflection or representation of society as a whole. What she is fighting against is any interpretation of bodily symbolism as exclusively aligned with the individual. In this we can see a similarity to or sympathy with projects such as Bourdieu's (see **Habitus**), but Douglas offers us explanations that Bourdieu does not. There are value judgements and qualitative distinctions in Bourdieu's work – high and low, desirable and worthless – but no place for ethical and moral content in the rationalism of the habitus. This is precisely what Douglas offers us, a way of accounting for ethically or morally 'good' and 'bad' – terms that are central to pollution and taboo and common to all societies. The moral and ethical aspects of embodiment are inseparable from issues of transgression.

Natural Symbols: Explorations in Cosmology (1970/1996) extends upon the themes and arguments of *Purity and Danger*, taking a closer look at the forms in which codifications of bodily symbolism appear. In it Douglas reiterates her argument from similarity, from the premise that all cultures – tribal, traditional, modern, industrial – have systems of cosmological symbols. These systems have embodied forms and effects. And they are different in their similarity, similar in their differences. For Douglas, given types of culture exhibit a characteristic symbolic expression. In it she argues that particular social formations will give rise to particular types of symbolic systems and characteristic forms of communication. And in each the body will be an important means of communicating that symbolism. The body is *the* natural symbol. The approach of *Natural Symbols* is to look at societies as a whole and to try to account for the importance of the symbolic within societies and how that is expressed on and through the body.

Douglas does have a tendency to homogenize across social formations, to point up differences in social behaviours between tribal people and city-dwellers and then collapse those differences into similarities. Her work has nevertheless formed the basis of much of the work on religion in relation to the body in society.

FURTHER READING

Specifically in relation to sociology and social theory, as distinct from our broader concern in this book with the body in society, Turner (1991) and Mellor and Shilling (1997) have written two of the key texts in relation to religion and the body. Coakley's collection (1997) is an eclectic mix of historical and cross-cultural approaches to the body in religion. Douglas' work, as noted above, is relatively approachable and well worth reading as a key thinker on the body with a specific interest in cosmologies (or religions).

REFERENCES

Coakley, S. (ed.) (1997) *Religion and the Body*. Cambridge: Cambridge University Press.

Douglas, Mary (1975) *Implicit Meanings: Essays in Anthropology*. London and Boston: Routledge and Kegan Paul.

Douglas, Mary (1996) *Natural Symbols: Explorations in Cosmology* (with a new Introduction). London: Routledge. First published 1970.

religion

Douglas, Mary (2000) *Purity and Danger: An Analysis of Concept of Pollution and Taboo.* London: Routledge. First published 1966.

Mellor, P.A. and C. Shilling (1997) *Re-forming the Body: Religion, Community and Modernity.* London: Sage.

Turner, Bryan S. (1991) *Religion and Social Theory,* 2nd edn. London: Sage. First published 1983.

Reproduction

Definition Reproduction is the process by which human beings (and other species) re-produce themselves. The male and female reproductive organs produce gametes or sex cells, namely ova and sperm. When an ovum and a sperm are brought together in the process of fertilization the joining of these two cells will repeatedly divide to create an embryo which, if implanted in the wall of a uterus will grow to become a foetus, and if gestated successfully for nine months will result in the birth of an infant. Each of these processes may occur as a result of sexual inter-course, but they may also occur in the context of various practices of Artificial Reproductive Technologies (ARTs), such as gamete donation, IVF procedures and surrogacy arrangements.

While reproduction is a biological process, like other socio-culturally significant biological processes (see **Death and Dying**) it is given meaning by and framed within socio-cultural norms and practices. As an expression of human sexuality, it is also subject to moral constraints within given social formations as defined within religious, legal and/or cultural codes. For example, being born within a recognized marital union is legally defined (legitimacy) and, even if it has less negative associations in Western societies than was once the case, entails a level of moral judgement on the parents and the child. Up until the late 1950s when the oral contraceptive pill was released in the developed world, reproduction was the likely result of heterosexual intercourse. The dominant social discourse in the West at that time, as derived from

Judeo-Christian morality, equated sexual activity with reproduction and imposed sanctions on both sex and reproduction outside of marriage (Solinger, 1992). The reality was more complicated. Contraception was available to married women but for social reasons based in gendered expectations of the time, not all doctors were willing to advise their use and none of the methods were foolproof (condoms, Dutch caps, spermicides, pessaries, abortifacients). Local forms of contraception also existed in tribal cultures but they too were not completely reliable. Abortion was practised both in developed and developing countries, but it was generally illegal or at least 'hidden' until the late twentieth century, when Western feminist movements, in particular, made women's reproductive choice part of its political agenda (Swain and Howe, 1995). From these examples one can see that the focus on the reproductive body was (and continues to be) almost exclusively a focus on the *female* reproductive body.

This has been the case across cultures for the obvious reason of the female body being the site of the creation of the new life. In traditional or tribal cultures reproduction is more than an individual action in the creation of a nuclear family unit; it is part of a process of social interconnection and kinship relations. Many tribal cultures treat children as the responsibility of the clan and, historically, in traditional social formations small children have been sent out to grow up in, and thereby create bonds with, other households (**Youth and Children**). Controlling the female reproductive body also becomes important in ensuring legitimacy, which is why proof of virginity on marriage often holds so much importance across cultures. By contrast, in communities in which the transmission of property is not an issue, but emphasis is placed rather on the production of labourers, hunters or gatherers to support the community, a premium is placed on proof of fertility rather than evidence of chastity in marriage negotiations.

Over the past 30 years, the reproductive body has become arguably the most medically 'gazed' into and intruded upon aspect of the human body (**Medicine and Science, Power**). The fascination with reproduction is not new: the preoccupation with the capacity to reproduce has been strong for millennia across cultures. What is new is the increasing biotechnologization of reproduction in the developed world. The technologization of human reproduction is largely in response to the inability of some people to reproduce, whether for biological or social reasons. Ironically, it is also directly linked to the ability of many women to delay or avoid reproduction thanks to the advent of the pill.

Where, once, infertile people were able to adopt infants, the supply of babies available for adoption dropped dramatically once single women were either able to prevent pregnancy or had the social and financial support to be able to keep their babies. International adoption addressed some of the demand for infants, but the availability of babies was often dependent on armed conflict or natural disasters, and increasing international regulation aimed at protecting women from exploitation and the outright trade in children does not make this an easy form of achieving 'reproduction'. Assisted Reproductive Technologies (ARTs) became better funded and more sophisticated from the early 1970s onwards, and methods involving ART techniques or contracting a surrogate are directly aimed at achieving reproduction for those unable to do so for reasons of medical or social infertility.[6]

ARTs include procedures such as artificial insemination (AI), in vitro fertilization (IVF) without gamete donation, IVF with gamete donation and both IVF-assisted and AI surrogacy arrangements. They also involve other technological interventions such as gamete selection (choosing specific embryos) and have taken reproduction out of the domestic sphere and into the laboratory. One need not be as reactionary as Francis Fukuyama (2002), whose idea of reproduction is bound to conservative notions of the nuclear family unit, to see that ARTs have and will continue to alter understandings of interpersonal relationships and to challenge what a family consists of. In ART processes the reproductive organs are chemically and physically manipulated in a number of ways to achieve conception and pregnancy: hyper-ovulation, sperm collection, fertilization, implantation, freezing of embryos, multiple embryo implantation, intra-cytoplasmic sperm injection and so on.

The technologization of reproduction is a process of what Elias (2000) termed rationalization that leads 'us to rationalize ourselves, our behaviour, to quantify and commercially value our actions and behaviours' (Cregan, 2006: 31). In it, the female body becomes a collection of 'organs without bodies' (Braidotti, 1989) and 'Women [are seen] as wombs and childbearing machines, instead of whole persons' (Gupta and Richters, 2008). Gupta and Richters write specifically about the way in which women who are poor and/or in developing countries are

---

[6]Medical infertility refers to a heterosexual couple who cannot conceive for one reason or another, including age. Social infertility generally refers to single women, gay men and lesbians who are incapable of supplying both gametes and/or are dependent on surrogacy arrangements to reproduce.

increasingly targeted for their reproductive capacity to supply infertile couples of the developed world through surrogacy arrangements. This is not only an issue in arrangements that involve obvious financial transactions, the technical processes of IVF encourage the increasing rationalization of our bodies and the commodification of childbearing.

The social complications that have arisen out of the biotechnologization of the reproductive body are many. Children born as the result of artificial insemination are increasingly demanding access to knowledge about their biological fathers, which in turn is problematic for those men who were sperm donors under conditions of complete privacy. There have also been known irregularities in unregulated AI with doctors providing the sperm or donors being allowed to make so many donations that the number of half-siblings becomes a social concern. This reflects the feelings of many locally adopted children of earlier generations and increasingly of the children internationally adopted since the Korean War, who seek out their birth families. This intensifies an understanding of kinship as genetic over and above the social, which is also implicated in the rationalization of the body into its constitutive parts (see also **Technology**).

So reproduction and the reproductive body in society take on a complex of associations that extend far beyond the individual creation of a child. These are issues of research and debate in the sociology and anthropology of family and kinship. They involve thinking through the meaning of genetics as opposed to social relations, particularly in relation to adoption and surrogacy. There are wider issues of the potential for exploitation of women, whether in developed countries with strict controls over gamete donation but strong cultural expectations of female altruism or in developing countries where poverty can lead women into agreeing to gestate a foreigner's child, often under pressure to alleviate the wider family's debts. Like paid organ donation, there are potential long-term harms to the surrogate in countries with poor access to healthcare.

The vast majority of the world's population still reproduces without technological intervention. That does not stop the technology from becoming a major influence in the way that reproduction is understood and undergone. The process of uncomplicated heterosexual reproduction is also increasingly technologized. Ultrasound imaging, genetic testing, monitoring during labour and a host of other technical interventions during pregnancy and birth have become normalized over the past 20 years. The medical gaze has taken reproduction out of the body and placed it onto the computer screen. Three hundred years ago doctors were marginal in the birthing experience and the process of pregnancy was in the pregnant woman's realm of expertise. Reproduction and the reproductive body are now medicalized to such a degree that women relate more easily to an abstract representation on a computer screen than to the subtle processes taking place within them.

FURTHER READING

For a historical contextualization of the experience and the meaning of pregnancy, Duden's (1991) book *The Woman Beneath the Skin* is an excellent and approachable narrative drawn from the notebooks of a doctor in eighteenth-century Germany, while her 1999 essay is broader in scope but no less contextualized. Solinger (1992) puts more recent historical examples of illegitimacy and pregnancy before reliable contraception in context. Ann Oakley's (1984) book on UK women's experiences of pregnancy and childbirth in more recent times is a landmark ethnographic study that has been at the centre of sociological debates around reproduction ever since. Similarly, Martin's US study (1992) is a qualitative inquiry into the experience of reproductive processes and women's negotiation of medical power. Franklin (1997) and Strathern (1992) both take an anthropological approach to the shifting meaning of kinship in relation to assisted reproductive techniques such as IVF. Shildrick (1997), influenced by Butler and other psychoanalytic feminists (**Performativity, Psychoanalysis**), analyses the construction of the female body within discourses around new reproductive technologies. While Fukuyama (2002) writes a conservative and reactionary view of the possible future of biotechnologies, Ettorre (2002) covers similar ground and finds the implications of genetic testing and screening during pregnancy socially problematic.

REFERENCES

Duden, Barbara (1991) *The Woman Beneath the Skin*, trans. T. Dunlap. Cambridge, MA: Harvard University Press.
Duden, Barbara (1999) 'The fetus on the "farther shore": Toward a history of the unborn', in *Fetal Subject: Feminist Positions*. Philadelphia: University of Pennsylvania Press.
Ettorre, E. (2002) *Reproductive Genetics, Gender and the Body*. London: Routledge.
Franklin, Sarah (1997) *Embodied Progress: A Cultural Account of Assisted Conception*. London: Routledge.

Fukuyama, F. (2002) *Our Posthuman Future: Consequences of the Biotechnology Revolution*. New York: Farrar, Straus & Giroux.

Martin, Emily (1992) *The Woman in the Body: A Cultural Analysis of Reproduction*. Boston: Beacon Press.

Oakley, A. (1984) *Woman Confined: Towards a Sociology of Childbirth*. Oxford: Martin Robertson.

Shildrick, Margritt (1997) *Leaky Bodies and Boundaries: Feminism, Postmodernism and (Bio)Ethics*. London: Routledge.

Solinger, R. (1992) *Wake Up Little Susie: Single Pregnancy and Race before Roe v. Wade*. New York: Routledge.

Strathern, M. (1992) *Reproducing the Future: Anthropology, Kinship and the New Reproductive Technologies*. Cambridge: Cambridge University Press.

Swain, S. and R. Howe (1995) *Single Mothers and Their Children: Disposal, Punishment and Survival in Australia*. Cambridge: Cambridge University Press.

Definition Sexuality is the capacity to feel and to express bodily desire. It is generally categorized in terms of identity: that is, one's sexual identity is positioned as a relational term that is attributed on the basis of the object of one's desires. The object(s) of one's desires may or may not accord with stereotypical sex roles that are based on gendered expectations of men and women. Attributions of, or identifications with, non-hetero-normative sexual identities have often been stigmatized, historically and culturally (see **Gender/Sex**, **Queer**,) and in many cases, criminally prosecuted.

The assumed and often compulsory sexuality of citizens in most, if not all, societies has been based on stereotypical sex roles. Hetero-sexuality, the attraction felt between opposite sexes (male and female), is the norm from which any 'other' is defined. Those 'others' are not so much the object of a love that dare not speak its name, as it was in Oscar Wilde's time, so much as it is heterosexuality that remains 'unspoken' and all other desires or loves are named in relation to it. However, hetero-normativity is far from being the only possible expression of sexuality for men and women. To list a few possibilities alphabetically, this includes people who identify as Asexual, Bisexual, Gay, Lesbian, Queer, Questioning (one's sexuality), Transgender and Undecided (see **Queer**). While those sexualities that were subject to criminal prosecution have been decriminalized in many (Western) countries, homosexuality in particular remains prosecutable in many other countries. Sexuality can also take forms which are widely condemned as aberrant or perverse across cultures and sexualities (for example, paedophilia and necrophilia).

Historically, all of the active sexual categories just named (except lesbianism) have been unlawful in Global Northern nations until relatively recently, although there is clear evidence of multiple sexualities existing for millennia. The Ancient Greeks are well known for their writings on homosexuality (Plato) and lesbianism (Sappho). Homosexuality, while generally seen in negative terms, is mentioned in a number of ancient religious texts. There is ample evidence of homosexuality in early modern England, in instances that show it was both tolerated as unremarkable and reviled as politically dangerous (Bray, 1982; Norton, 1992). The berdache is the name given to an accepted social category for transgender men and women in certain Native American tribes (Blackwood, 2002; Whitehead, 1981), who also engaged in same sex relationships, reinforcing and yet complicating normative sex roles. Similar social categories exist in other societies, for example the traditional hijra in India and the lady-boys of Thailand. While often tacitly or openly tolerated, non-normative sexualities also have a long history of discrimination and being socially reviled. In each of these examples, what is being policed here is the sexual conduct of bodies. Like Elias' manners (see **Civilizing Processes**), failure to conform – unsanctioned sexual bodily conduct – marks one as an outsider.

In many countries, where once-illegal sexualities have been decriminalized, the people who identify as being of a non-hetero-sexuality may still be considered socially aberrant, and treated with inequality before the law and the state. This is clear with respect to the status of pair-bonded relationships. For example, de facto heterosexual relationships may be recognized before the law and various rights legally ensured for those couples, while in the same legal system same-sex de facto couples may remain unable to access the same rights even after decades of union. Non-heterosexual marriage is possible in some countries, or in some states within countries, but even though such unions have been formalized in a number of jurisdictions this is not widespread.

Sexuality within any of the categories mentioned may vary widely on the basis of specific relationships that do not fit within these or any stable categories (Kane-Demaios and Bullough, 2006). Post-modern performativity of sexuality means that affective bonding, and where possible marriage, may occur across any and all of these boundaries (Hines and Sanger, 2010). Further, particular sexual practices that might be popularly associated with a given sexuality – for example gay men and anal intercourse – may in fact never be practised by individuals who identify with that sexuality, or conversely be practised across all the sexualities (including by women with sex toys). Sexuality is constructed as intimately connected with bodily practices, but those practices are not necessarily conveniently defined or experienced (Williams and Stein, 2002). Straight-identifying men have been shown to engage in homoerotic acts but also to refuse the identification of homosexual, both in wider society (Humphreys, 1975) but more persistently amongst prison populations.

The rejection of hetero-normative sexuality should not be assumed to entail a greater tolerance of all the sexual identity possibilities listed above. Historically, there has been antipathy between the political agendas of some groups of gay men and some groups of lesbians; there have been vocal criticisms of bisexuality from lesbians and gay men; there has been vilification of transgender women by lesbians and straight women; and so on.

As we can see from the examples of inequality before the law and intolerance at multiple levels, sexuality is not just a category of desire it is also a site of political agitation based in bodily practices. It is an area of attempted regulation, oppression and discrimination that has spawned resistance (see also **Queer**), both in group activism and at the level of the individual. Group action was highly visible during the 1980s in response to HIV/AIDS and the resulting demonization and discrimination experienced by gay men. As a disease, it was associated specifically with gay men's bodies, their bodily practices and their bodily degradation as a result of the progress of the disease (Aggleton and Homans, 1988; Lupton, 1994). This was despite the biological fact that the virus does not discriminate, its only object is surviving via any effective means of blood-borne transmission. Individual activism around sexualities can be seen in the move towards performing gender and sexuality (see **Gender/Sex**, **Performativity**). Both gender and sexuality, and the indeterminacy of association between them, can be said to be acts of post-modern activism through self-creation, by not remaining confined to one point on the continuum of sexuality

The variation in sexualities undoes many assumptions about bodies and biological determinants, and about sex roles, in showing how socially constructed sexualities and gender roles are, that bodies are not confined to deterministic notions of attraction. This is rebuffed by some psychologists and psychiatrists who attempt to find gay or lesbian brains or genes but we can very quickly see that any notion of determined sexuality, like any determinism, falls apart before the variation of attractions.

FURTHER READING

Laurence Stone's book (1979), though somewhat dated, is a core text in the history of normative (hetero)sexuality that includes some information on non-normative sexualities. More recent and very approachable is Springer's (1996) introduction to cyber-sexualities. There are several key cultural historical studies of homosexuality, which include Bray's (1982) overview of the meaning of homosexuality in sixteenth- and early-seventeenth century England, Norton's (1992) detailed study of late-seventeenth century London; and Weeks' reader (1991) was one of the first to contextualize homosexual bodies in society. The compilation by Gallagher and Lacquer (1987), gestures towards a history of the body in society as a sexual and sexualized object in the modern era. Orgel's (1996) study is of cross-dressing as allied to homosexuality in early modern British playhouses, whereas Hines and Sanger (2010) and Stryker and Whittle (2006) offer excellent overviews of issues around transgender identity and sexuality in the present. Williams and Stein (2002) is an excellent reader offering selections that cover an introduction to all the areas covered in this section.

REFERENCES

Aggleton, P. and H. Homans (eds) (1988) *Social Aspects of AIDS*. London: Falmer Press.

Bray, Alan (1982) *Homosexuality in Renaissance England*. London: Gay Men's Press.

Gallagher, Catherine and Thomas Laqueur (eds) (1987) *The Making of the Modern Body: Sexuality and Society in the Nineteenth Century*. Berkeley: The University of California Press.

Hines, S. and T. Sanger (2010) *Transgender Identities: Towards a Social Analysis of Gender Diversity*. New York: Routledge.

Kane-Demaios, J. and V. Bullough (2006) *Crossing Sexual Boundaries: Transgender Journeys, Uncharted Paths*. New York: Prometheus Books.

key concepts in
body and society

Lupton, D. (1994) *Moral Threats and Dangerous Desires: AIDS in the News Media.* London: Taylor & Francis.

Norton, Rictor (1992) *Mother Clap's Molly House: The Gay Subculture in England 1700–1830.* London: Gay Men's Press.

Orgel, Stephen (1996) *Impersonations: The Performance of Gender in Shakespeare's England.* Cambridge: Cambridge University Press.

Springer, C. (1996) *Electronic Eros: Bodies and Desire in the Post-Industrial Age.* London: Athlone.

Stone, Lawrence (1979) *The Family, Sex and Marriage in England 1500–1800,* abridged edn. London: Penguin.

Stryker, S. and S. Whittle (eds) (2006) *The Transgender Studies Reader.* London: Routledge.

Weeks, Jeffrey (1991) *Sexuality and its Discontents: Meanings, Myths and Modern Sexualities.* London: Routledge.

Williams C.L. and A. Stein (eds) (2002) *Sexuality and Gender.* Oxford: Blackwell.

Sport

Definition The differentiation between a sport, a game and a leisure activity is a site of dispute, particularly when professional and/or commercial concerns are involved. For the purposes of discussing the body in society, the sense of sport used here can be defined as an activity that incorporates particular physical skills, and that has an agreed framework within which the bodily actions of the player(s) are regulated. Further, sport is taken to imply a socio-political element and also to include earlier meanings of the word that contain a sense of entertainment and pleasure. A sport is also generally understood to be, but is not necessarily, competitive.

The rationalization of physical activities into mock-games or sports, with agreed structures or rules, can be found across time, place and culture. Sports may involve physical dexterity with an object, as in football or baseball, or they may rely on an individual's embodied strength, as in weight-lifting or boxing. They may be played in competing teams or in individualized tests of skill and ability. Sports can be categorized into various groups. These include team sports, individual sports, contact and non-contact sports, blood sports – which involve humans hunting and killing various types of animals, known as 'game' – aquatic sports and motor sports, which involve racing in cars or motorbikes.

While their contemporary association is with leisure activities, in many instances sports can be directly related to training up the body in ways that might, in other times, have been intended to develop skills for purposes other than pleasure and entertainment. That is, learning to accurately wield a tool through practice in a sporting context – whether it is a spear, a longbow or a rifle – or learning to embody specific capacities of endurance (running, wrestling) or agility (climbing, horse-riding). In other contexts, these abilities secure the survival of the group in having members prepared for success in battle and in hunting down food.

The Ancient Greeks considered sport and bodily health, training and fitness as central to education, sociality and by extension political health (Elias and Dunning, 2007). Sports were a part of their understanding of civilizing processes (**Civilizing Processes**) and the skills learned in sports were part of what the Greeks (and Romans) saw as setting them apart from 'barbarians'. However, as Elias argues, such contests were often intentionally violent and could prove to be both bloody and fatal (Elias and Dunning, 2007: 115). Men jousting in medieval tournaments were engaged in 'sports' with similar social, political and military functions. In many parts of Papua New Guinea (PNG), preparing for disputes with other clans and hunting food continues to be practised through traditional contests of skill (the Dani's mock-battles are one famous example).

At the same time, with the incursion of modernity into PNG, there is also a national obsession with modern sports that have long been abstracted from such practical purposes (football, cricket, rugby). Dunning argues that that abstraction is the result of a programmatic attempt at the sublimation of aggression into 'combat sports' (Elias and Dunning, 2007: 245). In nineteenth-century England this took the form of educationally sanctioned training in sports such as rugby, invented and codified (in 1848) at the eponymous school; and boxing, the rules of which were codified under the name of the Marquess of Queensberry in 1865 with the express intention of lessening the brutality of its playing by the introduction of gloves and other regularizing the practices.

From the examples given, we can see immediately that sports, both in the past and in the present, are interconnected with other categories in this book. Sport is deeply gendered (**Feminism, Gender/Sex, Sexuality**);

it has been used as a means of defining and excluding 'others' (**Colonialism/Post-colonialism, Difference, Nature/Culture**); as we have seen above, it has functioned as a means of transferring or suppressing violence (**Civilizing Processes, Violence**); it has been used to express nationalistic fervour (**Identity**); it has proved to be a means to self-construction (**Performativity**); and in modern societies it is increasingly a focus of discourses around public health in both positive and negative senses (**Anorexia/Bulimia/Obesity, Health and Illness, Modification/Dysmorphias**).

One of the first things we should notice from the examples above is that they all related to the activities of men. Women were largely excluded from sports until the late nineteenth century. Women might exercise in ways considered appropriate to what was conceived to be their more delicate nature and as may be beneficial to their health (**Nature/Culture**) – by walking and, amongst the upper classes, horse-riding. But as we saw in relation to **Gesture and Habits**, physical open-ness and exertion was considered unfeminine or at least lower class. Women supposedly did not need to be taught to sublimate their aggres-sion in more arduous activities because they were already considered to be passive and weak. The reality is, of course, that women were on bat-tlefields, both as extraordinary individuals (Joan of Arc), cross-dressed and passing as men, as well as camp-followers who might also take part in battles (Linebaugh and Rediker, 2000).

The exclusion of women from sports extended well into the twentieth century and similar bodily assumptions about physical frailty can still be heard in arguments around whether teenage girls should be allowed to play against boys in a range of contact sports, such as football. As health movements rose in the late nineteenth century, often related to or based in eugenics movements, women and girls were encouraged to take up 'appropriate' sports for the health, such as cycling and calisthenics. As Lenskyj (1986) shows, the health movements still argued for particular kinds of sports for women, on the basis of their not having harmful (mas-culinizing) effects on the mothers of the future. Just as women gained access to work, during World War II, so too there were opportunities for them to demonstrate their sporting capacities in the US All-American Girls Baseball League: however, like Rosie the Riveter, when the war ended women were expected to abandon sports for motherhood.

Sport became an open issue of gender discrimination for feminists in the 1960s and sporting leagues were set up in many developed countries, in reflection of the leagues of the highly socially visible male-dominated sports. Despite these moves, gender remains an issue in sport, in so far as women's leagues and women's sports are still treated (patronizingly) as being less worthy: they receive less coverage and lower funding than any male-dominated sport. There are aspects of women's sports that have proved more empowering, such as body-building, where women can reshape their bodies into heavily muscled forms subverting expectations and understandings of the woman as a weaker vessel. Gender is also a site of controversy at a genetic level in sport, as is shown in the very public arguments over whether Caster Semenya should be allowed to compete as a woman (**Gender/Sex, Genetics**). Semenya was widely reported to be genetically intersex (http://www.theage.com.au/world/world-champ-semenyas-gender-mystery-solved-20090911-fjjq.html), despite the fact that the medical results remain private and that her social identity is female.

The issue of the stratification of sports is complex and leads into other areas of discrimination on the basis of bodily attributes. In colonial contexts, sport has long been a site of segregation. An Australian Aboriginal cricket team from the Western District of Victoria toured England in 1868, but it was not on an equal footing; it was received, at best, as an anthropological exhibition and exotic oddity and, at worst, as a perversion of the game. Well into the 1980s, South African sporting teams were made up solely of whites, which led to riots in some of the countries they attempted to tour. In the US, until the 1950s, African-Americans were segregated into separate baseball leagues (the Negro Leagues) and the first African-American player to enter the major leagues in 1946, Jackie Robinson, was subjected to racist abuse. In the moment captured in the 1993 photograph on the cover of Bale and Cronin's collection (2003) on sport and post-colonialism, Indigenous Australian Rules player, Nicky Winmar, is responding to similar taunts from the opposing team's supporters. Winmar's stance is one of defiance, pointing exultantly to his bared chest, and has had a direct effect on the AFL's policies.

Notwithstanding that sports have been sites of racism, they have also provided important mechanisms for social mobility for athletes from minority groups. For example, US football and basketball scholarships have provided college educations and a pathway out of poverty for many African-American athletes. Similarly, Rugby Union has provided pathways for Maori and Pacific Islander athletes, and all football codes in Australia have offered opportunities for Aboriginal and Torres Strait

Islander players. However, this has proved something of a double-edged sword in practice, tending to reinforce racist stereotypes of the 'other' living in and through the body (**Colonialism/Post-colonialism, Nature/Culture**), as if purely by instinct and uninformed by intellect.

Sport is also a vehicle for identity, whether individual or massed. Sport can be a means of identity-formation for supporters and players alike, at both the personal and the national level. When team sports were uniformly local and amateur, individual supporters of a team stated a community allegiance to players they may see in action on a regular basis. Extending his arguments around state formation, Elias sees sports contested under national flags as a means to a particular form of masculine identity that reflects indicative stages of those civilizing processes. The intensified, globalized, commercialized post-modern societies of many developed nations have sports that are reflective of intensified globalization and massed professionalization. Individuals still claim membership of a community but, as with other forms of abstracted community that is no longer local, it may extend to teams on the other side of the planet who may never be seen live.

Nevertheless, in games or sports played under a national flag, elements of xenophobia and jingoism amongst supporters are brought out, particularly where long-held animosities exist. Serbian and Croatian supporters are often separated at International Open Tennis tournaments; European and World Cup football seasons regularly herald a spree of nationalistic violence on the streets of the host countries. The Olympics, which were re-founded in a spirit of amateur, apolitical goodwill have often been politicized. The notorious example of the politicization of the 1936 Berlin Olympics was at an overtly bodily level, as the contemporary propagandist documentaries, *Olympia: Parts 1 and 2* (1938), show. The intention was openly eugenicist and racist, based on theories of Aryan racial superiority and racial hygiene (Proctor, 1988). Sport has been used as a vehicle of imperial nationalism and has been turned back on the (former) empires teams in the avid support of post-colonial teams. The prime example of this is cricket, a game now dominated at the global level by teams from the former colonies of the British Empire (Maguire, 1994; Searle, 1990).

Sports also foster a very particular kind of phenomenological identity. Like a skilled musician who has practised her instrument until the appropriate bodily movements seamlessly flow as notes are read from the page, as one becomes skilled in a sport the appropriate movements on the playing field become so embodied they appear, and are felt to be, intuitive. This may be the case at the highest level of competitive sports, highly active or relatively passive. However, phenomenological or proprioceptive experience of sports is not confined to elite sportspeople who have made careers of their bodily abilities.

The phenomenological experience of sport is also a part of the identity formation of those who are skilled but who have been excluded from professional sports, as noted above, and those amateurs who may be less skilled but are passionate about their chosen sport. Sport as discussed under all the categories dealt with to this point has been focused on bodies that strive to compete and that exhibit a socially valued physical excellence. There are bodies that do not meet socially valued standards of physical excellence who have been excluded on that basis. We have already given two examples, of sexism and racism. Even for those who are not excluded and do succeed in amateur or professional sports, the pressures of competition can lead to attempts on the part of athletes to modify their bodies beyond the bounds of naturally occurring physical capacities. This is an extension of the body modification undertaken in standard training, from fuelling the bodily machine with regimens of targeted nutrients, and corrective surgeries such as knee replacements (**Cyborgs**), to re-balancing hormonal flows with steroids. It is not hard to believe that athletes will be attempting genetic enhancement before long.

Sports are often about the body beautiful. However, any discussion of sport and the body in society must deal with absences based on sexism and racism, it has to deal with the absence of physical excellence. The Paralympic Games were founded after World War II initially for physically disabled soldiers and with improved prosthetics some track and field athletes in these games are now capable of exceeding the times of able-bodied world records. The Special Olympics, for athletes with intellectual disabilities, are less competitive. These games retain that sense of amateur achievement, pleasure and enjoyment that is less visible in peak able-bodied sports and are socio-politically motivated to celebrate the diversity of bodily experience. Sports also function at another level of socio-political motivation, in their inclusion in public health campaigns. Many governments promote sport within schools more than as a means to training up young bodies to greater civility, but also as a part of preventive public health measures. Like other civilizing processes, sports can be seen to follow similar patterns of self-regulation, internalization of norms and reshaping of the mind as well as the body. Sports, in public health discourses, are re-framed as a means to a healthy life and one free of what are termed preventable diseases (for example, type 2 diabetes, coronary artery disease, high blood pressure). What this often means in practice is focusing on the weight of individual children who do not meet metrical standards for body shape and health (see **Anorexia/Bulimia/Obesity**).

FURTHER READING

A good place to start is any recent edition of Coakley's (2004) introductory reader on the sociology of sports. Shilling (2008) also has an excellent overview in a chapter on sports and their relationship to the body in society. For a comprehensive theoretical approach to the meaning of sport in everyday life, both in the past and the present, Elias and Dunning (2007) is excellent. Rippon (2006) is an explication of the famous example of the (Nazi) politicization of the 1936 Berlin Olympics, and racism in sports. Bale and Cronin (2003), the cover of which is mentioned above, provide an excellent collection of readings of sport from post-colonial perspectives that includes the exploitation of child-workers in former colonies in the service of sports industries. Lenskyj (1986) is an early but approachable and comprehensive treatment of sexism in the history of sports. Evans et al. (2004) are specifically interested in the uses of sport in education while Miah (2004) is concerned with the potential effects of gene technologies on sports and athletes. For a discussion of the commercialization of sport and the pressures athletes face see Blake (1996). Eichberg (1998) takes a sophisticated philosophical approach to extending the ideas on the meaning of sport in social formations found in Elias, Foucault and Habermas.

REFERENCES

Bale, J. and M. Cronin (eds) (2003) *Sport and Postcolonialism.* Oxford: Berg.

Blake, A. (1996) *The Body Language: The Meaning of Modern Sport.* London: Lawrence & Wishart.

Coakley, J. (2004) *Sport in Society: Issues and Controversies.* St Louis: Mosby.

Eichberg, H. (1998) *Body Cultures: Essays on Sport, Space and Identity.* London: Routledge.

Elias, Norbert and Eric Dunning (2007) *Quest for Excitement: Sport and Leisure in the Civilizing Process.* Oxford: Blackwell.

Evans, J., B. Davies and J. Wright (2004) *Body Knowledge and Control: Studies in the Sociology of Physical Education and Health.* London: Routledge.

Lenskyj, H. (1986) *Out of Bounds: Women Sport and Sexuality.* Toronto: The Women's Press.

Maguire, J. (1994) 'Globalisation, sport and national identities: "The empire strikes back"?', *Society and Leisure*, 16(2): 293–323.

Miah, A. (2004) *Genetically Modified Athletes*. London: Routledge.

Proctor, R. (1988) *Racial Hygiene: Medicine Under the Nazis*. Cambridge, MA: Harvard University Press.

Rippon, A. (2006) *Hitler's Olympics: The Story of the 1936 Olympic Games*. London: Pen and Sword Military.

Searle, C. (1990) 'Race before the wicket: Cricket, empire and the white rose', *Race & Class*, 31: 31–48.

Shilling, Chris (2008) *Changing Bodies: Habit, Crisis and Creativity*. London: Sage.

Technology

Definition Technology in the popular sense refers to the increasingly complex kinds of machinery that we encounter and use in our everyday lives. These may supplement or become a part of the human body (**Cyborgs**). In the sociological sense, technology also encompasses forms of productive 'technique' that may be more directly embodied, in the use of hand tools that have their origins in the earliest social formations. In both senses these are the outcomes of social processes that have direct effects on the human body.

Archaeological evidence shows that tool use was prevalent amongst the earliest humans: spears and axes extended the capacities of our bodies and, along with fire, allowed us to manipulate and affect the world around us. So, far from being an alien incursion impacting on the body, techniques and technologies that become extensions of our bodies appear inextricable from the rise of human social formations. What has changed across social formations is the intensity of the abstraction – the alienation from and the reconstitution of understandings of ourselves – involved in the use of those technological extensions. A handsaw into which a surgeon puts embodied force to cut through a bone feels a part of his or her arm in a way that a power-saw or a surgical laser, which are just as much extensions of that arm, does not. The surgeon's relation to his or her labour has changed with the technology and so too has the quality of the embodied relationship to the tool and the world (in this case, in the form of the body being operated upon). Human bodies, whether cyborg or not, interact with technology at many levels.

The computer I am writing on now is a technological intervention that is ubiquitous for anyone in a developed country under the age of 25. It is qualitatively different in its effects on my body from the pencil I learned to write with or the pens that were the highest technology available in my early schooling, which caused hand cramps but none of the pain in my neck or lower back that makes my embodied being intrude on my thoughts as I write. Lightweight mobile phones, similarly, have become widely available and also accessible around the globe, far more quickly than computer technologies. People in developing countries who have no access to a desktop or a laptop computer are able to enter into the world of electronically mediated and abstracted connections via a prepaid mobile, and even via the internet connectivity of their mobile, depending on the country's infrastructure. These technologies do not only affect the individual user's embodiment, they affect the quality of embodied interactions as a whole, as we can see in the recent political upheavals that have been organized via instant messaging and brought massed bodies out onto the streets (see **Media and Representation**).

Increasingly sophisticated technologies are affecting how we understand our bodies across a range of spheres (**Work**). That can be as basic as the outbreak of RSI when computers with fixed keyboards and screens became standard office equipment. All areas of life are affected by technological advance. We are becoming increasingly abstracted from our labour, which is taking place in concomitantly more abstracted forms. Robots are replacing workers in production-line processes. The 2008 children's film, Wall-E, puts a humorous spin on this by depicting a whole society of humans – who have fled Earth in a spacecraft after the complete environmental degradation of the planet – as morbidly obese, completely sedentary and, as a result, skeletally deficient consumers living on liquid food with no awareness of their surroundings beyond the video screens floating sixty centimetres in front of their faces. In a less flippant example, technologies are radically altering basic modes of human interaction from identity and community to personal relationships and sexual intimacy (Springer, 1996). For Haraway (see **Cyborgs**) and Balsamo (1996) these are exciting prospects for reimagining identity in a new form. The innovation of increasingly sophisticated versions of second life and other proprietary forms of group communication in the moment, are both seeing a shift in interaction and a repetition of the interpersonal dynamics that occur in 'first life', for example, playground or workplace bullying has moved into cyberspace.

In relation to the human body in general, as Foucault has proposed (**Medicine and Science, Power**), the shifting nature and form of technology have parallel effects on the ways in which we understand ourselves. As a practical example, let us take the shifting meaning and practice of anatomical dissection. Foucault argues that dissection is one stage in the creation of the medical 'gaze', that is, the seeing into the body and the importance of observation (visualization) from that time to the present within medical science. The means of visualization has changed from direct observation of the open body to other ways of 'seeing into' the human body. These technologies of visualization of what cannot be seen have become more sophisticated over time with microscopy, x-rays, radiographic scanning, heart monitoring, brain monitoring, electron-microscopy, magnetic resonance imaging, ultrasound, 3D ultrasound, and the gradual shift away from physical to virtual dissection. Surgery is increasingly done keeping the body surface intact, no longer relying on physical observation and the touch of the surgeon, visualized at a distance on computer screens and conducted using introduced cameras and remotely manipulated lasers.

Hand-held technologies can also have revolutionary effects at a public, political level. We can see, under **Media and Representation**, that mobile telephony with its capacity for broadcasting text and/or images almost instantly to an international audience, has been used in the promulgation of people power and revolutionary movements. Other technologies, in particular artificial reproductive technologies (ARTs), are shifting our understanding of much more fundamental concepts, by re-forming the meaning of kinship, of family, of individuality and, at base, what it means to be human (**Reproduction**). The effects of technologies on humans as individuals and collectively have not gone unchallenged. There are keen critics of technologies as expressions of scientific orthodoxies (**Medicine and Science**) and the gender blindness that has characterized those endeavours for centuries (**Feminism, Gender/Sex**) and this section should be read in conjunction with those entries.

FURTHER READING

Bell and Kennedy's (2000) reader includes a wide range of essays and excerpts that are relevant to technology and the body, including Haraway's 'Cyborg Manifesto'. Ott et al. (2002) give a history of the intermeshing of the human body with the earliest forms of technological supplements or replacements. Franklin (1997) gives a medical anthropologist's view of the experience of undergoing reproductive technologies and their effect on systems of kinship. Harding's (1986) book was one of the earliest feminist critical approaches to scientific knowledge production and remains influential. Shilling (2005) gives a social theory overview of the meaning of technologies in culture and society, specifically as they affect understandings of embodiment.

REFERENCES

Balsamo, A. (1996) *Technologies of the Gendered Body*. Durham: Duke University Press.

Bell, D. and B. Kennedy (2000) *The Cybercultures Reader*. London: Routledge.

Franklin, Sarah (1997) *Embodied Progress: A Cultural Account of Assisted Conception*. London: Routledge.

Harding, Sandra (1986) *The Science Question in Feminism*. Ithaca, NY: Cornell University Press.

Ott, K., D. Serlin and S. Mihm (eds) (2002) *Artificial Parts, Practical Lives: Modern Histories of Prosthetics*. New York: New York University Press.

Shilling, Chris (2005) *The Body in Culture, Technology and Society*. London: Sage.

Springer, C. (1996) *Electronic Eros: Bodies and Desire in the Postindustrial Age*. Austin: University of Texas Press.

Violence

Definition For the purposes of discussing violence in relation to the body in society, the term is understood to comprehend human actions that involve physical and/or psychological assault upon others, perpetrated in local, national or global contexts. Violence can occur at many different levels. It can be inflicted in private or in public, by individuals for individual reasons or by individuals, groups or states for socio-political reasons (see also **Pain, Private and Public**). Massed violence can be found in wars at any level, in police actions, and in popular uprisings such as revolutions. That is, violence may come from above, or below.

In Western cultures, violence at a personal level is frequently connected with biological, psychological and/or moral failings on the part of the individual who perpetrates the violence. At a biological level it may explained in terms of autonomic fight or flight responses (see **Emotion**); at a psychological level it might be explained in a number of ways, such as linking it to primal drives or underlying psychoses (**Psychoanalysis**); and at a moral level it can be seen as a failure of the individual to reflect the values of Western civilization. Elias argues that the ability to refrain from violence, for a person to exhibit self-control, is one of the core humanistic values that is incorporated in Western ideas of civilization (**Civilizing Processes**). Indeed, it is an ideal upheld in religious teachings well beyond the Judeo-Christian heritage (for example, Hinduism, Buddhism and Islam). Nevertheless, violence occurs on battlefields, in criminal acts, on the street, in workplaces, on sporting fields and in the home. How it is defined is less straightforward (Kelly and Radford, 1998) and ultimately dependent on who is constructing the definition.

The negative judgement of individual violence is in tension with the almost universal political justification of violence at the level of the state or the nation: that is in waging war. Elias explains this in his discussion of manners (**Civilizing Processes**) and the formation of nation-states as the endpoint of the process of self-control that we learn through manners, whereby the state becomes the only legitimate source of violence (1985). The other arena in which Elias saw (controlled) violence as having become socially acceptable through the adoption of self-control, although sublimated and defused, is on playing fields (see **Sport**).

In practice, there may be disagreements on who may or may not wage war, who is right and who is wrong in starting a war, whether particular wars are just, unjust or rogue actions, but violence is an understood component of any armed action. That is not to say that there are not biological, psychological and moral overtones to the representation and interpretation of individual acts of war, or of the various parties involved in a war. The reporting of armed conflicts through news media from either side of a dispute is sufficient evidence of that (**Media and Representation**). The incapacity to refrain from violence is often constructed as a quality of the un-civilized and un-restrained. At the national level this extends to the point where notions of savagery are deeply embedded in constructions of embodied conflicts in post-colonial or failed states (**Colonialism/Post-colonialism**). We can see this in language and imagery used in the media reporting and political representations of massed violence in civil conflicts in former African colonies (Rwanda, Somalia) and the localized or gang violence in the poorest sections of South American states (Brazil). Such associations are even embedded in our language for violent behaviour. For example, 'to run amok' originates in colonialist observations, in the late eighteenth century, of young Malaysian men in a state of violent spiritual frenzy (*mengamok*) that was seen locally as a socio-culturally understood state of possession, and in the colonial eye as an expression of (socio-cultural) primitivism. The term in English continues to mean indiscriminate and irrational violence and is also the diagnostic name for a psychotic psychiatric condition (Saint Martin, 1999). The phrase running amok, then, holds within it an ascription of uncontrolled violence that is specifically related to a non-Western way of being.

The differentiation between developed and developing countries in the available means for enacting violence in war plays into old prejudices (**Race/Ethnicity**) whereby (bodily) savagery is allocated to those who have few other means to fight. The military of developed countries use highly abstracted methods of killing: like surgeons using laser or keyhole surgery, post-modern soldiers are rarely called upon to engage in combat in which their bodies are in direct contact with another human being. Fewer soldiers are required in most conflicts and those that are deployed are provided with sophisticated protective measures. They are provided with combat gear to protect their bodies as far as possible, they use weapons that allow them to attack at a distance, travel in armoured vehicles and have support from air forces that can attack at even greater distances. Bodies at war for wealthy and/or developed countries are highly technologized and rationalized. High-tech weapons allow mass destruction to be visited in short sharp blows – even without resorting to nuclear weapons. As the number of those dying on the side of the well-prepared in wars is proportionately less the significance of their deaths appears to become far greater. Historically, the bodies of the slain have always held a high social significance, but no longer are 'our fallen' permitted to remain on a foreign shore, remains must be retrieved at all costs. Their bodies are sacred: the enemies' are not (Cregan, 2007).

By contrast, combatants in developing countries, of whom the professional military are often a minority, may have guns but they are also likely to be reliant on the cheapest available weapons, such as machetes. The depiction of child soldiers in developing countries is an example of the attribution of embedded ideas about inherent violence: whole populations are demonized because of the use of the only means at hand to wage war (Shepler, 2005). There are dual ideas at play here: those who induct children into armed conflicts are portrayed as cynical, abusive and evil and the children are depicted as corrupted and damaged innocents

(Betancourt, 2010). The reality more probably lies somewhere in between, with children over the age of 10 being capable of making a rational political decision to take up arms and the groups into which they are inducted performing a kinship network in situations where children may have already been living outside such networks (Uppard, 2003).

Approval or disapproval of state-supported violence at the local level in the suppression of civil unrest or police actions against citizens protesting unpopular legislation – for example, cuts to the funding of Higher Education – rather depends on where one is standing: that is, behind or in front of the barricades. So, as noted earlier, the definition of violence often depends on who is constructing the systems that are put in place to control it. As with other dominant and/or discursive constructions (**Discourse**), historically this has meant that violence has been clearly gendered. As we saw from Elias, men are expected to displace violence on the sporting field: within that is a basic and popular assumption that aggression is a masculine trait that needs to be civilized. Basic assumptions about what is appropriate to masculinity therefore underpin social and legislative reactions to violence, and its toleration, at all levels (Breines et al., 2000). To return to the individual or 'private' realm, violence perpetrated upon women and children, within a family (also called domestic violence) or on the street (see also **Youth and Children**) is a key point of social research amongst feminists (**Feminism, Gender/ Sex**), and is generally seen as an outcome of patriarchal norms. The tacit toleration of violence against women in legal judgements – if not necessarily in the legislation itself – becomes most obvious in cases where women's sexual history is used to mitigate the violent actions perpetrated upon them or where women mitigate their own experiences of sexual assault (Lees, 1997). The construction and the perception of violence, then, depends very much on the bodies upon whom it is being perpetrated, whether at the local or at the national level.

FURTHER READING

See also the readings for **Civilizing Processes** and **Sport**.

For discussions of violence in relation to child soldiers, Betancourt et al. (2010) show the difficulties of reintegrating former child soldiers into mainstream society from a social psychology point of view, as does Shepler (2005) from a more sociological perspective. Uppard (2003) problematizes the view of child soldiers as non-agents. Breines et al. (2000) report on the dominance of masculinities in the perpetuation of violence, while Kelly and Radford (1998) and Lees (1997) discuss the implications of violence against women. Saint Martin (1999) places the psychological definition of 'running amok' in a cultural context.

REFERENCES

Betancourt, T. et al. (2010) 'Past horrors, present struggles: The role of stigma in the association between war experiences and psychosocial adjustment among former child soldiers in Sierra Leone', *Social Science and Medicine*, 70(1): 17–26.

Breines, L., R. Connell and I. Eide (2000) *Male Roles, Masculinities and Violence*. Paris: UNESCO.

Cregan, K. (2007) 'Remembering the dead', in *Globalism Institute Annual Report 2006*. Melbourne: RMIT University.

Kelly, L. and J. Radford (1998) 'Sexual violence against women and girls', in R. Emerson and R. Dobash (eds) *Rethinking Violence Against Women*. London: Sage.

Lees, S. (1997) *Ruling Passions: Sexual Violence, Sexual Reputation and the Law*. Buckingham: Open University Press.

Saint Martin, M. (1999) 'Running amok: A modern perspective on a culture-bound syndrome', *Primary Care Companion to the Journal of Clinical Psychiatry*, 1(3): 66–70.

Shepler, S. (2005) 'The rites of the child: Global discourses of youth and reintegrating child soldiers in Sierra Leone', *Journal of Human Rights*, 4(2): 197–211.

Uppard, S. (2003) 'Child soldiers and children associated with fighting forces', *Medicine, Conflict and Survival*, 19(2): 121–7.

Definition Work has two inter-related meanings. Work is an act, our physical (and/or mental) labour to produce something. Work also indicates a form of employment, the complex within which we perform that labour. In writing these words, my employment is as an academic and author, and I am undertaking mental (thinking) and physical (typing)

(Continued)

The consideration of work in relation to the body in society intersects with many of the categories within this book. As noted above, body modification and body enhancements through weight training or beauty regimes (Gimlin, 2002), and the innumerable ways in which the body is the site of professional expertise and labour – '*bodies-working-on-bodies*' (Shilling, 2011: 336) – are examples of how other sections of this book involve a nexus between work and the human body. However, the focus in this section is on work as the labour of 'our' bodies. Historically, work has been an indicator of social stratum (**Class/Caste**). Women's ability to undertake work, based on their social status as women, has varied across time, space and culture (**Feminism, Gender/Sex**). Similarly, men and women have been excluded from work on the basis of their background (**Colonialism/Post-colonialism, Race/Ethnicity**), their perceived capabilities (**Ageing and Childhood, Disability/Ability**) or their personal lives (**Modification/Dysmorphias, Queer**). In Bourdieu's terms, work is an embodied practice which is inseparable from our social, cultural, political and spatial existence (**Habitus**).

So, work is a site at which our embodied being is assessed and which in turn contributes to the shaping of our bodies. The more physically demanding work is the more likely it is to encourage the development of specific patterns of musculature: this is true for both men and women. Work has a direct effect on the embodiment of individuals. It also has effects at a structural level. That is, as work patterns change, forms of employment alter and the institution of labour regulations ensures that time is spent away from work in leisure pursuits. Bourdieu (1984) found, in *Distinction*, that people from different social strata spent not only their work in quite different forms of labour but that they also chose to undertake different forms of leisure pursuits, which in turn had effects on their embodied being. He was looking at a very particular historical moment where the demarcation between the leisure pursuits of the classes was clearly defined, but what he found was that there were observable differences in body shapes between those who laboured physically and those who worked in offices, with a reversed relationship in their leisure pursuits (physical activity was a leisure pursuit for the rich, sedentary relaxation for the working class). In a general sense, his point holds, for manual labour is likely to contribute to different patterns of muscular and skeletal formation from those developed by bench-pressing weights in a gym or competitive ballroom dancing.

As noted above, work can be a site at which discrimination is enacted on a bodily basis. Where labour is closer to the ground, that is, where everyone's labour is important to the survival and prosperity of the community, women and children are as likely as men to work in any capacity where they are capable. That work might take place in a household or family business, or it may take place outside the home. Historically, in agriculture and in cottage industries, the whole household contributed to the constitution of the workforce. In contemporary developing countries, that remains a necessity for people living in poverty, with everyone contributing to the production of food in agricultural societies while in urban or semi-urban situations, the cheapest labourers (children) are often those most likely to be able to contribute cash income into the household (ILO, 1999; see also **Youth and Children**).

In developing and developed countries, embodied gender remains a powerful factor in work (Adkins, 1995): overall, women remain lower paid than men performing the same or equivalent work (Dex, 1985). Women are denied access to or are allowed limited entry into particular workforces (for example, the armed forces) specifically on the basis of embodiment. However, as we have just seen, in different historical and cultural contexts women have been at least equal contributors to communities in terms of labour. Prior to the eighteenth century in England, the wives of artisans and guildsmen regularly worked alongside their husbands and as widows were able to carry on the business (Fraser, 1985). What remains unaccounted for in talking about labour as work, in the sense of employment, is the unpaid labour that is carried out across social or cultural settings. That unpaid labour is highly gendered (see ILO annual statistics, http://www.ilo.org/global/statistics-and-databases/lang-en/index.htm) and age-related, with women carrying higher domestic labour loads and the elderly taking responsibility for unpaid child-minding, whether it is in developing or developed countries.

Work has also been a means of controlling sections of the population. In colonial empires, the colonized people were generally debarred from forms of work that entailed responsibility or public power. For example, under many colonial regimes locals were barred from holding particular forms of employment, the apartheid system of South Africa being an obvious case. Similar discriminatory practices have existed elsewhere: for example, as part of the segregation practices of the Deep South of the US; within the British, French and Dutch imperial colonies until independence; and Jews were restricted by law from many fields of employment in countries across Europe, up to the middle of the twentieth century. Elias' move out of Germany was at least in part because the Nazis' discrimination against Jews in higher education. Such examples turned on the power of racist discrimination.

So work has been a site of discrimination and exclusion on the basis of embodied differences (**Difference**). To the examples given above, can be added discrimination and exclusion on the basis of sexual preferences, gender identity (**Queer**) and non-normative appearance (**Appearance and Beauty**). Many countries now have specific workplace legislation that forbids the exclusion of people from work on discriminatory bases (such as age, gender, sexual preference, ethnicity and disability). Nevertheless, in doing so embodied being remains or becomes a more intensified marker of one's social being. Legislation to monitor bodies at work also extends into the 'manners' displayed in the workplace, such that not only is exclusion from the workplace a focus, so is the inter-relating of bodies within the workplace.

In many instances this will be on the basis of Occupational Health and Safety (OHS) legislation, which regulates bodies with constant checks on safety and surveillance of workplace practices. Protective clothing to minimize injury to the body is mandatory in many workplaces. In these and other ways the body has become subject to surveillance technologies in the workplace (**Power**). The provision of ergonomic furniture is an acknowledgement of the bodily effects of sedentary work but at the same time readjusts the body. Workers are trained in body techniques in every workplace imaginable, from how to lift weights to how *not* to physically interact with other workers. Workers' physical behaviour towards each other, whether in bullying legislation or sexual harassment, is an overweening concern in modern workplaces. Bodily risks of every kind are guarded against.

Bourdieu's habitus still has something to say about work and how it contributes to the general definition or construction of our embodied being. In shifting to more sedentary paid employment more emphasis is put on the body-work – sport and exercise – we might do to maintain our physical forms. Work is paired with leisure, but leisure is becoming an industry in itself in which the body becomes the product we both manufacture and consume. The more developed, technological and sophisticated work practices become, the less clear those traditional ascriptions of blue-collar or working-class employments pertain. Manual labour still exists, but in the developed world the range of employment that can be described in these terms is rapidly shrinking. What is clear is that work and the body are indissociable and that the symbolic, phenomenological and practical effects on embodiment are more complex.

FURTHER READING

Wolkowitz (2006) is one of the best places to start for a view of the body and work that problematizes common understandings of the body in work. Adkins (1995) and Dex (1985) each give a sound inter-pretation of the gendered effects of work, with ample evidence to back their cases. Fraser (1985) was one of the first feminist historians to give a broad overview of women's lives in context, in this instance in early modern Britain. For a recent collection of essays on bodies-working-on-bodies see the special edition of *SHI* edited by Twigg et al. (2011).

REFERENCES

Adkins, L. (1995) *Gendered Work: Sexuality, Family and the Labour Market.* Buckingham: Open University Press.
Dex, S. (1985) *The Sexual Division of Work.* Brighton: Wheatsheaf Books.
Fraser, A. (1985) *The Weaker Vessel.* London: Vintage.
Gimlin, D. (2002) *Body Work: Beauty and Self-Image in American Culture.* Berkeley: University of California Press.
Shilling, C. (2011). 'Afterword: Body work and the sociological tradition', *Sociology of Health and Illness,* 33(2): 336–40.
Twigg, J., C. Wolkowitz, R.L. Cohen and S. Nettleton (eds) (2011) Special Issue: Body Work and Health in Social Care: Critical Themes, New Agendas. *Sociology of Health and Illness,* 33(2).
Wolkowitz, C. (2006) *Bodies at Work.* London: Sage.

Youth and Children

Definition As noted under **Ageing and Childhood**, under the UN Convention on the Rights of the Child, childhood is defined as spanning the period from birth to 18 years of age. Whether all people between those ages are children – in the sense of being vulnerable and lacking agency – is debatable. Many in the social sciences prefer to use the term 'youth' to avoid the infantilizing connotations that are conveyed by the term childhood.

Here, the distinction is made rather between children and youth in terms of their bodily attributes, and contingent or historical notions of childhood as a comparative life stage are discussed more fully elsewhere (see **Ageing and Childhood**). Here we will look at the several key concepts that are raised in relation to the bodies of children and youth. For the sake of simplicity in discussing our two groups we will take children to mean persons from infancy to the onset of puberty. We will understand youths to mean those persons who are post-pubescent but not yet legal natural persons with the full rights and responsibilities of citizens. The distinction is somewhat flexible but can generally be understood to span from birth to 11 or so and the teenage years respectively.

The bodies of children and youth are open to very particular types of social control. In the earliest years of life, children's bodies are subjected to training regimes aimed at the control of their bodily functions. They are also the objects of control in relation to their daily activities (social and educational) and are increasingly focused upon in terms of not only basic health but also in terms of setting up bodily regimes for a long-term healthy life. Infants' bodies are regularly monitored – both in the developed and the developing world – against a range of indices (weight, height) and with the expectation of docility in the face of wider social expectations (immunization).

Developmentalism is the term used to characterize the broad understanding of the child's or youth's body (and mind) as something that is in the process of being formed – and that the processes and progress of that formation can be positively or negatively affected. Developmentalism

key concepts in body and society

is most closely associated with the work of the French educational psy-
chologist Piaget, and is a theoretical approach that arose out of both
disciplinary models. It therefore has direct links to the biomedical and/
or biopsychosocial body (see **Medicine and Science**) and is a theoretical
grounding found not only within the practices of schools and particularly entry level teaching but also in public health initiatives promoted
by governments and medical bodies. Age and weight charts, appropriate
ages and stages for developing particular capacities (language, gross and
fine motor skills) are all part of the developmentalist approach to children, which inevitably centres on managing a child's body. So, there is a
strong emphasis on the child's body as an object of physical observation
and surveillance (see also **Discourse**) within developmentalism. In this
way of understating children as a social category, the child's body is
something to be measured, compared, controlled and actively formed.
The child's body should be involved in education and play – or play as
education – and not exposed to pursuits or pressures that belong to the
adult world. Examples of this approach to children and youth can be
found not only in baby-health centres but also in campaigns about the
negative effects of alcohol on the brains of teenagers, and research into
young males' incapacity to effectively use rational judgement or to be
prone to risk-taking behaviour.

Another influential approach, to the definition of children and their
relationship to their bodies, comes out of sociological (Alanen, 1988)
and liberal political theory. This concentrates more on the child's or
youth's ability to control and consciously use their own bodies. From
this point of view the child's ability to self-determine is uppermost. That
self-determination might be found in a child in a developed country
being able to make representations for themselves in the public sphere
(legal actions, medical procedures, political campaigns, youth parliaments,
etc.) or to enjoy balancing education and play (which includes all forms
of extra-curricular pursuits). In developing countries, self-determination
may involve a child's need to find a balance between being responsible
for contributing to the family unit by undertaking paid labour and the
pursuit of an education. In countries that are experiencing social and
political unrest, this may even extend to children taking part in war: that
is, putting their bodies on the line in armed or hand-to-hand conflict.

On the developmentalist continuum youth are, similarly, objects of
control but they are also accorded capacities children are not. Legally,
youths are expected to have the rational capacities to avoid breaking the
law and at the same time they are 'minors' and not accorded full standing

under the law. Youths are therefore subject to higher penalities for breaking the law but treated more leniently as not yet capable of fully responsible decision-making. With respect to bodies, this has practical applications in the ways youth are treated by legal bodies or peace-keepers. Youth are the subject of social anxiety and moral panics, as members of gangs or as child soldiers.

On the other hand, youth may also be seen as capable of self-determination. They may have the right to 'choice' in the management of their own bodies (medically) in how they use their bodies (sexually), and in where they place their bodies (in protests). The bodies of youths are causes of concern for their likelihood to put themselves at risk of physical harm (train-surfing, joy riding, extreme sports). The bodies of youths are also the key concern of eating disorders, which is an extension of the concerns over healthy development (see **Anorexia/Bulimia/Obesity**).

FURTHER READING

See also the readings for **Ageing and Childhood**.
Alanen (1988) was one of the first sociologists to call for the rethinking of childhood, shortly after which she co-founded the journal *Childhood*, and she remains a central figure in the field. Wyness (2006) gives a good overview of the sociology of childhood and youth since Alanen's work first appeared. Similar work has been under way in anthropology, which has brought to the discussion a wide body of evidence of the cultural specificity of most of the Western/UN ideas of childhood. Lancy (2008) and Montgomery (2009) are but two of an increasing number of anthropologists questioning the effects of the normalization of a culturally and historically contingent notion of childhood to societies with different understandings.

REFERENCES

Alanen, L. (1988) 'Rethinking childhood', *Acta Sociologica*, 31(1): 53–67.
Lancy, D.F. (2008) *The Anthropology of Childhood: Cherubs, Chattels, Changelings*. Cambridge: Cambridge University Press.
Montgomery, H. (2009) *An Introduction to Childhood: Anthropological Perspectives on Children's Lives*. Chichester: Wiley Blackwell Publishers.
Wyness, M. (2006) *Childhood and Society: An Introduction to the Sociology of Childhood*. New York: Palgrave Macmillan.

Glossary

Abject and abjection

Abject refers to phenomena or properties that are considered to be impure or polluting in a given social formation. Mary Douglas describes many of the bodily excretions that are (variably) considered abject in particular cultures, such as bodily wastes (urine, faeces, dead skin) and bodily excretions (menstrual blood, mucous). Abjection is the wider process of theorizing the rejection of phenomena which is more associated with the work of Julia Kristeva, particularly in *The Powers of Horror*. See **Death and Dying**.

Biomedicine

Biomedicine is the sociological term for the contemporary construction of Western medical knowledge. That is, biomedicine is a scientific endeavour that understands the body as a biological mechanism which can be maintained and repaired. This mechanistic, or dualistic, view of the body tends to underestimate the effects of social context and cultural influences in health and illness. See **Dualism, Health and Illness** and **Medicine and Science**.

Biopower

Biopower is Foucault's term for the regulation of the body through social, political and cultural fields of knowledge (epistemes), the most important of which is medicine. So, biopower is exerted through the medical 'gaze', and through surveillance techniques that foster self-regulation, as explained in relation to the 'panopticon'. See **Discourse, Medicine and Science** and **Power**.

Body projects

Body projects is a term coined by Chris Shilling for the kinds of modifications to the body that have become increasingly popular since the 1980s. That is, treating the body as something that can be altered for personal (often aesthetic) reasons. The means for doing so include cosmetic surgery, tattooing, piercing, exercise, dieting, etc. It has connections with post-modern ideas of self-creation and Giddens' notion of post-modern forms of identity. See **Identity** and **Modification/Dysmorphias**.

Body techniques

Body techniques are the ways we shape our bodily behaviours to meet the rules of our social context, that is, through manners. This is closely allied to the work of Norbert Elias and his history of Western European manners. It is also the term used for the conscious shaping of body habits as discussed in an early essay of Marcel Mauss (1979). See **Civilizing Processes** and **Gesture and Habits**.

Body work

The process by which body projects are enacted, that is, through the physical actions required to carry out the chosen body project.

Boundary crossing

This is a term developed by Mary Douglas that is built around the importance given social groups' place on what is allowed to permeate bodily boundaries. In her earlier work she argued that those items we consider most profane often challenge the boundaries of the body: what is sacred leaves the bodily boundaries intact. Douglas refined and revised this idea, after studying the pangolin cult of the Lele, to say that the same moment or object of bodily boundary crossing could be *both* sacred and profane. See **Cyborgs, Food and Eating**, and **Religion**.

Embodiment

This concept underpins all the categories dealt with in this book. The sense in which it is understood here is as the way of approaching the human body as an object to social and cultural importance, and most importantly as how bodies are lived and experienced. More precisely, it is used in terms of Bourdieu's description of embodiment or *hexis* as the bodily expression of habitus (see below).

Habitus and Hexis

As formulated by Bourdieu (1977, 1990a), habitus is the social, cultural and physical environment that we as social beings inhabit, through which we know ourselves and others identify us. Our habitus is made up of all the kinds of social connections, achievements, attainments and attachments one acquires from birth, whether by formal or informal means. These include, but are not limited to, the level of education one has reached, the kind of work one does, the sort of entertainments one enjoys, the places one goes, the cultural pursuits one takes part in or values, the class one identifies with, and so on. Bodily hexis, or embodiment, is the political expression of all the factors that make up one's habitus that are embodied or embedded in our physical being. See also **Habitus**.

Masks of ageing

The idea of social masks is a commonplace, that is, we display ourselves differently or present varying aspects of our social selves in different situations and for different audiences. Masks of ageing is a term specifically associated with Hepworth and Featherstone's discussion of ageing and the drive in contemporary developed societies to hide the physical signs and bodily effects of ageing, in ways that conflict with the inner experience of ageing. See **Ageing and Childhood**, and **Youth and Children**.

Medicalization

The process by which bodily functions and processes become understood as matters of treatment under medical control. For example, childbirth is to all intents and purposes a natural bodily process but it has become medicalized to the extent that birth and reproduction have become a medical specialty and women are alienated from the lived experience of their bodies during pregnancy. See **Medicine and Science**.

Modernity

Modernity is generally understood as the historical era in Western Europe, the precise dates of which are often disputed but are generally held to have occurred between 1500 and the late twentieth century (up to 1989). Modernity is characterized by the move away from traditional social formations based around sovereign rule and agrarian economies (the Early Modern period, 1500–1789), towards industrialization, secularization and the slow and uneven rise of the nation-state (Classical Modernity, 1789–1914) and the period between World War I and the fall of the Berlin Wall (Late Modernity, 1914–1989 – see also **Postmodernity** below). Not to be confused with Modernism, an aesthetic and cultural movement that rose towards the end of the nineteenth century and held sway into the mid to late twentieth century.

Moral Panic

This is a term that comes from the work of Stanley Cohen (1980), who wrote on the social dynamics of massed reactions of populations based on fears about supposedly threatening out-groups or scapegoats. It is a process by which individuals or groups are characterized as dangerous to the social and moral fabric. Witch-hunts are a prime example of a moral panic as are their twentieth-century parallels in the fears over communism. The term is used to describe a massed reaction of groundless fears to a perceived (rather than actual) threat.

Post-modern, post-modernity

This is a sometimes disputed term used to differentiate contemporary social and cultural forms from modernity. Some theorists dispute that we moved beyond the modern era of industrialization into a period in which modes of identity related to national boundaries have disappeared, preferring to describe this as a phase of Late Modernity. Post-modernity is intended to capture a disenchantment with ideology and a heightened sense of individuality in social formations. Not to be confused with Post-modernism, an aesthetic and cultural movement which is largely concerned with the mixing and matching of styles from any aesthetic movement or culture in a parodic or ironic commentary on life and meaning. See **Introduction**.

Post-structuralism

Post-structuralism is a theoretical movement that rose in France in the late 1960s and 1970s with which theorists such as Foucault and Derrida are identified. It was a rejection of the formalist assumptions that underpinned structuralism and part of the wider questioning of fixed meanings that was taking place in the wake of the riots of 1968. See **Discourse**.

Sick role

This is the process by which a person is positioned as a passive consumer of medical treatment and by which they embody the role of the sick person. It originated in the work of Talcott Parsons (1937).

Structuralism

A French theoretical movement based in the structural linguistics of Ferdinand Saussure, that rose in the 1950s and 1960s. It was concerned with the connections, or disconnections, between meaning and the signs intended to convey meaning, in an attempt to explain human culture. See **Post-structuralism** above.

Bibliography

Adkins, L. (1995) *Gendered Work: Sexuality, Family and the Labour Market*. Buckingham: Open University Press.

Aggleton, P. and H. Homans. (eds) (1988) *Social Aspects of AIDS*. London: Falmer Press.

Ahmed, S. (2000) *Strange Encounters: Embodied Others in Post-Coloniality*. London: Routledge.

Ahmed, S. and J. Stacey (eds) (2001) *Thinking Through the Skin*. London: Routledge.

Alanen, L. (1988) 'Rethinking childhood', *Acta Sociologica*, 31(1): 53–67.

Anderson, B. (1991) *Imagined Communities*. London: Verso.

Annandale, E. (1998) *The Sociology of Health and Medicine*. Cambridge: Polity.

Arber, S. and J. Ginn (1995) *Connecting Gender and Ageing: A Sociological Approach*. Buckingham: Open University Press.

Ariès, Phillipe (1962) *Centuries of Childhood: A Social History of Family Life*, trans. Robert Baldick. New York: Alfred A. Knopf.

Ariès, Phillipe (1974) *Western Attitudes to Death from the Middle Ages to the Present*. Baltimore: Johns Hopkins University Press.

Ariès, Phillipe (1981) *The Hour of Our Death*, trans. H. Weaver. London: Allen Lane.

Ariès, Phillipe (1985) *Images of Man and Death*, trans. J. Lloyd. Cambridge, MA: Harvard University Press.

Armstrong, D. (1983) *The Political Anatomy of the Body*. Cambridge: Cambridge University Press.

Armstrong, D. (2005) 'The rise of surveillance medicine', *Sociology of Health and Illness*, 17: 393–404.

Astell, M. (1694) *A Serious Proposal to the Ladies for the Advancement of Their True and Greatest Interest*. London: R. Wilkin.

Australian Human Rights Commission (1997) *Bringing Them Home: The Report of the National Inquiry into the Separation of Aboriginal and Torres Strait Islander Children from their Families*. Sydney: Human Rights and Equal Opportunity Commission.

Baclawski, K. (1995) *The Guide to Historic Costume*. London: B.T. Batsford.

Baehr, H. and A. Gray (eds) (1996) *Turning it On: A Reader in Women and Media*. London: Arnold.

Baikie, K.A. and K. Wilhelm (2005) 'Emotional and physical health benefits of expressive writing', *Advances in Psychiatric Treatment*, 11: 338–46.

Bakhtin, Mikhail (1984) *Rabelais and His World*, trans. Hélène Iswolsky. Bloomington: Indiana University Press.

Bale, J. and M. Cronin (eds) (2003) *Sport and Postcolonialism*. Oxford: Berg.

Balsamo, A. (1996) *Technologies of Gendered Bodies: Reading Cyborg Women*. Durham, NC and London: Duke University Press.

Barbalet, J. (1998) *Emotion, Social Theory and Social Structure: A Macrosociological Approach*. Cambridge: Cambridge University Press.

Barnard, M. (ed.) (2007) *Fashion Theory: A Reader*. London: Routledge.

Barthes, R. (1983) *The Fashion System*, trans. M. Ward and R. Howard. New York: Farrar, Straus & Giroux.

Bauby, J-D. (1997) *The Diving Bell and the Butterfly*. London: Harper Perennial.

Bell, D. and B. Kennedy (2000) *The Cybercultures Reader*. London: Routledge.

Bendelow, G. and S. Williams (eds) (1997) *Emotions in Social Life*. London: Routledge.

Berger, J. (1972) *Ways of Seeing*. Harmondsworth: Penguin

Betancourt, T. et al. (2010) 'Past horrors, present struggles: The role of stigma in the association between war experiences and psychosocial adjustment among former child soldiers in Sierra Leone', *Social Science and Medicine*, 70(1): 17–26.

Birke, L. (1999) *Feminism and the Biological Body*. Edinburgh: Edinburgh University Press.

Blackwood, E. (2002) 'Sexuality and gender in certain native American tribes: The case of cross-gender females', in C.L. Williams and A. Stein (eds) *Sexuality and Gender*. Oxford: Blackwell.

Blaikie, A. (1999) *Ageing and Popular Culture*. Cambridge: Cambridge University Press.

Blake, A. (1996) *The Body Language: The Meaning of Modern Sport*. London: Lawrence & Wishart.

Bogdan, R. and S. J. Taylor (1975) *Introduction to Qualitative Research Methods*. New York: Wiley-Interscience.

Bordo, Susan (1993) *Unbearable Weight: Feminism, Western Culture and the Body*. Berkeley: University of California Press.

Bordo, Susan (1999) *The Male Body: A New Look at Men in Public and in Private*. New York: Farrar, Straus & Giroux.

Bourdieu, Pierre (1977) *Outline of a Theory of Practice*, trans. Richard Nice. Cambridge: Cambridge University Press. First published 1972.

Bourdieu, Pierre (1984) *Distinction: A Social Critique of the Judgement of Taste*, trans. Richard Nice. Cambridge, MA: Harvard University Press. First published 1979.

Bourdieu, Pierre (1990a) *The Logic of Practice*, trans. Richard Nice. Stanford: Stanford University Press. First published 1980.

Bourdieu, Pierre (1990b) *In Other Words: Essays Towards a Reflexive Sociology*, trans. M. Adamson. Cambridge: Polity Press.

Bourdieu, Pierre (1998) 'Is a disinterested act possible?', in *Practical Reason: On the Theory of Action*. Cambridge: Polity Press, pp. 75–91.

Braidotti, R. (1989) 'Organs Without Bodies', *Differences: A Journal of Feminist Cultural Studies* 1: 147–61.

Brain, V. (1979) *The Decorated Body*. London: Harper & Row.

Branson, Jan and Don Miller (1995) *The Story of Betty Steel: Deaf Convict and Pioneer*. Petersham, NSW: Deafness Resources Australia.

Bray, Alan (1982) *Homosexuality in Renaissance England*. London: Gay Men's Press.

Braziel, J.E. and K. LeBesco (2001) *Bodies Out of Bounds: Fatness and Transgression*. Berkeley: University of California Press.

Breines, L., R. Connell and I. Eide (2000) *Male Roles, Masculinities and Violence*. Paris: UNESCO.

Bremmer, J. and H. Roodenberg (eds) (1992) *A Cultural History of Gesture*. Ithaca, NY: Cornell University Press.

Bronwell, K. and C. Fairburn (eds) (2002) *Eating Disorders and Obesity: A Comprehensive Handbook*, 2nd edn. New York: The Guilford Press.

Bryson, Anna (1990) 'The rhetoric of status: Gesture, demeanour and the image of the gentleman in sixteenth and seventeenth-century England', in L. Gent and N. Llewellyn (eds), *Renaissance Bodies: The Human Figure in English Culture c.1540–1660*. London: Reaktion Books, pp. 136–53.

Burke, E. (2009) 'Pro-anorexia and the internet: A tangled web of representation and (dis)embodiment', *Counselling, Psychotherapy, and Health*, The Use of Technology in Mental Health Special Issue, 5(1): 60–81.

Burkitt, I. (1999) *Bodies of Thought: Embodiment, Identity and Modernity*. London: Sage.

Butler, Judith (1990) *Gender Trouble: Feminism and the Subversion of Identity*. New York: Routledge.

Butler, Judith (1993) *Bodies that Matter: On the Discursive Limits of 'Sex'*. New York: Routledge.

Butler, R. and H. Parr (eds) (1999) *Mind and Body Spaces: Geographies of Illness, Impairment and Disability*. London: Routledge.

Bynum, Carolyn Walker (1991) *Fragmentation and Redemption: Essays on Gender and the Human Body in Medieval Religion*. New York: Zone Books.

Calhoun, Craig (1993) 'Habitus, field and capital: The question of historical specificity', in C. Calhoun, E. LiPuma and M. Postone (eds), *Bourdieu: Critical Perspectives*. London: Polity Press.

Caplan, J. (ed.) (2000) *Written on the Body: The Tattoo in European and American History*. London: Reaktion Books.

Cartright, L. (1995) *Screening the Body: Tracing Medicine's Visual Culture*. Minneapolis: University of Minnesota Press.

Cixous, H. (1991) *'Coming to Writing' and Other Essays*. Cambridge, MA: Harvard University Press.

Coakley, J. (2004) *Sport in Society: Issues and Controversies*. St Louis: Mosby.

Coakley, S. (ed.) (1997) *Religion and the Body*. Cambridge: Cambridge University Press.

Cohen, S. (1980) *Folk Devils and Moral Panics: The Creation of the Mods and Rockers*. London: Routledge.

Connell, R.W. (1995) *Masculinities*. Cambridge: Polity.

Cooley, C.H. (1902) *Human Nature and the Social Order*. New York. Charles Scribner and Sons.

Counihan, C. and S. Kaplan (eds) (1998) *Food and Gender: Identity and Power*. Amsterdam: Harwood Academic Publishers.

Craik, J. (2005) *Uniforms Exposed: From Conformity to Transgression*. Oxford: Berg.

Cregan, K. (2005) 'Ethical and social issues of embryonic stem cell technology', *Internal Medicine Journal*, 35(2): 126–7.

Cregan, K. (2006) *The Sociology of the Body: Mapping the Abstraction of Embodiment*. London: Sage.

Cregan, K. (2007a) 'Early modern anatomy and the Queen's body natural: The sovereign subject', *Body & Society*, 13(2): 47–66.

Cregan, K. (2007b) 'Remembering the dead', in *Globalism Institute Annual Report, 2006*. Melbourne: RMIT University.

Cregan, K. (2008) 'The informal sector', in P. James, Y. Nadarajah, K. Haive and K. Cregan, *Community Sustainability, Community Livelihoods: Learning for Wellbeing, Resilience and Sustainability in Papua New Guinea*, Ministerial Report for the Department For Community Development, Papua New Guinea.

Cregan, K. (2009) *The Theatre of the Body: Staging Life and Embodying Death in Early Modern London*. Turnhout, Belgium: Brepols.

Cregan, K. and P. James (2002) 'Stem-cell alchemy: Techno-Science and the new philosopher's stone', *Arena Journal*, 19: 61–72.

Croakley, J. (1994) *Sport in Society: Issues and Controversies*. St Louis: Mosby.

Crossley, N. (2001) *The Social Body: Habit, Identity and Desire*. London: Sage.

Csordas, T. (ed.) (1994) *Embodiment and Experience: The Existential Ground of Culture Itself*. Cambridge: Cambridge University Press.

Cunningham, H. (1995) *Children and Childhood in Western Society Since 1500*. London: Longman.

Davis, F. (1994) *Fashion, Culture and Identity*. Chicago: University of Chicago Press.

Davis, K. (1995) *Reshaping the Female Body: The Dilemma of Cosmetic Surgery*. New York: Routledge.

De Beauvoir, S. (1972) *The Second Sex*. Harmondsworth: Penguin.

Descartes, R. (1980) *Discourses on Method*. Harmondsworth: Penguin.

Dex, S. (1985) *The Sexual Division of Work*. Brighton: Wheatsheaf Books.

Dickenson, Donna (2002) 'Commodification of human tissue: Implications for feminist and development ethics', *Developing World Bioethics*, 2(1): 55–63.

Diprose, R. (1994) *The Bodies of Women: Ethics, Embodiment and Sexual Difference*. London: Routledge.

Dixon, J. and D.H. Broom (2007) *The Seven Deadly Sins of Obesity: How the Modern World is Making Us Fat*. Sydney: UNSW Press.

Douglas, Mary (1975) *Implicit Meanings: Essays in Anthropology*. London and Boston: Routledge and Kegan Paul.

Douglas, Mary (ed.) (1984) *Food in the Social Order*. New York: Russell Sage Foundation.

Douglas, Mary (1996) *Natural Symbols: Explorations in Cosmology* (with a new Introduction). London: Routledge. First published 1970.

Douglas, Mary (2000) *Purity and Danger: An Analysis of Concept of Pollution and Taboo*. London: Routledge. First published 1966.

Duden, Barbara (1991) *The Woman Beneath the Skin*, trans. T. Dunlap. Cambridge, MA: Harvard University Press.

Duden, Barbara (1999) 'The fetus on the "farther shore": Toward a history of the unborn', in *Fetal Subject: Feminist Positions*. Philadelphia: University of Pennsylvania Press.

Duncombe, J. and D. Marsden (1993) 'Love and intimacy: The gender division of emotion and "emotion work"', *Sociology*, 27: 221–42.

Durkheim, E. (1952) *Suicide*. London: Routledge & Kegan Paul. First published 1897.

Edgerton, S.Y. Jr. (1985) *Pictures and Punishment: Art and Criminal Prosecution During the Florentine Renaissance*. Ithaca, NY: Cornell University Press.

Eichberg, H. (1998) *Body Cultures: Essays on Sport, Space and Identity*. London: Routledge.

Elias, Norbert (1983) *The Court Society*, trans. E. Jephcott. New York: Pantheon.

Elias, Norbert (1985) *The Loneliness of the Dying*, trans. E. Jephcott. London: Continuum.

Elias, Norbert (1986) *Quest for Excitement: Sport and Leisure in the Civilizing Process*. Oxford: Blackwell.

Elias, Norbert (1991) 'Human beings and their emotions', in M. Featherstone, M. Hepworth and B. Turner (eds) *The Body: Social Process and Cultural Theory*. London: Sage.

Elias, Norbert (2000) *The Civilizing Process: Sociogenetic and Psychogenetic Investigations* (revised edition), trans. E. Jephcott. E. Dunning, J. Goudsblom and S. Mennell (eds) Oxford: Blackwell Publishers.

Ellingson, L. (2006) 'Embodied knowledge', *Qualitative Health Research*, 16(2): 298–310.

Elliott, A. (2008) *Making the Cut: How Cosmetic Surgery is Transforming our Lives*. London: Reaktion Books.

Ellis, H. (1936) *Studies in the Psychology of Sex, Vol. 2: Sexual Inversion*. New York: Random House.

Epstein, J. and K. Straub (eds) (1991) *Body Guards*. New York: Routledge.

Ettorre, E. (2002) *Reproductive Genetics, Gender and the Body*. London: Routledge.

Evans, J., B. Davies and J. Wright (2004) *Body Knowledge and Control: Studies in the Sociology of Physical Education and Health*. London: Routledge.

Falk, Pasi (1994) *The Consuming Body*. London: Sage.

Fanon, F. (2004) *The Wretched of the Earth*, trans. R. Philcox. New York: Grove Press. First published 1961.

Fausto-Sterling, A. (1993) 'The five sexes: Why male and female are not enough', *The Sciences*, May/April: 20–25.

Featherstone, M. (1982) 'The body in consumer culture', *Theory, Culture & Society*, 1: 18–33.

Featherstone, M. (ed.) (2000) *Body Modification*. London: Sage.

Featherstone, M. and A. Wernick (eds) (1995) *Images of Ageing*. London: Routledge.

Featherstone, Mike, Mike Hepworth and Bryan Turner (eds) (1991) *The Body: Social Process and Cultural Theory*. London: Sage.

Feher, Michael (ed.) (1989) *Fragments for a History of the Human Body*, Parts 1–3. New York: Zone Books.

Fields, B.J. (1990) 'Slavery, race and ideology in the United States of America', *New Left Review*, 181: 95–118.

Finkelstein, Joanne (1991) *The Fashioned Self*. London: Polity.

Foucault, Michel (1975) *The Birth of the Clinic: An Archaeology of Medical Perception*, trans. A.M. Sheridan Smith. New York: Random House.

Foucault, Michel (1980) 'Governmentality', in *Power/Knowledge: Selected Interviews and Other Writings 1972–1977*. New York: Vintage.

Foucault, Michel (1988a) *Madness and Civilization: A History of Insanity in the Age of Reason*, trans. R. Howard. New York: Vintage Books.

Foucault, Michel (1988b) *Politics, Philosophy, Culture: Interviews and Other Writings, 1977–1984*, trans. A. Sheridan and others, ed. L.D. Kritzman. New York: Routledge.

Foucault, Michel (1990) *The History of Sexuality, Volume 1*, trans. R. Hurley. Harmondsworth: Penguin.

Foucault, Michel (1991) *Discipline and Punish: The Birth of the Prison*, trans. A. Sheridan. London: Penguin.

Foucault, Michel (1994) *The Archaeology of Knowledge*, trans. A.M. Sheridan Smith. London: Routledge.

Fox, N., K. Ward and A. O'Rourke (2005) 'Pro-anorexia, weight-loss drugs and the internet: An "anti-recovery" explanatory model of anorexia', *Sociology of Health and Illness*, 27(7): 944–71.

Fox, Renée and Judith Swazey (1992) *Spare Parts*. New York: Oxford University Press.

Frank, A. (1995) *The Wounded Storyteller: Body, Illness & Ethics*. Chicago: Chicago University Press.

Franklin, Sarah (1997) *Embodied Progress: A Cultural Account of Assisted Conception*. London: Routledge.

Fraser, A. (1985) *The Weaker Vessel*. London: Vintage.

Freedman, E. (ed.) (2007) *The Essential Feminist Reader*. New York: Random House.

Friedan, B. (1963) *The Feminine Mystique*. New York: W.W. Norton and Co.

Freund, P.A. and M. McGuire (1999) *Health, Illness and the Social Body*. London: Prentice Hall.

Fukuyama, F. (2002) *Our Posthuman Future: Consequences of the Biotechnology Revolution*. New York: Farrar, Straus & Giroux.

Gaines, J. and C. Herzog (eds) (1990) *Fabrications: Costume and the Female Body*. New York: Routledge.

Gallagher, Catherine and Thomas Laqueur (eds) (1987) *The Making of the Modern Body: Sexuality and Society in the Nineteenth Century*. Berkeley: The University of California Press.

Gans, H.J. (2005) 'Race as class', *Contexts*, 4(4): 17–21.

Garber, M. (1992) *Vested Interests: Cross-Dressing and Cultural Anxiety*. London: Routledge.

Gatens, Moira (1983) 'Critique of the sex/gender distinction', in J. Allen and P. Patton (eds), *Interventions after Marx*. Sydney: Intervention.

Gatens, Moira (1995) *Imaginary Bodies: Ethics, Power and Corporeality*. London: Routledge.

Gay, P. (1995) *The Freud Reader*. London: Vintage.

Giddens, A. (1991) *Modernity and Self-Identity: Self and Society in the Late Modern Age*. Cambridge: Polity Press.

Gilman, Sander (1985) *Difference and Pathology: Stereotypes of Sexuality, Race and Madness*. Ithaca, NY: Cornell University Press.

Gilman, Sander (1988) *Disease and Representation: Images of Illness from Madness to AIDS*. Ithaca, NY: Cornell University Press.

Gilman, Sander (1999) *Making the Body Beautiful: A Cultural History of Aesthetic Surgery*. Princeton: Princeton University Press.

Gimlin, D. (2002) *Bodywork: Beauty and Self-Image in American Culture*. Berkeley: University of California Press.

Gittings, Clare (1984) *Death, Burial and the Individual in Early Modern England*. London: Croom Helm.

Godelier, M. (1999) *The Enigma of the Gift*, trans N. Scott. Chicago: University of Chicago Press.

Goffman, E. (1963) *Behaviour in Public Places*. New York: The Free Press.

Goffman, E. (1971) *The Presentation of Self in Everyday Life*. Harmondsworth: Penguin.

Goudsblom, Jan and Stephen Mennell (eds) (1998) *The Norbert Elias Reader*. Oxford: Blackwell.

Great Britain, House of Commons, Select Committee on Health (1998) *The Welfare of British Child Migrants*. London: HMG Stationery Office.

Greenblatt, Stephen (1980) *Renaissance Self-Fashioning: from More to Shakespeare*. Chicago: University of Chicago Press.

Greer, G. (1970) *The Female Eunuch*. London: Paladin Grafton Books.

Grosz, Liz (1994) *Volatile Bodies: Toward a Corporeal Feminism*. Bloomington: Indiana University Press.

Grosz, Liz (1995) *Time, Space and Perversion: The Politics of Bodies*. New York: Routledge.

Gupta, J.A. and A. Richters (2008) 'Embodied subjects and fragmented objects: Women's bodies, assisted reproduction and the right to self-determination', *Journal of Bioethical Inquiry*, 5(4): 239–49.

Hallam, E., J. Hockey and G. Howarth (1999) *Beyond the Body: Death and Social Identity*. London: Routledge.

Hancock, P., B. Hughes, E. Jagger, K. Paterson, R. Russell, E. Tulle-Winton and M. Tyler (2000) *The Body, Culture and Society*. Buckingham: Open University Press.

Haraway, Donna (1991) *Simians, Cyborgs and Women: The Reinvention of Nature*. London: Free Association Books.

Haraway, Donna (1997) *Modest_Witness@Second_Millennium.FemaleMan©_Meets_OncoMouse™: Feminism and Technoscience*. New York and London: Routledge.

Hardey, M. (2002) '"The story of my illness": Personal accounts of illness on the internet', *Health*, 6(1): 31–46.

Harding, Sandra (1986) *The Science Question in Feminism*. Ithaca, NY: Cornell University Press.

Hargreaves, J. (1994) *Sporting Females*. London: Routledge.

Hepworth, J. (1999) *The Social Construction of Anorexia Nervosa*. London: Sage.

Hepworth, M. (2000) *Stories of Ageing*. Buckingham: Open University Press.

Hester, R. and H. Parr (eds) *Mind and Body Spaces: Geographies of Illness, Impairment and Disability*. London: Routledge.

Heywood, C. (2001) *A History of Childhood: Children and Childhood in the West from Medieval to Modern Times*. Cambridge: Polity.

Hines, S. and T. Sanger. (2010) *Transgender Identities: Towards a Social Analysis of Gender Diversity*. New York: Routledge.

Hobson, J. (2005) *Venus in the Dark: Blackness and Beauty in Popular Culture*. London: Routledge.

Hochschild, A.R. (1983) *The Managed Heart: The Commercialization of Human Feeling*. Berkeley: University of California Press.

Hochschild, A.R. (1998) 'The sociology of emotion as a way of seeing', in G. Bendelow and S. Williams (eds), *Emotions in Social Life: Critical Themes and Contemporary Issues*. London: Routledge.

Hockey, E. and A. James (1993) *Growing Up and Growing Old: Ageing and Dependency in the Life Course*. London: Sage.

Hogle, L. (1999) *Recovering the Nation's Body: Cultural Memory, Medicine and the Politics of Redemption*. New Brunswick: Rutgers University Press.

Hollander, A. (1980) *Seeing Through Clothes*. New York: Avon Books.

Howson, A. (2004) *The Body in Society: An Introduction*. Cambridge: Polity.

Howson, A. (2005) *Embodying Gender*. London: Sage.

Humphreys, L. (1975) *Tearoom Trade: A Study of Homosexual Encounters in Public Places*. Chicago: Aldine Publishing Company. First published 1970.

Illich, I. (1976) *Medical Nemesis: The Expropriation of Health*. Harmondsworth: Penguin.

Illich, I. (2001) *Limits to Medicine*. New York: Marion Boyars.

International Labour Organization (1999) *ILO Convention No. 182 on the Worst Forms of Child Labour*. Geneva: ILO. Available at: http://www.ilo.org/ilolex/cgi-lex/convde.pl?C182 (accessed May 2011).

Irigaray, L. (1980) 'When our lips speak together', *Signs*, 6: 69–79.

James, A. and A. Prout (eds) (1997) *Constructing and Reconstructing Childhood: Contemporary Issues in the Sociological Study of Childhood*. London: Falmer Press.

James, A., C. Jenks and A. Prout (1998) *Theorizing Childhood*. Cambridge: Polity.

Jankowski, T. (1992) *Women in Power in the Early Modern Drama*. Chicago: University of Illinois Press.

Jenks, C. (1996) *Childhood*. London: Routledge.

Jenkins, Richard (ed.) (1998) *Questions of Competence: Culture, Classification and Intellectual Disability*. Cambridge: Cambridge University Press.

Jewson, Norman (1976) 'The disappearance of the sick man from medical cosmologies: 1770–1870', *Sociology*, 10: 225–44.

Jones, Ann Rosalind and Peter Stallybrass (2000) *Renaissance Clothing and the Materials of Memory*. Cambridge: Cambridge University Press.

Jordanova, Ludmilla (1989) *Sexual Visions: Images of Gender in Science*. Madison: University of Wisconsin Press.

Jupp, P. (2006) *From Dust to Ashes: Cremation and the British Way of Death*. Basingstoke: Palgrave Macmillan.

Kane-Demaios, J.A. and V.L. Bullough (eds) (2006) *Crossing Sexual Boundaries*. New York: Prometheus Books.

Kelly, L. and J. Radford. (1998) 'Sexual violence against women and girls', in R. Emerson and R. Dobash (eds), *Rethinking Violence Against Women*. London: Sage.

King, Margaret L. (2007) 'Concepts of childhood: What we know and where we might go', *Renaissance Quarterly*, 60: 371–407.

Krafft-Ebing, R. von (1965) *Psychopathia Sexualis*. New York: G.P. Putnam's & Sons.

Kristeva, Julia (1980) *Powers of Horror: An Essay on Abjection*, trans. L. Roudiez. New York: Columbia University Press.

Kroker, A. and M. Kroker (1988) *Body Invaders: Sexuality and the Postmodern Condition*. Basingstoke: Macmillan.

Kübler-Ross, E. (1997) *On Death and Dying*. New York: Scribner.

Küchler, S. and D. Miller (eds) (2005) *Clothing as Material Culture*. New York: Berg.

Kymlicka, W. (2001) *Politics in the Vernacular: Nationalism, Multiculturalism, Citizenship*. Oxford: Oxford University Press

Lancy, D.F. (2008) *The Anthropology of Childhood: Cherubs, Chattels, Changelings*. Cambridge: Cambridge University Press.

Laqueur, Thomas (1992) *Making Sex: Body and Gender from the Greeks to Freud*. Cambridge, MA: Harvard University Press.

Leder, D. (1990) *The Absent Body*. Chicago: University of Chicago Press.

Lees, S. (1997) *Ruling Passions: Sexual Violence, Sexual Reputation and the Law*. Buckingham: Open University Press.

Lemma, A. (2010) *Under the Skin: A Psychoanalytic Study of Body Modification*. New York: Routledge.

Lenskyj, H. (1986) *Out of Bounds: Women Sport and Sexuality*. Toronto: The Women's Press.

Lestringant, F. (1994) *Mapping the Renaissance World: The Geographical Imagination in the Age of Discovery*, trans. David Fausett. Berkeley: University of California Press.

Linebaugh, P. and M. Rediker (2000) *The Many-Headed Hydra: Sailors, Slaves, Commoners and the Hidden History of the Revolutionary Atlantic*. Boston: Beacon Press.

Lingis, A. (1994) *Foreign Bodies*. New York: Routledge.

Lloyd, G. (1993) *The Man of Reason: Male and Female in Western Philosophy*. London: Routledge.

Lockwood, M. (2002) *Twice Dead: Organ Transplants and the Reinvention of Death*. Berkeley: University of California Press.

Lovell, Terry (2000) 'Thinking feminism with and against Bourdieu', in B. Fowler (ed.), *Reading Bourdieu on Society and Culture*. Oxford: Blackwell Publishers.

Luke, Carmen (1989) *Pedagogy, Printing, and Protestantism: The Discourse on Childhood*. New York: State University of New York Press.

Lupton, D. (1994a) *Moral Threats and Dangerous Desires: AIDS in the News Media*. London: Taylor & Francis.

Lupton, D. (1994b) *Medicine as Culture*. London: Sage.

Lupton, D. (1995) *The Imperative of Health: Public Health and the Regulated Body*. London: Sage.

Lupton, D. (1996) *Food, the Body and the Self*. London: Sage.

Lurie, A. (1992) *The Language of Clothes*. London: Bloomsbury.

Macnaughton, P. and J. Urry (2001) *Contested Natures*. London: Sage.

Maguire, J. (1994) 'Globalisation, sport and national identities: "The empire strikes back"?', *Society and Leisure*, 16(2): 293–322.

Martin, Emily (1991) 'The egg and the sperm: How science has constructed a romance based on stereotypical male–female roles', *Signs: Journal of Women in Culture and Society*, 16: 485–501.

Martin, Emily (1992) *The Woman in the Body: A Cultural Analysis of Reproduction*. Boston: Beacon Press.

Mason, L. (ed.) (2002) *Food and the Rites of Passage*. Totnes: Prospect Books.

Mauss, Marcel (1979) *Sociology and Psychology: Essays*, trans. B. Brewster. London: Routledge & Kegan Paul.

Mauss, Marcel (1990) *The Gift: The Forms and Reasons for Exchange in Archaic Societies*, trans. W.D. Halls, Foreword by Mary Douglas. New York and London: W.W. Norton and Co.

Mead, G.H. (1962) *Mind, Self and Society*. Chicago: University of Chicago Press. First published 1934.

Mellor, P.A. and C. Shilling (1997) *Re-forming the Body: Religion, Community and Modernity*. London: Sage.

Memmi, A. (1991) *The Colonizer and the Colonized*. Boston: Beacon Press. First published 1965.

Memmi, A. (2006) *Decolonization and the Decolonized*, trans. R. Bonnono. Minneapolis: University of Minnesota Press.

Mennell, Stephen (1991) 'On the civilising of appetite', in M. Featherstone, M. Hepworth and B. Turner (eds), *The Body: Social Process and Cultural Theory*. London: Sage, pp. 126–56.

Mennell, Stephen (1996) *All Manners of Food: Eating and Taste in England and France from the Middle Ages to the Present*, 2nd edn. Urbana: University of Illinois Press.

Merleau-Ponty, Maurice (1984) *Sense and Non-Sense*, trans. H.L. Dreyfus and P.A. Dreyfus. Evanston, IL: Northwestern University Press. First published 1961.

Merleau-Ponty, Maurice (2001) *Phenomenology of Perception*, trans. C. Smith. London: Routledge. First published 1962.

Miah, A. (2004) *Genetically Modified Athletes*. London: Routledge.

Miller, D. (1982) 'Artifacts as products of human categorisation processes', in I. Hodder (ed.), *Symbolic and Structural Archaeology*. Cambridge: Cambridge University Press. pp. 89–98.

Miller, L. (2006) *Beauty Up: Exploring Contemporary Japanese Body Aesthetics*. Berkeley: University of California Press.

Millett, K. (1970) *Sexual Politics*. New York: Doubleday.

Mitchell, J. (1974) *Psychoanalysis and Feminism*. London: Allen Lane.

Montgomery, H. (2009) *An Introduction to Childhood: Anthropological Perspectives on Children's Lives*. Chichester: Wiley Blackwell Publishers.

Mosse, G.L. (1996) *The Image of Man: The Creation of Modern Masculinity*. Oxford: Oxford University Press.

Nairn, T. (1977) *The Break-Up of Britain: Crisis and Neonationalism*. London: New Left Books.

Nazroo, J. (2001) *Ethnicity, Class and Health*. London: Policy Studies Institute.

Nettleton, S. (2006) *The Sociology of Health and Illness*. Cambridge: Polity.

Nettleton, S. and U. Gustafsson (eds) (2002) *The Sociology of Health and Illness Reader*. Oxford: Polity.

Norton, Rictor (1992) *Mother Clap's Molly House: The Gay Subculture in England 1700–1830*. London: Gay Men's Press.

Oakley, A. (1972) *Sex, Gender and Society*. London: Temple Smith.

Oakley, A. (1979) *Becoming a Mother*. Oxford: Martin Robertson. (Under the title *From Here to Maternity*. Harmondsworth: Penguin, 1981. Reprinted with new Introduction, 1986.)

Oakley, A. (1981) *Doing Feminist Research*. London: Routledge & Kegan Paul.

Oakley, A. (1984) *Woman Confined: Towards a Sociology of Childbirth*. Oxford: Martin Robertson.

O'Brien, P. and M. Sullivan (2005) *Allies in Emancipation: Shifting from Providing Service to Being of Support*. Melbourne: Dunmore Press.

Oliver, M. (2009) *Understanding Disability: From Theory to Practice*, 2nd edn. London: Macmillan.

O'Neill, J. (2004) *Five Bodies: Refiguring Relationships* (revised edn). London: Sage.

Orbach, S. (1986) *Fat Is A Feminist Issue*. London: Arrow Books.

Orgel, Stephen (1996) *Impersonations: The Performance of Gender in Shakespeare's England*. Cambridge: Cambridge University Press.

Ortner, Sherry (1974) 'Is female to male as nature is to culture?', in M.Z. Rosaldo and L. Lamphere (eds) *Woman, Culture and Society*. Stanford, CA: Stanford University Press. pp. 67–87.

Ott, K., D. Serlin and S. Mihm (eds) (2002) *Artificial Parts, Practical Lives: Modern Histories of Prosthetics*. New York: New York University Press.

Oudshoorn, N. (1994) *Beyond the Natural Body: An Archaeology of Sex Hormones*. London: Routledge.

Pande, A. (2010) 'Commercial surrogacy in India: Manufacturing a perfect 'mother-worker', *Signs: Journal of Women in Culture and Society*, 35(4): 969–92.

Panjari, M., S. Davis, P. Fradkin and R. Bell (2011) 'Breast cancer survivors' beliefs about the causes of breast cancer', *Psycho-Oncology*, DOI: 10.1002/pon.1949.

Parens, E. (ed.) (2006) *Surgically Shaping Children: Technology, Ethics and the Pursuit of Normality*. Baltimore: Johns Hopkins University Press.

Parsons, T. (1937) *The Structure of Social Action*. New York: McGraw-Hill.

Paulicelli, E. and H. Clark (2009) *The Fabric of Cultures: Fashion, Identity, and Globalization*. New York: Taylor & Francis.

Pierce, C.S. (1994) *Writing on Signs: Writings on Semiotic*, in J. Hoopes (ed.) Chapel Hill, NC: University of North Carolina Press.

Pilcher, J. and I. Whelehan (2004) *50 Key Concepts in Gender Studies*. London: Sage.

Pilnick, A. (2002) *Genetics and Society: An Introduction*. Buckingham: Open University Press.

Pollock, Linda (1983) *Forgotten Children: Parent–Child Relations from 1500 to 1900*. Cambridge: Cambridge University Press.

Proctor, R. (1988) *Racial Hygiene: Medicine under the Nazis*. Cambridge, MA: Harvard University Press.

Prout, Alan (ed.) (2000) *The Body, Childhood and Society*. Basingstoke: Macmillan

Rippon, A. (2006) *Hitler's Olympics: The Story of the 1936 Olympic Games*. London: Pen and Sword Military.

Robbins, Derek (2000) *Bourdieu and Culture*. London: Sage.

Roberts, E. (1984) *A Woman's Place: An Oral History of Working-Class Women, 1890–1940*. Oxford: Basil Blackwell.

Romanoff, D. and B. Thompson (2006) 'Meaning construction in palliative care: The use of narrative, ritual and the expressive arts', *The American Journal of Hospice and Palliative Medicine*, 23(4): 309–16.

Rothman, S. and D. Rothman (2003) *The Pursuit of Perfection: The Promise and Perils of Medical Enhancement*. New York: Vintage.

Said, Edward (1978) *Orientalism*. New York: Pantheon Books.

Saint-Martin, M. (1999) 'Running amok: A modern perspective on a culture-bound syndrome', *Primary Care Companion to the Journal of Clinical Psychiatry*, 1(3): 66–70.

Sanders, C. and D. Vail (2008) *Customizing the Body: The Art and Culture of Tattooing*. Philadelphia: Temple University Press.

Saussure, F. (1983) *Course in General Linguistics*, trans. and ed., R. Harris. Peru, IL: Open Court Publishing.

Sawday, J. (1995) *The Body Emblazoned: Dissection and the Human Body in Renaissance Culture*. London: Routledge.

Scarry, Elaine (1985) *The Body in Pain: The Making and Unmaking of the World*. Oxford: Oxford University Press.

Scheper-Hughes, N. (2000) 'The global traffic in human organs', *Current Anthropology*, 41: 191–224.

Scheper-Hughes, N. and L. Wacquant (eds) (2002) *Commodifying Bodies*. London: Sage.

Schiebinger, L. (1993) *Nature's Body: Gender in the Making of Modern Science*. Boston: Beacon Press.

Schutz, A. (1967) *The Phenomenology of the Social World*. Evanston, IL: Northwestern University Press. First published 1932.

Searle, C. (1990) 'Race before the wicket: Cricket, empire and the white rose', *Race & Class*, 31: 31–48.

Seear, K. (2009) '"Nobody really knows what it is or how to treat it": Why women with endometriosis do not comply with healthcare advice', *Health, Risk and Society*, 11(4): 367–85.

Seidman, S. (ed.) (1996) *Queer Theory/Sociology*. Oxford: Blackwell.

Sennett, Richard (1994) *Flesh and Stone: The Body and the City in Western Civilization*. New York: W.W. Norton & Company.

Sennett, Richard (1974) *The Fall of Public Man*. Cambridge: Cambridge University Press.

Seymour, Wendy (1998) *Remaking the Body: Rehabilitation and Change*. Sydney: Allen & Unwin.

Shakespeare, Tom (ed.) (1998) *The Disability Studies Reader: Social Science Perspectives*. London: Cassell.

Shakespeare, Tom (2006) *Disability Rights and Wrongs*. London: Routledge.

Shepler, S. (2005) 'The rites of the child: Global discourses of youth and reintegrating child soldiers in Sierra Leone', *Journal of Human Rights* 4(2): 197–211.

Shildrick, Margritt (1997) *Leaky Bodies and Boundaries: Feminism, Postmodernism and (Bio)Ethics*. London: Routledge.

Shilling, Chris (1993) *The Body and Social Theory*. London: Sage.

Shilling, Chris (2005) *The Body in Culture, Technology and Society*. London: Sage.

Shilling, Chris (2008) *Changing Bodies: Habit, Crisis and Creativity*. London: Sage.

Shilling, Chris (2011) 'Afterword: Body work and the sociological tradition', *Sociology of Health and Illness*, 33(2): 336–40.

Snyder, L. (2000) *Speaking Our Minds: Personal Reflections from Individuals with Alzheimer's*. New York: W.H. Freeman and Co.

Solinger, R. (1992) *Wake Up Little Susie: Single Pregnancy and Race before Roe v. Wade*. New York: Routledge.

Sontag, Susan (1991) *Illness and Metaphor and AIDS and its Metaphors*. Harmondsworth: Penguin.

Spark, C. (2005) 'Learning from the locals: Gajdusek, Kuru and cross-cultural interaction in Papua New Guinea', *Health and History*, 7(2): 80–100.

Spivak, G.C. (1988) 'Can the subaltern speak', in C. Nelson (ed.), *Marxism and the Interpretation of Culture*. Chicago: University of Illinois Press. pp. 271–313.

Springer, C. (1996) *Electronic Eros: Bodies and Desire in the Post-Industrial Age*. London: Athlone.

Stone, L. (1977) *The Family, Sex and Marriage in England: 1500–1800*. Harmondsworth: Penguin Books.

Stone, Lawrence (1979) *The Family, Sex and Marriage in England 1500–1800* (abridged edn). London: Penguin.

Strathern, A.J. (1996) *Body Thoughts*. Ann Arbor: University of Michigan Press.

Strathern, M. (1991) *The Gender of the Gift: Problems with Women and Problems with Society in Melanesia*. Berkeley: University of California Press.

Strathern, M. (1992) *Reproducing the Future: Anthropology, Kinship and the New Reproductive Technologies*. Cambridge: Cambridge University Press.

Strong, R. (2003) *Feast: A History of Grand Eating*. London: Pimlico.

Stryker, S. and S. Whittle (eds) (2006) *The Transgender Studies Reader*. London: Routledge.

Swain, S. and R. Howe (1995) *Single Mothers and Their Children: Disposal, Punishment and Survival in Australia*. Cambridge: Cambridge University Press.

Sydie, R.A. (1987) *Natural Women/Cultured Men: A Feminist Perspective on Sociological Theory*. Milton Keynes: Open University Press.

Synnott, Alan (1993) *The Body Social: Symbolism, Self and Society*. London: Routledge.

The Modern World Encyclopaedia: Volumes I–IX (1935). London: Hazell, Watson & Viney for The Home Entertainment Library.

Titmuss, R. (1997) *The Gift Relationship: From Human Blood to Social Policy*, eds A. Oakley and J. Ashton. New York: The New Press. First published 1970.

Trevor-Roper, H. (1983) 'The invention of tradition: The Highland tradition of Scotland', in E. Hobsbawm and T. Ranger (eds), *The Invention of Tradition*. Cambridge: Cambridge University Press.

Tuhiwai Smith, L. (1999) *Decolonizing Methodologies: Research and Indigenous Peoples*. London and New York: Zed Books.

Turner, Bryan S. (1991) *Religion and Social Theory*, 2nd edn. London: Sage. First published 1983.

Turner, Bryan S. (1996) *The Body and Society: Explorations in Social Theory*. 2nd edn. London: Sage. First published 1984.

Turner, Bryan S. with Samson, Colin (1995) *Medical Power and Social Knowledge*, 2nd edn. London: Sage. First published 1987.

Turner, Victor (1982) *From Ritual to Performance: The Human Seriousness of Play*. New York: Performing Arts Journal Publications.

Twigg, J. (2006) *The Body in Health and Social Care*. London: Palgrave Macmillan.

Twigg, J., C. Wolkowitz, R.L. Cohen and S. Nettleton (eds) (2011) Special Issue: Body Work and Health in Social Care: Critical Themes, New Agendas, *Sociology of Health and Illness*, 33(2).

United Nations (1989) UN Convention on the Rights of the Child. Available at: http://www2.ohchr.org/english/law/crc.htm (accessed May 2011).

Uppard, S. (2003) 'Child soldiers and children associated with fighting forces', *Medicine, Conflict and Survival*, 19(2): 121–7.

Urla, J. and A.C. Swedlund (2000) 'The anthropometry of Barbie: Unsettling ideals of the feminine body in popular culture', in L. Schiebinger (ed.), *Feminism and the Body*. Oxford: Oxford University Press.

Valentine, G. (1999) 'What it means to be a man: The body, masculinities, disability', in R. Hester and H. Parr (eds) *Mind and Body Spaces*. London: Routledge.

Weeks, Jeffrey (1991) *Sexuality and its Discontents: Meanings, Myths and Modern Sexualities*. London: Routledge.

Whitehead, H. (1981) 'The bow and the burden strap: A new look at institutionalized homosexuality in native North America', in S. Ortner and H. Whitehead (eds) *Sexual Meanings: The Cultural Construction of Gender and Sexuality*. Cambridge: Cambridge University Press. pp. 80–115.

WHO (1948) *Constitution of the World Health Organization*. Available at: http://www.who.int/governance/eb/who_constitution_en.pdf

WHO Expert Consultation (2004) 'Appropriate body-mass index for Asian populations and its implications for policy and intervention strategies', *Lancet*, 363(9403): 157–63.

Wilkinson, J. (2005) *Suffering: A Sociological Introduction*. Cambridge: Polity.

Williams, C.L. and A. Stein (eds) (2002) *Sexuality and Gender*. Oxford: Blackwell.

Williams, S. (2003) *Medicine and the Body*. London: Sage.

Williams, Simon and Gillian Bendelow (1998) *The Lived Body: Sociological Themes, Embodied Issues*. London: Routledge.

Wolf, N. (1990) *The Beauty Myth*. London: Vintage.

Wolkowitz, C. (2006) *Bodies at Work*. London: Sage.

Wollstonecraft, M. (1792) *A Vindication of the Rights of Woman: With Strictures on Political and Moral Subjects*. London: T. Fisher Unwin.

World Health Organization (WHO), Data and Statistics. Available at: http://www.who.int/research/en/index.html

World Health Organization (WHO) Global Database on Body Mass Index. http://apps.who.int/bmi/index.jsp (accessed 6 June 2011).

Wyness, M. (2006) *Childhood and Society: An Introduction to the Sociology of Childhood*. New York: Palgrave Macmillan.

Youngner, S.J., R. Fox and L. O'Connell (1996) *Organ Transplantation: Meanings and Realities*. Madison: University of Wisconsin Press.